DEATH LITURGY AND RITUAL

Death Liturgy and Ritual is a two-volume study of Christian funerary theology and practice, presenting an invaluable account of funeral rites and the central issues involved for compilers and users. Paul Sheppy writes from direct experience of conducting funerals and of drafting liturgical resources for others.

In *Volume II: A Commentary on Liturgical Texts*, Sheppy reviews a wide range of current Christian funeral rites and examines how they reflect both the Church's concern for the death and resurrection of Christ and the contemporary secular demand for funerals which celebrate the life of the deceased.

The companion volume, *Volume I: A Pastoral and Liturgical Theology*, proposes that the Church ought to construct its theological agenda in dialogue with other fields of study. Sheppy argues for a Christian statement about death that finds its basis in the Paschal Mystery, since human death must be explained by reference to Jesus' death, descent to the dead, and resurrection. Using the three phases of van Gennep's theory of rites of passage, the author shows how the Easter triduum may be seen as normative for Christian liturgies of death.

PAUL SHEPPY is a Baptist minister in pastoral charge of a congregation in Reading, England. From 1987 to 2002 he was a member of the Joint Liturgical Group of Great Britain, serving as its Secretary from 1994. During the latter period, he was a member of the English Language Liturgical Consultation. He has been a member of the Churches' Funerals Group since 1997 and continues to serve as a Trustee of the Joint Liturgical Group.

LITURGY, WORSHIP AND SOCIETY

Series editors
David Leal, Brasenose College, Oxford, UK
Bryan Spinks, Yale Divinity School, USA
Paul Bradshaw, University of Notre Dame, UK and USA
Gregory Woolfenden, Ripon College, Cuddesdon, Oxford, UK
Phillip Tovey, Diocese of Oxford and Oxford Brookes University, UK

This new series comes at a time of great change in liturgy and much debate concerning traditional and new forms of worship, the suitability and use of places of worship, and wider issues concerning the interaction of liturgy, worship and contemporary society. Offering a thorough grounding in the historical and theological foundations of liturgy, books in the series explore and challenge many key issues of worship and liturgical theology which are currently in hot debate – issues set to make a significant impact on the place of the church in contemporary society. Presenting an ecumenical range of books, comparing and contrasting liturgical practices and concerns within various traditions and faiths, this series will appeal to those in university and theological colleges; adult education colleges; those on other ministry or lay ministry training courses; and practitioners and those involved in worship in churches across a broad ecumenical range.

Forthcoming titles in the series include

Inculturation of Christian Worship
Exploring the Eucharist
Phillip Tovey

West Syrian Liturgical Theology
Baby Varghese

Rituals and Theologies of Christian Baptism
Beyond the Jordan
Bryan D. Spinks

Daily Liturgical Prayer
Origins and Theory
Gregory W. Woolfenden

The Liturgies of Quakerism
Pink Dandelion

Death Liturgy and Ritual
Volume II

A Commentary on Liturgical Texts

PAUL P.J. SHEPPY

ASHGATE

Published by
Ashgate Publishing Limited
Gower House
Croft Road
Aldershot
Hants GU11 3HR
England

Ashgate Publishing Company
Suite 420
101 Cherry Street
Burlington, VT 05401-4405
USA

Ashgate website: http://www.ashgate.com

British Library Cataloguing in Publication Data
Sheppy, Paul
  Death liturgy and ritual
  Vol. 2: commentary on liturgical texts. – (Liturgy,
  worship and society)
  1.Death – Religious aspects – Christianity 2.Liturgics
  3.Funeral rites and ceremonies
  I.Title
  265.8'5

Library of Congress Cataloging-in-Publication Data
Sheppy, Paul P.J.
  Death liturgy and ritual / Paul P.J. Sheppy.
      p. cm. – (Liturgy, worship and society series)
  Includes bibliographical references and index.
  Contents: v. 2. A commentary on liturgical texts.
  ISBN 0-7546-3899-5 (hbk. alk. paper) – ISBN 0-7546-3900-2 (pbk. : alk paper)
    1. Funeral service. 2. Death–Religious aspects–Christianity. I. Title. II. Series.

BV199.F8S53 2003
265'.85–dc21

                                                                            2003052240

ISBN 0 7546 3899 5 (Hbk)
ISBN 0 7546 3900 2 (Pbk)

Printed and bound in Great Britain by MPG Books Ltd, Bodmin, Cornwall

To the memory of my dear friend and colleague, whose scholarship, charity and skill with words combined in the liturgical texts he drafted.

To Michael Vasey

Eternal Memory

Contents

Acknowledgements

Books do not just happen. This book certainly has not. Many people have combined to help me in writing it; among them have been funeral directors and officiants, liturgists, the dying and the bereaved. There have been the congregations of which I have been privileged to be part and the communities in which I have lived. Simply to tell someone that you are interested in death produces some sort of interest – even if only a confirmation of your oddity!

To some friends, however, a special word of thanks should be spoken. The members of the Department of Theology and Religious Studies at the University of Leeds nurtured me in my doctoral research; to Al McFadyen and Philip Mellor I owe an enormous debt. Colleagues in Societas Liturgica have offered me opportunities to present papers to liturgical scholars for comment and correction; to Donald Gray, Robert Gribben and Richard Rutherford, I offer particular thanks. The Churches' Group on Funerals at Cemeteries and Crematoria has provided me with knowledgeable and encouraging friends who have urged me on when otherwise I might have faltered; Peter Jupp, John Lampard and Geoffrey Rowell have inspired with their own tireless studies as well as their kindly words.

To Sarah Lloyd, the series editor, and the team at Ashgate I owe the debt of time – I have delayed for too long and yet still have asked for more. They have been generosity itself. Betty Brown read the complete text before I sent it to the publishers. She saved me from more errors than I imagined possible, and I can only apologise to her that there was so much for her to do.

To the Benedictine community at Douai Abbey are due my thanks for days when I needed the stillness that final proofing and indexing requires. In particular, I would like to thank Fr Oliver Holt, the Guestmaster, who welcomed me and enabled me to feel part of the special world that St Benedict envisioned.

Beyond these, additional words must be said. To those closest to me – my wife and our daughter and son, who have put up with death and funerals, waking and sleeping – what can I say? "Sorry," seems far too little.

Bring us, O Lord God,
at our last awakening
into the house and gate of heaven,
to enter into that gate
and dwell in that house,
where there shall be
no darkness nor dazzling,
but one equal light;
no noise nor silence,
but one equal music;
no fears nor hopes,
but one equal possession;
no ends nor beginnings,
but one equal eternity;
in the habitations of thy glory and dominion,
world without end.
Amen.

John Donne

CHAPTER 1

Introduction to Volume II

A brief recapitulation

In Volume I (pastoral and liturgical theology), I sought to trace some of the contemporary issues which Christian funerary liturgy faces. We might summarise the discussion thus far as having identified two main areas requiring our response: the nature of death and human existence and the social observance of death and bereavement. To put it another way, death and dying raise questions of individual and social anthropology.

I have suggested that Christian funeral rites ought first to display a Christological response to death. To questions of what it means to be human, what it means to die, and how we ritualise death, Christian answers begin with the life, death and resurrection of Jesus. The way in which we formulate our answers will shape what we do in our funeral rites.

An agenda for Volume II

In Volume II, we shall consider a number of liturgical texts currently in use in a variety of Christian traditions and geographical locations. As well as describing these texts, I shall want to ask how what is written and enacted handles the nature of death and the passage of the dead and of the bereaved into the Paschal Mystery, which (as I have argued earlier) is the location of God's great and final word against death.

The questions we need to ask of the texts cover such issues as:

— What kind of anthropological view does the rite take?

— Does the text suggest a rite of passage, or does it simply mark a closure? Does it suggest that the rite takes a retrospective or a prospective view of the occasion? Is death seen as the end or as a gateway?

— How is the balance held between expressing the common nature of our mortality and the individuality of this particular human life now ended?

— Is judgement or hope the principal eschatological note?

— Where does the priority of focus lie between deceased and bereaved? Does the text suggest or exclude the idea that something is being transacted for the one who has died?

— How does the text reveal a Christological response to these questions?

The limits of Volume II

These questions arise from the central argument of Volume I: death raises a primary question about God, and the death of Jesus offers the best way of approaching that question. It is hardly right to subject to those criteria rites which do not share that faith. We shall, therefore, look only at Christian rites.

Moreover, we shall only look at those rites that exist in a written tradition; this is in full knowledge of the fact that Christian funerary practice exists far beyond that compass. In many ways I regret this self-imposed limitation, since it eliminates the black churches.[1] Many of their rites demonstrate a very keen sense of separation, transition and incorporation and a strong sense of journeying into glory. However, in the context of a liturgical and ritual approach, a vast study of the ritual components of a huge number of funerals would be needed to produce a choreography that might correspond to more formal ways of encoding liturgy. Such an approach is beyond the scope of this book.

I have selected rites that are in current (or recent) use. The historical tradition is not without interest; indeed, it has drawn attention from scholars from across the world. To attempt to add to their work here would, in my view, be impertinent.

I have drawn largely from liturgies in the Western Church. The Orthodox tradition is represented by one text and I attempt an explanation for this limitation when I deal directly with that text. I have tried to draw from texts across the world; apart from the English Free Church tradition (which has its own unique flavour), there are three texts from Britain, three from North America, three from Oceania, three from India and two from Africa.

The structure of Volume II

The commentary will begin with that Orthodox text. Its distinctiveness will make an effective contrast with the subsequent commentary which begins by looking at the English language rites of the oldest continuing Western tradition – that of the Roman Catholic Church. We shall then consider various rites of the Anglican Communion. The commentary will move to rites from what we might call Churches of the Reformation: Lutheran, Presbyterian and Free Churches. A final section will include the rites of ecumenical groupings.

The book concludes with some general reflections and questions arising from the work.

---

[1]   By "black churches", I mean not the ancient churches of Africa or India, but those churches arising from the European/American slavery market that carried the African experience into the New World.

CHAPTER 2

The Orthodox

Introduction

To suggest that in the compass of a few pages one can describe the funeral rites of the Orthodox churches is folly of the highest order. Leaving aside the fundamental division between Chalcedonian and non-Chalcedonian churches, each Orthodox Church is, in effect, a national church. While the central core of the rites stretches back to the liturgies of Basil and Chrysostom, the national and regional customs modify it in countless ways.

What this commentary attempts, therefore, is a review of just one text published in *The Great Book of Needs* by the St. Tikhon's Seminary Press in 1999. Moreover, the commentary looks only at the rites used at the funeral of a lay-person. The variations for monks, priests and bishops are indeed of the greatest interest, but the text here under consideration is (for obvious reasons) the most commonly used and what is used at these other rites is additional to what occurs in the lay-person's rites. In these is found the core.

For Orthodox Christians, death is viewed through the lens of the resurrection of Christ and the promised resurrection of all the departed. It is not, therefore, an end; rather, it is a time of repose – a *dormition* (sleeping). In the funeral service two things are believed to happen. The prayers of the living bring joy to the departed; the prayers and hymns provide a means of expressing grief and faith in the promise of eternal life through Christ Jesus. The funeral ends as the faithful take the departed to their rest in the anticipation of that day when the Lord will awaken them from their *dormition*.

The Orthodox pay great attention to the preparation of the body for burial.[1] And it is burial that the Orthodox choose. The Church's canon law declares that the body of a deceased Christian must be returned to the earth. This is not simply about the example of Christ's burial, there are other concerns. Not least among these is the understanding that the Christian, who in the Holy Liturgy has received Christ, is thereby sanctified. The body of that Christian in burial sanctifies in its turn the ground where it is laid, signifying and making real the salvation of the whole earth. The sealing of this is effected by the grave marker or monument which bears the image of the Cross.

The Funeral Service may be preceded by the Office of the Parting of the Soul from the Body, if the family or close friend of those who are dying can summon a priest (and

---

[1] This does not mean that, for example, organ donation is not permitted. It does mean that the body is visible; the coffin is not closed until after the Last Kiss.

a cantor) to the bedside.[2] After the Funeral Service the *Panichida* or *Lite* may be observed.[3] The days of observation are: the ninth, the fortieth and the year's end.

The Great Book of Needs (1999)

The Funeral Service is essentially the Matins service, with the canon and other hymns selected from the Matins for Great Saturday (Holy Saturday) – the day of Christ's burial.

At the House

The rites begin with a service at the house. The priest censes the body and begins in the customary manner:

> Blessed is our God, always, now and ever, and unto the ages of ages.

Those present respond by singing the Amen and Holy God. The Reader says the remainder of the opening, concluding "for Thine is the Kingdom".
They then sing to tone 4 several *troparia*, beginning

> With souls of the righteous departed, give rest to the soul of Thy servant, O Saviour, preserving it in the blessed life which is with Thee, O Lover of Mankind.

and concluding

> O Virgin, who only art pure and undefiled, who didst bear God without seed:
> Do thou pray that this his (her) soul may be saved.

The deacon then says the Litany as the singers respond to each petition with a threefold "Lord, have mercy", and after the last petition "Grant it, O Lord". The priest then secretly says the prayer, "O God of spirits and all flesh", finishing with the exclamation:

> For Thou art the Resurrection and the Life, and the Repose of Thy servant N, who has fallen asleep, O Christ, our God, and unto Thee do we send up glory, together with thy Father Who is without beginning, and Thy Most-holy, Good, and Lifegiving Spirit, now and ever, and unto the ages of ages.

The deacon cries out, "Wisdom" and the choir sings the hymn to the *Theotokos*. After the singing of the *Gloria* and threefold *Kyrie*, the priest dismisses those gathered.

---

[2] In practice it is not often possible in modern societies, where death is remote and families are scattered, to make the necessary arrangement for this rite.

[3] It may also be observed on the evening before the funeral. It is a memorial service at which *kolivo* is served and prayers are said. *Kolivo* is a mixture of wheat or barley mixed with sugar, honey and dried fruit. It recalls the text, "Unless a grain of wheat falls into the earth and dies, it remains alone; but if it dies, it bears much fruit" (Jn 12.24). Candles should be distributed to all who attend as a sign of Christ, the Light of the World in whose resurrection the Christian hopes.

The Procession to Church

All should now be prepared for the beginning of the candle-lit procession to church. Once again, the preface is sung from "Blessed is our God" and "Holy God". The coffin (still open) is now brought to the church and placed according to local custom. As the procession enters the church Ps 90[91] is sung,[4] followed by the acclamation drawn from Pss 118[119] and 1:

> Blessed art Thou, O Lord, teach me thy statutes. The undefiled in the way: Alleluia.

The Service in Church

The first *stasis* of the "undefiled" is sung in tone 6 with the following introduction:

> Blessed are the undefiled in the way,
> who walk in the Law of the Lord.
> **Alleluia.**

> Blessed are they that search out His testimonies:
> with their whole heart shall they seek after Him.
> **Alleluia.**

> For they that work no iniquity
> have walked in His ways.
> **Alleluia.**

The remainder of the first *stasis* is resumed and the deacon says the Little Litany for the Departed. The priest secretly utters the prayer, "O God of spirits and all flesh," with the exclamation as before. The second *stasis* (in tone 5) is begun and introduced as follows:

> Thy hands have made me and fashioned me;
> give me understanding and I will learn Thy commandments.
> **Have mercy upon Thy servant.**

> They that fear shall see me and be glad,
> for on Thy words have I set my hope.
> **Have mercy upon Thy servant.**

> I have known, O Lord, that Thy judgements are righteousness,
> and with truth Thou hast humbled me.
> **Have mercy upon Thy servant.**

The deacon repeats the Little Litany for the Departed, followed by the prayer secretly uttered and the exclamation. The singers now begin the third *stasis* (in tone 3) with the following introduction:

---

[4] Note that *The Great Book of Needs* (as is the Orthodox custom) adopts the liturgical numbering of the LXX.

> Look upon me and have mercy on me,
> according to them that love Thy name.
> **Alleluia.**
>
> Order my steps according to Thy word,
> and let no iniquity have dominion over me.
> **Alleluia.**
>
> Deliver me from the false accusation of men,
> and I will keep Thy commandments.
> **Alleluia.**

The third *stasis* is resumed with an extended conclusion at the end of which the deacon repeats the Little Litany for the Departed and the prayer and exclamation follow.

Troparia are sung seeking forgiveness for sin and introducing Ps 50[51], followed by the Canon of the Departed and a series of six odes with the refrain:

> Give rest, O Lord, unto the soul of Thy servant who has fallen asleep.

The odes precede the Little Litany, the secret prayer and the exclamation. The kontakion is now sung in full:

> With the Saints, give rest, O Christ, to the soul of Thy servant, where sickness is no more, neither sorrowing nor sighing, but life everlasting.
>
> (*Ikos*) Thou only art immortal, Who hast created and fashioned man. For out of the earth were we [mortals] made, and unto earth shall we return again, as Thou didst command when Thou madest me, saying unto me: "For earth thou art and unto the earth shalt thou return," whither we [mortals] all shall go, making as our funeral dirge the song: Alleluia. Alleluia. Alleluia.
>
> With the Saints, give rest, O Christ, to the soul of Thy servant, where sickness is no more, neither sorrowing nor sighing, but life everlasting.

The choir intones odes 7 to 9, followed by the Little Litany, secret prayer and exclamation.

The *idiomela* of John the Monk precede the singing of the beatitudes, which conclude with stanza to the *Theotokos*:

> How didst thou spill out milk from thy breasts, O Virgin?
> How didst thou nourish the Nourisher of Creation?
> He knoweth Who didst spill out water from the rock;
> streams of water for a thirsting people, as it was written.

The deacon now calls the congregation to attend and then cries, "Wisdom". The Epistle is read from 1 Thess 4.13-17. Again the deacon calls for attention and the Gospel is introduced with Alleluias; the passage read is Jn 5.24-30. A litany follows, seeking repose and remission of sins for the departed. The presiding priest or bishop then repeats the prayer, "O God of spirits and all flesh" out loud; other clergy present say it secretly.

The Last Kiss
There now follows the Last Kiss, which is accompanied by the *Stikhera* beginning

> Come, brethren, let us give the last kiss unto the dead, giving thanks unto
> God, For he (*she*) has vanished from among his (*her*) kinsmen and hastens to
> the grave. For him (*her*) there is no anxiety concerning vain things and the
> much-suffering flesh. Where now are his (*her*) kinsmen and his (*her*) friends?
> Behold, we are parted. Let us pray unto the Lord that He will give him (*her*)
> rest.

and ending

> By the prayer of her that gave Thee birth, O Christ, and of The Forerunner, of
> the Apostles, Prophets, Hierarchs, Venerable Ones and the Righteous, and of
> all the saints, give rest unto Thy servant who has fallen asleep.

The *Trisagion* and Lord's Prayer follow, then the troparia beginning "With the souls of
the righteous departed". The deacon says the litany and the priest secretly utters "O God
of spirits and all flesh" followed by the exclamation.

Dismissal
The deacon calls "Wisdom" and the choir sing the hymn to the *Theotokos*. The priest
then makes the dismissal in these words:

> May He Who rose from the dead, Christ our True God, by the prayers of His
> most-pure Mother; of the holy, glorious and all-praised Apostles of our
> venerable and Godbearing Fathers; and of all the Saints, establish the soul of
> His servant *N*, who has been taken away from us, in the abodes of the
> Righteous, and give him (*her*) rest in the bosom of Abraham and number him
> (*her*) with the Righteous; and that He will have mercy on us, as He is Good
> and the Lover of Mankind.
> **Amen.**

The bishop (or presiding priest) proclaims three times:

> May thy memory be eternal, O worthily-blessed and ever-memorable brother
> (*sister*).

Prayer of Absolution
A short parting prayer may conclude the rite, but increasingly the extensive prayer of
absolution is said:

> May our Lord Jesus Christ, by His divine grace, and also by the gift and
> power given unto His holy Disciples and Apostles, that they should bind and
> loose the sins of men (for He said unto them, "Receive the Holy Spirit.
> Whosoever's sins you remit, they are remitted unto them; and whosoever's
> sins you retain, they are retained". And "whatsoever you shall bind *or loose*
> on earth shall be bound *or loosed* in Heaven") and which also has been
> handed down to us from them as their successors, absolve this my spiritual

child, *N*, through me who am unworthy, from all things wherein, as a human, he (*she*) sinned against God, whether by word or by deed, whether by thought and with all his (*her*) senses, whether voluntarily or involuntarily, whether by knowledge or by ignorance. And if he (*she*) be under the ban or excommunication of a Bishop or of a Priest; or if he (*she*) has brought upon himself (*herself*) the curse of his (*her*) father or mother; or has fallen under his (*her*) own curse; or has transgressed by any oath; or has been bound, as a human, by any sins whatsoever, but has repented of these with a contrite heart, may He absolve him (*her*) also from all these faults and bonds. And may all those things that proceed from the infirmity of *human* nature be given over unto oblivion and may He forgive him (*her*) everything, for the sake of His Love for Mankind, through the prayers of our most-holy and most-blessed sovereign Lady, the Theotokos and ever-Virgin Mary, of the holy, glorious and all-praised Apostles, and of all the Saints. Amen.

That is as about as comprehensive an absolution as any sinner could require! As a closing prayer, it completes the rite with total effect.

The Procession to the Grave

Those present take the body to the grave singing the *Trisagion, Kyrie* and Lord's Prayer. The coffin is placed in the grave. The bishop (or presiding priest) takes earth and casts it on the remains in the form of the Cross, with the words:

> The earth is the Lord's and the fullness thereof, the world and all that dwell therein.

Oil is poured from the shrine lamp and the ashes from the censer are scattered over the coffin with the words of Ps 24.1 – the earth is the Lord's and the fullness thereof. The oil as a sign of the mercy of God,[5] the ashes as a reminder – "dust thou art, and to dust shalt thou return". The grave is filled the Troparia beginning "With the souls of the righteous departed" are sung.

Summary

As always, the overwhelming impression of the Orthodox is the rootedness in scripture and tradition. The centrality of the Trinity, and of the Christ who goes to death and is raised from it, is absolute. The open coffin confronts us with our mortality, which cannot (indeed, must not) be concealed.

The extended preparation with the repeated prayers and acclamations combine to deliver a sense of the unending liturgy of heaven into which the faithful are drawn and upon whose threshold the departed stand. The understanding of death as dormition gives to the rites that transitional phase which is often simply reproduced as confusion.

The prayer of absolution prepares the deceased for incorporation into the realms of the blessed and the rites accompanying the burial (oil and ashes) speak of frailty shown mercy in final echo of the hope of the Christian of resurrection to eternal life.

---

[5]   Olive oil in Greek is cognate with the appeal "Have mercy" (*elaion: eleison*).

The body-soul anthropology is part of the liturgical and theological tradition which informs all Orthodox liturgy (as it does much of the liturgy of the Churches of the West). Yet the totality of death is clearly demonstrated in these rites and the hope of a future blessed in Christ shines as an example to those of us from other traditions.

"Eternal Memory".

CHAPTER 3

The Roman Catholic Church

Order of Christian Funerals (1990)

In 1990 the *Order of Christian Funerals* (*OCF*) was published upon the approval of the Bishops' Conferences of England and Wales and of Scotland and their instruction that its use would be mandatory and exclusive from Easter Sunday 1991. In this they followed their American brethren. The American Bishops' Conference approved *OCF* for mandatory and exclusive use as from All Souls Day 1989.

OCF is based on the revised Roman Rite published and authorised in the pontificate of Paul VI. The British edition was prepared by the Liturgy Office of the Bishops' Conference of England and Wales and the International Commission on English in the Liturgy (ICEL). ICEL undertook the translation of the Roman Ritual and the general preparation of the texts. The liturgies are therefore ICEL texts. The national Liturgy Office produced the necessary detailed revision for approval by the Bishops' Conference. A similar process occurred in the USA and in each of the national Bishops' Conferences.

The first thing that strikes one about *OCF* is its size. The British edition is a two-volume work, with a page size greater than ten inches by six and a total of nearly 670 pages.[1]

The physical bulk of the volumes was determined by the decision about how to present the funeral rites with the various options. Previously, other churches had normally produced a core liturgy with additional readings and prayers in separate sections or appendices. The drawback with this form of book is that the officiants need to flip back and forward as they adapt the main service to the particular circumstances.[2] *OCF*'s way of dealing with the problem of options is to lay out every possibility in full in separate liturgies. This makes for much of the material being printed several times over. The advantage sought is that once the priest has selected the appropriate rite he can follow the chosen option from beginning to end without the need for thumbs, pieces of ribbon, or slips of paper to keep the place.

---

[1] In early 1991 the bishop of Leeds summoned the priests of his diocese to a day conference at which they were to be introduced to the liturgies of *OCF* by a member of the national Liturgy Office. I was privileged to be a guest, as a doctoral student of the University of Leeds. When the time for questions and comment came, scarcely a priest who spoke refrained from criticizing the publication's size. There was a strong feeling that what had been produced was a magnificent (and expensive) lectern/altar book. They asked for something less vulnerable to graveside committals in the wind and rain, something more portable. More than one priest suggested laminated cards for use in the open. The liturgies were of great interest, but the size of the book was intimidating.

[2] This may be a small price to pay when *OCF*'s solution to the matter is held in the hands – for it cannot be held in one hand at the graveside. The only way that an officiant using *OCF* can have a hand free to raise in blessing or to make any other gesture is to have a lectern or an acolyte holding the book.

The resultant duplication and reduplication make the book unwieldy and repetitive for the commentator. I propose to look at what I judge to be the main lines in each of the rites. *OCF* divides its liturgical provisions into five main parts: funeral rites (vigil, funeral, committal), funeral rites for children (vigil, funeral, committal) funerals for catechumens, office for the dead, additional texts. I shall follow the same scheme, but after I have looked at the main developments, I shall simply refer to significant variations in the various options provided.

The guiding principle in the preparation of these funeral rites was the Liturgical Constitution arising from Vatican II, which said of the burial rite that "it should express more clearly the paschal nature of Christian death".[3]

In the commentary provided in 1964 with the Constitution this was explained a little more fully:

> Death, for believers, is a participation in the paschal mystery. Baptism has initiated a movement that will terminate in death, which, after Christ's example, is a passage from this world to the Father. Sorrow accompanies death; but the thought of, and union with, the agony of the redeemer fill it with hope in the resurrection.[4]

Part I: Funeral Rites
VIGIL AND RELATED RITES AND PRAYERS
OCF's rites start with preparation for the funeral itself. This is done by means of vigil rites in which a watch is kept by the body before the funeral liturgy.

Prayers after Death
After an invitation to silent prayer, there is a short Gospel reading.[5] The Lord's Prayer precedes prayers for the deceased and those who mourn. The prayer for the deceased asks that forgiveness may be granted to her/him and claims the promise "to Abraham and his children for ever" in a short quotation from the *Magnificat*.[6]

The *Magnificat* is the canticle of the evening office, which traditionally used the theme of evening rest as a metaphor for death. Its place in this opening rite is thus evocative of the daily prayers of the church as the faithful on earth enter into the worship of heaven. The deceased is now on her/his final journey to join in that ceaseless activity to which this canticle refers both in itself and its customary *locus* in the evening liturgy.

Comfort and refuge are sought for those who mourn, and the death and resurrection of Christ are set forth as the ground for hope of reunion "with those we love".[7]

The reference to the death and resurrection echoes an acclamatory couplet from the eucharistic prayer of the Mass:

---

[3] *Constitutio liturgica* (1964: article 81).
[4] *Constitutio liturgica cum commentario* (1964: 156). Commentary by P. Journel.
[5] The passages offered are Matt 18.19-20 (where two or three meet in my name, I shall be there with them); Jn 11.21-24 (at the death of Lazarus: I am the resurrection); Lk 20.35-38 (God is the God, not of the dead, but of the living). *OCF*: 25-26.
[6] *OCF*: 27.
[7] *OCF*: 27.

> Dying, you destroyed our death,
> rising, you restored our life.[8]

As with the prayer for the deceased, the reference here to the continuing worship of the church places this office into a more familiar context than simply the dread of death.

Blessings are pronounced. A first blessing is spoken for the deceased.[9] This is followed by the couplet that is at the heart of Catholic remembrance of the dead:

> Eternal rest grant unto him/her, O Lord.
> And let perpetual light shine upon him/her.

There follows a blessing spoken to the congregation, and invoking the peace and love of God.

The rite is intended for use at the first pastoral visit, and it is suggested that the priest can use this occasion for preliminary consideration of how the funeral should be planned.

Gathering in the Presence of the Body

This rite is intended for use with the family as it first gathers around the body. After the sign of the cross, a verse of scripture is read, and the body is sprinkled with holy water in an evocation of the deceased's baptism.[10] A psalm is then sung or said, followed by the Lord's Prayer and a concluding prayer.[11] The same forms of blessing are used as in the rite *Prayers after Death*.

Vigil for the Deceased

This is the principal rite for use before the funeral. It may take place at the home, or in a chapel of rest, or in the church. At the church it should be celebrated well before the funeral. The focus of the vigil is the reading of scripture and includes a first reading, a responsorial psalm and the gospel.

The vigil begins with a greeting and an invitation to silent prayer. The silence is concluded with an opening prayer which links the death of the one for whom the vigil is held with the death and resurrection of Christ.

The Liturgy of the Word offers a vast selection for the various readings. The preferred passages are printed in full.[12] Among the texts are several relating to the Final

---

[8] In the eucharistic prayer of the Mass the congregational acclamation concludes: "Lord Jesus, come in glory."

[9] An option is provided for children from Mk 10.14.

[10] Matt 11.28-30 (Come to me, all you who labour) and Jn 14.1-3 (Do not let your hearts be troubled) are suggested, though other words may equally well be used. At the aspersion, texts are used speaking of the Lord as shepherd (Ps 23), or of baptism in Christ, or of the baptised as the temple of God.

[11] The psalms proposed are selections from Pss 130, or 115 and 116. I shall use the non-liturgical numbering of the psalms in all my references to the Psalter in this review of *OCF*.

[12] The texts are interchangeable for all the funeral rites. Here the preferred choices are: 2 Cor 5.1, 6-10 (an everlasting home in heaven); Ps 27 (the Lord is my light); Lk 12.35-40 (the sudden return of the householder).

OT: Job 19.1, 23-27; Wisd 3.1-9 (*or* 1-6, 9); Wisd 4.7-15; Isa 25.6a, 7-9; Lam 3.17-26; Dan 12.1-3; 2 Macc 12.43-46.

Judgement – a reminder of death as gateway to judgement as well as to the presence of God. The rubric which follows reads:

A homily on the readings is then given.

The pastoral notes accompanying the vigil rite add that this homily is given "to help those present find strength and hope in God's saving word". The emphasis on proclamation follows the *Liturgical Constitution* of Vatican II, which urged that all liturgical reform should be marked by active congregational participation, more interesting use of the Bible, and intelligibility of symbol and gesture.

The pattern of prayers of intercession (here taking the form of a litany), Lord's Prayer, concluding prayer, and blessing, established in the previous rites, now follows.

Vigil for the Deceased with Reception at the Church

This rite is a fuller version of the one just described. It is for use where the body of the deceased is brought into church, so that it may be placed at rest before the altar – usually overnight. The rite suggests that those who have received Christ at the altar in bread and wine are now themselves received there by Christ. The Easter Candle is lit – both as a visual reminder of Ps 27.1 and as a proclamation of the link between the death of the faithful and the Paschal Mystery.

The main difference between the present order and the simple Vigil is in the introductory rites, which include the reception of the body. The coffin is sprinkled at the door to the Church with holy water (baptism) and the Easter Candle lit. Where it is the local custom a pall is placed on the coffin along with a Bible, a Book of the Gospels, or a cross.[13] The coffin is then taken in procession to the altar.[14]

Where the body is to be received into church without a vigil, *A Simple Form of Reception at the Church* is provided.[15] This is the same as the *Vigil and Reception* but without the Liturgy of the Word.

NT: Acts 10.34-43 (*or* 34-36, 42-43); Rom 5.5-11; Rom 5.17-21; Rom 6.3-9 (*or* 3-4, 8-9); Rom 8.14-23; Rom 8.31b-35, 37-39; Rom 14.7-9, 10b-12; 1 Cor 15.20-23, 24b-28 (*or* 20-23): 1 Cor 15.51-57; 2 Cor 4.14-5.1; 2 Cor 5.1, 6-10; Phil 3.20-21; 1 Thess 4.13-18; 2 Tim 2.8-13; 1 Jn 3.1-2; 1 Jn 3.14-16; Rev 20.11-21.1; Rev 21.1-5a, 6b-7.

RESPONSORIAL PSALMS: Pss 23; 25; 27; 42 and 43; 63; 103; 116; 122; 130; 143.

ALLELUIA VERSES AND VERSES BEFORE THE GOSPEL: Matt 11.25; Matt 25.34; Jn 3.16; Jn 6.39; Jn 6.40; Jn 6.51a; Jn 11.25-26; Phil 3.20; 2 Tim 2.11b-12a; Rev 1.5a, 6b; Rev 14.13.

GOSPEL: Matt 5.1-12a; Matt 11.25-30; Matt 25.1-13; Matt 25.31-46; Mk 15.33-39 (16.1-16); Lk 7.11-17; Lk 12.35-40; Lk 23.33, 39-43; Lk 23.44-46, 50, 52-53 (24.1, 6a); Lk 24.13-35 (*or* 13-16, 28-35); Jn 5.24-29; Jn 6.37-40; Jn 6.51-58; Jn 11.17-27 (*or* 21-27); Jn 11.32-45; Jn 12.23-28 (*or* 23-26); Jn 14.1-6; Jn 17.24-26; Jn 19.17-18, 25-30.

[13] It is important to note that the General Introduction to *OCF* makes the very clear and crucial observation: "Only Christian symbols may rest on or be placed near the coffin during the funeral liturgy. Any other symbols, for example, national flags, or flags or insignia of associations, have no place in the funeral liturgy" (*OCF*: 11).

[14] The preferred readings at the Liturgy of the Word are: 1 Jn 3.1-2; Ps 103; Jn 14.1-6.

[15] *OCF*: 63ff.

Gathering of the Family and Transfer of the Body to the Church or to the Place of Committal

This rite is for use on the day of the funeral as the family meet together. The introductory note comments that:

> The procession to the church is a rite of initial *separation* [my stress] of the mourners from the deceased; the procession to the place of committal is the journey to the place of final separation of the mourners from the deceased. . . Reverent celebration of the rite can help reassure the mourners and create an atmosphere of calm preparation . . .

A short introduction of a verse of scripture, and silent prayer is followed by Ps 130 or Pss 115 and 116 (or any other from the list provided for use at the Vigil).[16] A litany rehearses the salvation history of the deceased through the story of the Passion, and ends with the Lord's Prayer, and a concluding prayer. The priest then extends an Invitation to the Procession with the words of Ps 121:

> The Lord guards our coming in and our going out.
> May God be with us today
> as we make this last journey with our brother/sister.

The Procession begins with the words of Ps 122:

> I rejoiced when I heard them say:
> 'Let us go to God's house.'

The Funeral Liturgy follows.

The use of vigil rites and rites of preparation is important in the van Gennep scheme of things. The separation of death is undertaken carefully; and the ritual expression, far from emptying what occurs of meaning, gives to those who participate the framework within which meaning can be discerned and expressed. The old tradition of the funeral procession is not easily replicated in those situations where the home, the church and the place of committal are at a distance from one another. Nonetheless, the ritual nature of processing reinvigorates the funeral rites, and provides a cord upon which the beads of the various services can be threaded to form a coherent unity.

FUNERAL RITES

There are two liturgies provided for funerals. The first is a liturgy for a Funeral Mass; the second is for a Funeral outside Mass. The preferred form is a Funeral Mass. Where this is not possible, the introductory note urges that family and friends should arrange for the celebration of Mass as soon as possible after the Funeral.[17] The intention is to demonstrate the unity of the faithful in Christ: the living by means of Christ in the sacrament, the dead by the resurrection.

---

[16]   Pss 23; 25; 27; 42 and 43; 63; 103; 116; 122; 130; 143.
[17]   *OCF*: 80, paragraph 137.

Funeral Mass

Where the body has already been received into Church, Mass begins in the normal way as set out in the Roman Missal. Where the body has not been received into Church, the introductory rite follows the pattern of reception to be found in the Vigil and Reception.

The Liturgy of the Word follows the pattern for Mass; readings should be selected as the pastoral circumstances suggest.

Once again, *OCF*'s rubric is clear: a homily is to be given after the reading of the Gospel. There then follow the general intercessions. Two litanies are provided: Form A offers specific petitions for a deacon and for a bishop or priest. This follows ancient tradition; but ancient tradition raises a question. On what grounds should a differentiation be made in death between one Christian and another? If, as the note in the General Introduction observes, secular dignities and orders are not to be observed in the funeral liturgy, why should ecclesiastical honours be noted? In the vision of the heavenly Jerusalem which John the Divine describes in the book of the Revelation, religion is at an end, and so are all its impedimenta.[18]

> I saw no temple in the city, for its temple is the Lord God the Almighty and the Lamb. (Rev 21.22)

The question of hierarchy is one that causes considerable awkwardness within *OCF*, as we shall see when we come to consider the funeral rites for children and for the catechumenate. This is but the first instance. There is not much notion here of Death the Leveller.

Form B of the intercessions is less concerned with ecclesiastical matters, and the prayers include a petition for justice and peace. However, in both forms A and B the major concern is to pray for the deliverance of the deceased from eternal punishment, and to seek for the congregation a like reception into the company of all the saints.

The concluding prayer summarises the intercessions and leads to the Liturgy of the Eucharist. It is not within the scope of this book to comment on the liturgy of the Mass, and so we move directly to the final action of the service in Church: the final commendation.

An invitation to silent prayer begins the final commendation, although there is provision for a member or friend of the family to speak in remembrance of the deceased first of all. Five forms of the invitation are printed in *OCF*.[19] A and B articulate with particular clarity the separating nature of death and of the funeral rites. C uses the language of falling asleep in Christ. After silence, the coffin may be aspersed and

---

[18] The old argument was that the clergy would be recognised as clergy in heaven. From the perspective of the judgement, the argument has strong biblical warrant with the repeated warning to pastors that they will be called to account for those in their care (Cf., for example, Ezek 34; 1 Cor 4.1-2; Jas 3.1; 1 Pet 5.1-4.) But there is no suggestion that the priestly office and cure of souls exist beyond death. What need will there be for it? There will be no need of sacraments when the ceaseless, eternal, co-inherent and immediate presence of God is directly known by the blessed. What then is the meaning of the intercession for a bishop or priest "that he may be given a place in the liturgy of heaven" (*OCF*: 94)? In heaven, ecclesiology is at an end.

[19] *OCF*: 97. Invitations D and E are special options; A, B and C are general in scope. D is for use prior to burial, E for use prior to cremation.

incensed. *A Song of Farewell* speaks of the joys of heaven, and a final prayer of commendation is spoken.

The commendatory prayer occurs in two forms. The first speaks of "the sure and certain hope" of the resurrection, and asks that the gates of paradise may be opened for the deceased. The second seeks forgiveness and everlasting peace. It is noteworthy that, while form B of the prayer commends "the soul of *N*" to God, form A simply commends "our brother/sister *N*". It would be unwise to attach any significance to the lack of reference to the soul in form A. It is simply an alternative form of commendation. There follows the call to process to the place of rest. The traditional funeral anthems are available for singing:

> May the angels lead you to paradise;
> may the martyrs come to welcome you
> and take you into the holy city,
> the new and eternal Jerusalem.

or

> May choirs of angels welcome you
> and lead you to the bosom of Abraham;
> and where Lazarus is poor no longer
> may you find eternal rest.

A verse form is also available, or a suitable psalm may be used.

These anthems are particularly apposite to the liturgical action. The procession that leaves the deceased in the grave gives way to the procession of angels and martyrs who lead the faithful to God. This marks a genuine move through transition to incorporation.

FUNERAL LITURGY OUTSIDE MASS

The rite is similar to that of the Funeral Mass.[20] A liturgy without Mass need not, of course, mean a liturgy without communion. A priest may preside at a communion when Canon Law precludes a Mass.[21] Equally, if there is no priest present but there is eucharistic bread available, a eucharistic minister may preside at a sharing of the communion. If there is no communion, a concluding prayer precedes the prayer of commendation.

Where there has been a communion, a post-communion prayer is said. Four forms are offered. One of these is for a catechumen; once again the hierarchical tone is introduced in a rite that is supposed to express the unity of the Church. The effect is at least inharmonious, and for some may be disturbing. The final commendation is the same as that provided for the Funeral Mass.

---

[20]   At the intercessions there are no distinctive prayers for deacons, priests or bishops, since a Funeral Mass will almost inevitably mark the death of a member of the clergy.

[21]   Three reasons are offered for the use of this rite: when a Funeral Mass is not permitted by Canon Law – solemnities of obligation, Holy Thursday and the Easter Triduum, Sundays of Advent, Lent and Easter; if a priest is not available; if pastoral reasons make it more appropriate (see *OCF*: 103, paragraph 188).

THE RITE OF COMMITTAL – A GENERAL COMMENT

It is at the rite of the committal that the commentator's nightmare is realised. There are seven different rites of committal provided in *OCF* for the funeral of an adult. Similarly, there are seven different rites of committal for the funeral of a child. The multiplicity is initially bewildering and almost bizarre. Yet the pastoral notes preceding the rite give an explanation for the variety.

Basically the rites divide into two groups of three with a separate seventh liturgy. The first group relates to committal at the cemetery, the second group to committal at the crematorium. The place of the rite for the burial of ashes is self-explanatory.

The introductory notes to the rites of committal indicate that in each group of rites the first form is for use when there has been a full funeral liturgy already. The second is for use where the funeral liturgy thus far has made no final commendation of the deceased. The third is for use where the funeral liturgy is to take place in its entirety at the place of disposal. In its comment on the third form of service *OCF* notes:

> Many mourners who are not members of the Church, and who may not regard themselves as religious, are often among the most assiduous in attending funerals. While it may not have been the wish, either of the deceased or of the community, that the funeral should be celebrated in this way, arrangements are often made with the funeral director before contact has been made with the Church. It is important that the priest or minister bring out the particular insights and interpretations which Christian faith brings to bear on the reality of death and the experience of bereavement.[22]

There are two assertions here that may need some qualification. The first suggests a particular assiduity in attending funerals among those professing no religious faith. Formal affiliation is not the only form of religious belief. Whilst most people (including churchgoers) may live on a day-to-day basis without an immediate awareness of God, death poses a challenge to day-to-day living. Death says, "Day-to-day living does not go on for ever." Once that has been said, questions of transcendence begin very quickly to force themselves upon the mind. It is precisely because death raises the question of God that the priest or minister has the opportunity to speak of Christian faith in relation to death, and in particular to the death and resurrection of Jesus.

The second statement demanding some comment is the remark that funerals are often arranged without reference to the Church. Those charged with the responsibility for making of funeral arrangements may not themselves have any church connections. It is hardly surprising that in the first instance they turn to those whose professional business it is to deal with the arrangement of funerals and the other official business arising from death. Maura Naylor noted in her doctoral thesis for the University of Leeds that clerical frustration with funeral directors was mirrored almost exactly by the experience of funeral directors who frequently had to deal with incompetence and intransigence among clergy.[23]

---

[22] *OCF*: 125, paragraph 229.

[23] Naylor (1989). Conversations with undertakers and funeral directors suggest that ministers do not often make an early call to the offices of their local undertakers when they arrive in the parish. Frequently the first contact is when a funeral has been arranged by a mourner with the undertaker, simply because the new minister is not yet known in the community. There is more to the business of funerals than reaction

In commenting on the rite of committal, I intend only to look at the main line in the *Rite of Committal at a Cemetery*. Since the five rites that follow are variations on the theme, we need only note that they amend one another by the use of material already discussed.[24] It will remain then to say something very briefly about the *Rite for the Burial of Ashes*.

RITE OF COMMITTAL AT A CEMETERY
The rite begins with an invitation to pray:

> Our brother/sister *N.* has gone to his/her rest in the peace of Christ. May the Lord now welcome him/her to the table of God's children in heaven. With faith and hope in eternal life, let us assist him/her with our prayers.

This invitation to help the deceased is one of the clearer indications in *OCF*'s liturgies so far of a phase of transition within the funeral rites. We might have expected to find far more explicit references to transition, since the Roman Catholic Church has more clearly defined its teaching on the progress of the faithful departed than have the churches of the Reformation. The purgatorial emphasis is less immediately discernible than one might have anticipated.

The opening verses of scripture speak of the welcome in heaven for the faithful and the sureness of salvation through Christ the first-born from the dead.[25] A prayer is then said at the grave; five options are given, of which four offer a blessing of the grave. Prayers B and D speak of the sleep of the deceased. This appears to be a departure from the language of purgatory. Prayer E offers at its conclusion an alternative view, though still a traditional one – the separation of soul and body:

> In a spirit of repentance
> we earnestly ask you
> to look upon this grave and bless it,
> so that, while we commit to [the earth/its resting place]
> the body of your servant *N.*
> his/her soul may be taken into paradise.

The prayer of committal allows for the possibility of burial at sea in all three options. The third form is specifically for such a burial, and is particularly noteworthy with its references to the primordial sea of chaos, to the stilling of the storm, and to the waters of baptism:

> Lord God,
> by the power of your Word
> you stilled the chaos of the primeval seas,

---

to death after the event. Part of good pastoral practice is early contact with those other professionals with whom pastors do their work.
[24] Official Catholic reserve about the appropriateness of cremation as a means of disposal is now at an end. Although separate rites are offered for use in the crematorium, there is little creativity about the provision. However, *OCF*'s rites are no different in this respect from other rites covered in this commentary.
[25] Matt 25.34; Jn 6.39; Phil 3.20; Rev 1.5-6.

you made the raging waters of the Flood subside,
and calmed the storm on the sea of Galilee.

As we commit the body of our brother/sister *N.* to the deep,
grant him/her peace and tranquillity
until that day when he/she and all who believe in you
will be raised to the glory of new life
promised in the waters of baptism.

This is a vivid and powerful text whose effect is made by linking chaos with death and tranquillity with new life. In so doing, it offers a remarkably good example of how to handle the awkward stage of transition in this rite of passage.

After the committal, intercessions are made both for the deceased and the bereaved. These are followed by the Lord's Prayer and concluding prayers which complete the act of separation and speak of the blessedness of the kingdom. The blessing is pronounced and the rites are at an end.[26]

RITE FOR THE BURIAL OF ASHES

One of the difficulties attached to cremation is the disposal of remains. While families often find upkeep of graves a difficult business, especially when they are scattered, there is still for many the need to have a marker. Crematoria generally have some provision for this, but this does not always meet the needs of the family and friends. Where a previous member of the family (spouse, parent, or child) has been buried but the present deceased is to be cremated, the best choice for the family may be to have the ashes interred at the previously existing grave. This rite provides for this kind of situation. There is nothing particularly noteworthy about a rite whose shape I reproduce below:

—   Invitation

—   Scripture Verse

—   Prayer of Committal

—   Lord's Prayer

—   Blessing

Part II: Funeral Rites for Children

These rites follow the same pattern as the ordinary Funeral Rites. Differences in choices of scripture and in prayers for the parents and other members of the family form most of the variations from the rites already described. Probably the most notable issue is the contentious pastoral decision to differentiate between children baptised and those not baptised. In the general introductory notes to the rites this explanation appears:

Funeral rites may be celebrated for children whose parents intended them to be baptized but who died before baptism. In these celebrations the Christian community

---

[26]   The conclusion of these rites does not necessarily mark the end of ritual engaged upon in relation to the dead, however. As with the rite of a Funeral without Mass, there may be a Mass after the funeral. Further, there is the Office of the Dead, which forms an important part of the Church's life of prayer.

entrusts the child to God's all-embracing love and finds strength in this love and in Jesus' affirmation that the kingdom of God belongs to little children (cf. Matt 19:14).[27]

Here, a little disguised (though not very well), is an echo of the doctrine of limbo. The texts are unwilling to affirm gladly that God welcomes children baptised or not, but make vague noises about leaving it to God. Surely, all judgement belongs to God, and polite murmurings do not hide the divisiveness of what is said here. Throughout the rites, different prayers and gestures are made for baptised and unbaptised children.[28] At certain points in the funeral liturgies, the coffin may be sprinkled.[29] This is a gesture denied to the unbaptised, since aspersion is a reference to baptism. Never mind that the child died before her/his parents could have her/him baptised, the unbaptised are without caste.[30]

---

[27] *OCF*: 220, paragraph 334, which has the following footnote attached to it: "In the general catechesis of the faithful, priests and other ministers should explain that the celebration of the funeral rites for children who die before baptism is not intended to weaken the Church's teaching on the necessity of baptism."

[28] In the Vigil rites at paragraphs 349 and 351.
In the Funeral Liturgy at paragraphs 375, 377, 379, 383, 388, 390, 392, 396, 399, 401, 407, 410, 413, 417. In the Committal rites at the Cemetery at paragraphs: 425, 434, 438, 441, 443, 444, 446, 452, 454, 456, 458 463. Similarly in the Committal rites at the Crematorium.

[29] Paragraphs, 375, 390, 396, 415, 436 and parallels.

[30] The distinction between baptised and unbaptised children also occurs in the provision of scripture readings. They are listed in the American edition of *OCF* at pages 247 and 265. The omission of NT epistle readings for the unbaptised indicates that a Funeral Mass will not normally be provided for such an infant. The texts omitted from the Psalter are those psalms which speak of God as shepherd, of the longing confidence of the psalmist in God, of creation's praise for God. The omissions among the Gospel texts include the Marcan text "Let the children come to me", the Johannine texts from the eucharistic discourse of chapter six with their reference to the promise of eternal life, and the text from the Lazarus story. The exclusions demonstrate what appears to be a lack of pastoral sensitivity. Of them all, the most extraordinary is the Marcan Gospel text.
I spoke to a senior monsignor about this differentiation. He agreed that the distinctions jarred, but added that his attitude was that rubrics were simply stage directions and formed no substantial part of the liturgy. He had been present at the funeral of an unbaptised child very soon after the introduction of *OCF*. He said that the tension in the congregation had been almost unbearable and that he had decided there and then to ignore the rubrics. Since the instructions about sprinkling or not sprinkling and about praying this or that prayer were in the rubrics, they formed nothing to which he was required by Canon Law to adhere. His own pastoral practice was to treat every child as baptised. Many parish priests take the same line.
That pastorally sensitive priests are driven to such mental gymnastics by a rite promulgated in 1989/1990 reflects one of two things. Either the Church is holding true to a theological dogma knowing the pastoral cost, yet believing the theological principle to be paramount; or a theological tenet has blunted pastoral sensitivity. Theological acuity is important, but people come first – especially in rites of passage. Many will find the differentiation between baptised and unbaptised children uncongenial. Someone defending the position would argue that truth is more important than congeniality. One response might be that truth is more than propositional accuracy. Christian truth is concerned with love for neighbour and enemy lived out in gentleness and forgiveness. Cf. Jn 8.11b.
Of course, the Catholic position on the baptism of infants gained its greatest advocate in Augustine of Hippo who saw baptism as effective in washing away sin, and defended the baptism of infants on the grounds of original sin. If one is unconvinced by Augustine's baptismal theology at this point, the rubrics of *OCF* are likely to be equally disappointing.

Part III: Funerals for Catechumens

The rites for the funerals of catechumens are not reproduced in full, but guidelines are given in general notes. Once again, differences are drawn which seem to me to be pastorally insensitive. Officiants are reminded:

> In choosing texts and elements of celebration, the minister should bear in mind that the catechumen had not yet celebrated the sacraments of initiation.[31]

It is permissible to place a cross on the coffin, or a bible or book of the Gospels, and the Easter candle may be lit, but the coffin may not be sprinkled with holy water. The catechumen was signed with the cross on admission to the catechumenate, so a cross on the coffin is acceptable.[32] The bible is permitted since "Christ's followers live by the word of God and . . . fidelity to that word leads to eternal life".[33] The Easter candle can be reinterpreted for the poor catechumen. "At its highest level of symbolism, the Easter candle is baptismal". That is a resonance denied in this instance, but other levels of meaning can be offered instead – for example, "Christ's undying presence" among the faithful.[34] But holy water and a pall on the coffin are denied to the deceased catechumen:

> Blessed or holy water reminds the assembly of the saving waters of baptism. Consequently, this symbol is inappropriate for the catechumen.
>
> The Pall, a reminder of the baptismal garment, is similarly unsuitable. [35]

The official line is that a Christian funeral is not being denied to the catechumen. Rather, only those who are fully members of the Church may receive the Church's full rites at death. Yet at paragraph 517, in the note referring to the placing of the bible on the coffin, the explicit presumption is that catechumens may be included among the followers of Christ. They are counted, therefore, as sharers in eternal life. However, the funeral that they will receive (while being a Christian one) will not be the fullness of what the Church offers. To withhold in death what the believer earnestly desired by being a member of the catechumenate is, at the least, questionable.

Nowhere in the text is there the slightest suggestion that the catechumen is not an inheritor of the kingdom. The judgement relates to membership of the Church. Since church has no place beyond death, it would surely be better to draw no distinction against those who are, as the introductory note observes, "Christ's followers".

Part IV: The Office of the Dead

What are offered in the Office of the Dead are variations to the daily offices of Morning and Evening Prayer. The main interest in each case comes at the intercessions. In Morning Prayer, this is to be found in the fourth petition of the litany; in Evening Prayer, in the fifth petition.

---

[31] *OCF*: 366, paragraph 514.

[32] *OCF*: 367 paragraph 518.

[33] *OCF*: 367 paragraph 519. It is worth noting what Jesus said about searching the scriptures and any consequent guarantee of eternal life (Jn 5.39).

[34] *OCF*: 367 paragraph 520.

[35] *OCF*: 368, paragraphs 521 and 522.

The morning petition reads:

> You delivered the three young men from the blazing furnace;
> free the souls of the dead from the punishments their sins have deserved.
> **Lord, bring us to life in Christ.**

Here is the traditional Catholic understanding that the prayers of the living can affect the progress of the dead. It is a transitional statement reflecting the ancient use of the Church. The traditional Protestant stance is that it is too late to pray that there will be a change in the eternal destiny of the dead after their death.[36]

At Evening Prayer, the following petition is made:

> You restored sight to the man born blind
> and opened the eyes of his faith;
> reveal your face to the dead
> who have not seen your glory.
> **Lord, you are our life and our resurrection.**

Part V: Additional Texts

All but two of the additional texts offered are prayers of intercession. Forty-seven prayers are provided for the dead, fifteen for the mourners. This accurately reflects the emphasis of *OCF*, which sees funeral rites as moving the dead from the world of the living into the judgement hall of God and the hope of salvation.[37]

Three prayers from those for the dead demand special attention: one for "A deceased non-Christian married to a Catholic" and two for "One who died by suicide".

> *A deceased non-Christian married to a Catholic*
> Almighty and faithful Creator,
> all things are of your making,
> all people are shaped in your image.
> We now entrust the soul of N. to your goodness.
> In your infinite wisdom and power,
> work in him/her your merciful purpose,
> known to you alone from the beginning of time.
> Console the hearts of those who love him/her
> in the hope that all who trust in you
> will find peace and rest in your kingdom.
> We ask this through Christ our Lord.
> **Amen.**

---

[36] The proof text invariably advanced is Heb 9.27 – with emphasis given to the phrase "and then the judgement".

[37] We have already noted the hierarchical nature of *OCF*. In the case of *Prayers for the Dead*, distinctions are drawn between Popes and bishops, diocesan and other bishops, priests and deacons, religious and secular, baptised and unbaptised. In the list of *Prayers for the Mourners* there is also to be found the distinction between a baptised and an unbaptised child. Of course, since the rites have already drawn the distinction, there is necessarily a need to offer special consolation for parents of the unbaptised.

What is interesting about this prayer is its generosity of spirit in rites which elsewhere make so many distinctions and differences. The Catholic openness in this regard makes the earlier discriminatory attitude so much harder to bear.

> *One who died by suicide*
> God, lover of souls,
> you hold dear what you have made
> and spare all things, for they are yours.
> Look gently on your servant N.,
> and by the blood of the cross
> forgive his/her sins and failings.
> Remember the faith of those who mourn
> and satisfy their longing for that day
> when all will be made new again
> in Christ, our risen Lord,
> who lives and reigns with you for ever and ever.
> **Amen.**

> *One who died by suicide*
> Almighty God and Father of all,
> you strengthen us by the mystery of the cross
> and with the sacrament of your Son's resurrection.
> Have mercy on our brother/sister N.
> Forgive all his/her sins and grant him/her peace.
> May we who mourn this sudden death be comforted
> and consoled by your power and protection.
> We ask this through Christ our Lord.
> **Amen.**

Given the Roman Catholic Church's long opposition to Christian burial for suicides, these two prayers are remarkable simply by their presence. It would be unjust to conclude that the phrase asking for the forgiveness of sins and failings is a direct and intentional reference to the act of suicide as a mortal sin. However, the inference may be drawn by some, and the wording might have been better recast. In the first prayer we might have read:

> and by the blood of the cross
> grant him/her the life of your kingdom.

In the second prayer the phrase "Forgive all his/her sins" need simply be omitted. A separate prayer, seeking the forgiveness of sins "for N and for us all", could then have been drafted to meet the necessary point that we all stand in need of forgiveness – the living and the dead.

The prayer for a stillborn child and those who mourn also demands brief comment:

Lord God,
ever caring and gentle,
we commit to your love this little one,
quickened to life for so short a time.
Enfold him/her in eternal life.
We pray for his/her parents
who are saddened by the loss of their child.
Give them courage
and help them in their pain and grief.
May they all meet one day
in the joy and peace of your kingdom.
We ask this through Christ our Lord.
Amen.

As it stands, this prayer is marked by a weakness and by a short phrase of real skill. The weakness is simply remedied. Whenever prayers are being said relating to a stillborn child or to a child dying near the time of birth, the name of the child is of great importance. Loss of a child in these circumstances is for many the most difficult of all bereavements to suffer. The name of the child should be used wherever possible. This prayer will be pastorally more effective where this is done. However, it has the stunning phrase: " quickened to life for so short a time." Parents to whom I have spoken find that it articulates much of what they feel.

It is in the additional texts that many from non-Roman traditions will find much of immediate practical use. This is probably true of the funerary texts of most traditions. Pastors will look through the lists of prayers for special circumstances and find treasures in the work of other churches. The time spent on drafting such material is of incalculable ecumenical benefit and pastoral care across ecclesiastical boundaries will inevitably be enriched.

Summary

The strengths of *OCF* are in its central focus on the deceased, which is clearly expressed throughout all the rites, and the strong sense of a rite of separation. Pastoral care to the bereaved is delivered precisely in allowing the fullest possible expression of the importance of the one who has died.

The expression of the Paschal Mystery as the hope of the living and the dead permeates the rites. The strong sense that Mass is normative exemplifies this Christological emphasis – even if this is not specifically linked to the sense of passage that funeral rites ought to express. Moreover, the frequent use of baptismal imagery reminds us that the Christian life begins ritually in death – the death of Christ, which itself is a birth to new life.

There is not as clear a sense of transition as the processional nature of the rites and the doctrine of purgatory might lead us to expect. The liturgically alert officiant will probably enable mourners to negotiate this phase of the passage by the way the rite is enacted. Paper liturgy (the text on the page) is often deceptive. It may suggest more than actually occurs; equally, it may inadequately describe what is enacted. We can never take the texts alone for the liturgical reality. Great texts can be marred; poor texts may be rescued.

Despite this, the hierarchical formation of the rites presents a serious problem for the present commentator. Whilst it accurately reflects the nature of the Catholic Church, it intrudes with considerable pastoral insensitivity.[38] My conversations with Catholic parish clergy reveal a similar unease on this point.

Nonetheless, *OCF* represents a major international liturgical achievement. It was one of the last texts to receive approval from the Congregation for Divine Worship. The work of ICEL and the national Bishops' Conferences produced in *OCF* rites worthy of the tradition in its post-Conciliar flowering.[39]

---

[38] Some years ago, there appeared in the *Independent* newspaper a letter on the hierarchical nature of the Roman Catholic church from one of its people. The specific subject of the letter was a declaration of Pope John Paul II's about the ordination of women to the priesthood, but the general remark holds good. Its thrust has an especial force when Death the Leveller arrives. I reproduce here the relevant paragraph of Vincent McLaughlin's letter: "The argument that Jesus did not envisage the ordination of women on the grounds that the NT reports no example of his ordaining a woman is a risky one: the NT reports no instance of Jesus ordaining *anyone* to the priesthood. On the contrary, the only priesthood the NT knows is the priesthood of Jesus himself and of *all* the people of God. The silence of Roman Catholic authorities, papal or episcopal, when their attention is drawn to this fact is deafening" (*Independent*, London, 1 June 1994). Nothing has changed since McLaughlin wrote.

[39] *Liturgiam Authenticam*, published in 2000, has changed the way that liturgical texts may be prepared. The obsequies of *Comme le prévoit* appear to have been said. The present writer prays for its resurrection.

CHAPTER 4

The Anglican Communion: Selected Rites[1]

Introduction

Although the Anglican Communion finds its origins in England in the reign of Henry VIII in the first half of the sixteenth century and its Primate holds his see in Canterbury, it is a mistake to imagine that the Anglican Communion and the Church of England are one and the same thing. The Archbishop of Canterbury is the spiritual leader of a communion claiming to be as universal as that of his separated brother in Rome.

However, whereas the Roman funeral rites published as *The Order of Christian Funerals* are effectively the same in the United States of America as they are in England and Wales, and Scotland, the same unanimity is not to be found in the funeral rites of the Anglican Communion.[2] It is therefore my intention to comment upon a number of texts currently in use or of great historical significance. The following will be cited:

— the early English text established in the *Book of Common Prayer* (1662);

— the latest texts of the Church of England contained in *Common Worship* (2000);

— the *Revised Funeral Rites 1987* of the Scottish Episcopal Church;

— the texts found in *A New Zealand Prayer Book* (1989) from the Church of the Province of New Zealand;

— the texts of the Anglican Church of Australia;

— the texts of the Episcopal Church in the United States of America;

— the texts of the Anglican Church of Canada;

— *An Anglican Prayer Book* (1989) of the Church of the Province of Southern Africa;

— the texts of the Anglican Chruch of Kenya;

— the texts of the Marthomas Syrian Church.

---

[1] For a wider and more detailed review of rites before 2000 see "Sterbebegleitung und Begräbnis in der anglikanischen Tradition", in Becker, H.-J., Fugger, D., Pritzkat, J., and Suss, K. (eds) *Liturgie im Angesicht des Todes.* Vol. 5: *Reformatorische Traditionen der Neuzeit* (Sheppy: 2003b)

[2] *The Order of Christian Funerals* was produced by the International Committee on English in the Liturgy. It was approved for use in the United States of America in 1985, in England and Wales in 1986, and in Scotland in 1987.

The Church of England

The Book of Common Prayer (1662)[3]

Although not a contemporary text, this is effectively the *Ur*-text for Anglican funerals and is still used – sometimes in the modified form of 1928 and sometimes in the form found in *Common Worship* (2000).

Three sets of texts are provided which may be used in the context of dying and death: the Visitation of the Sick, the Communion of the Sick, and the Burial of the Dead. Of these, the second provides resources for use at a home communion: a Collect, and two proposed readings – Epistle (Heb 12.5) and Gospel (Jn 5.24). Various rubrics give practical and pastoral advice. The service may be used with the dying, but is not restricted to this use. Indeed, on most occasions, it is used for those who are too unwell or infirm to attend church.

THE VISITATION OF THE SICK

Nor is the service provided for visitation of the sick simply intended for use with the dying. However, it does offer a "commendatory prayer for a sick person at the point of departure". It is derived from the ancient prayer *Deus, apud quem omnia morientia vivunt*, which came from the Gelasian sacramentary into English use by way of the Sarum Rite.

In this form of the prayer, Cranmer established several motifs which were to inform the funeral service: death as the separation of body and soul and as the gateway to judgement; the need for the living to prepare for their own death by an amendment of life; and an appeal to the mercy of God displayed in the death of Christ (the blood of the Lamb). None of the stances taken by this prayer is particularly surprising in the context of Cranmer's day. We would expect to encounter a body-soul anthropology and a strong eschatological note of judgement with the accompanying call to repentance and cry for mercy. While there is a retrospective note, it is clearly not a "celebration of the life" of the one about to die. Rather, we are confronted with a strong penitential note. Moreover, the prayer is not specifically personal. There is no mention of a Christian name; the reference is to "our dear *brother*". The note is general rather than individual.[4] For those living in the twentieth and twenty-first centuries, the language seems impersonal – even remote. However, Cranmer's intention is to remind us of our common mortality. The prayer assumes that death is frequently ("daily") encountered; there is no privacy or sequestration of death here. Cranmer's context differs from ours; yet we ought not to assume that his call to see death as a gateway to judgement and a call to repentance can be set aside.

---

[3]   Hereafter referred to as *BCP1662*.
[4]   Other forms of this prayer did name the deceased. Cranmer presumably decided that it would be wiser to avoid any suggestion of prayers for the dead. The emphases of the sixteenth century were no longer politically acceptable.

The prayer clearly assumes a sense of process (or passage) in dying and death, but we shall need to look at the burial service before coming to any further conclusion.

THE BURIAL OF THE DEAD[5]

The 1662 *Order for the Burial of the Dead* is quite different in style from its predecessor of 1549. Like the 1552 service, it eschews any eucharistic celebration and avoids petitions for the deceased. The theological atmosphere is dark, and this tone is established from the outset. Previous rites had started with an initial rubric indicating that the officiant was to meet the corpse "at the Church stile". This rubric is placed second after a clear definition of those to whom the Church may offer its ministry.

> *Here is to be noted, that the Office ensuing is not to be used for any that die unbaptized, or excommunicate, or have laid violent hands upon themselves.*

Matters of baptism and excommunication may well have been occasioned by two different concerns. By 1662, Baptists had arrived from the European mainland. Their practice of the baptism of believers meant that adherents with families would have repudiated paedo-baptism. Such people could no longer look for the hospitality of the established church in the burial of their dead – assuming, of course, that they wished it. In the course of the establishment of the Church of England the weapon of excommunication had been increasingly used as a political instrument. In previous generations, churchyards had been the last resting place of all in the parish. Catholics were now excluded from grounds and churches that had been seized from Rome in the English Reformation. They could not be buried where their families had been laid to rest. The prohibitions regarding the burial of the unbaptised and the excommunicated had doubtless always been in force (as had the ban on those who had committed suicide). What is noteworthy is this explicit reference to Canon Law in the rubric.

It is worth observing here that, although the opening rubrics speak of the service taking place in the church or at the grave, the rubrics that follow in the 1662 order describe the reading of scripture as taking place while the prayers are said at the graveside. In fact, various factors produced different practices.

BCP1662 assumed a parish church with its own yard in which the dead would be buried. The industrialisation of the nineteenth century and the urbanisation that followed it led to a separation of the church from the place of disposal. By the twentieth century, the service might take place in the parish church or in a chapel at the cemetery or crematorium – or, increasingly, at the Funeral Director's chapel of rest. The committal frequently occurred at a geographical distance from the local church, and so the unity of the rite was imperilled. Further, burial became a far less common form of disposal than cremation, so that at the committal words about committing the body to the ground had to be amended.

---

[5]   The funeral rite found in *BCP1662* presumes burial as the mode of disposal. More than 200 years were to pass before cremation became legal in Britain. Even after its introduction, it was for a considerable time resisted by the Churches. They argued that, since Christ had been buried, this was the appropriate means of dealing with the Christian dead. This may be something of an historical over-simplification. Cremation was quite common in 1st and 2nd century Rome and therefore may have been an option for at least some early Christians.

None of these changes could have ever been in the mind of those who wrote the 1662 liturgy, and it is a testimony to the strength of the rite and the conservatism of religious forms that the order of *BCP1662* has survived for so long.

The rite is extremely brief; its structure very simple:

— Opening Sentences of Scripture
— Psalmody
— A Reading from the New Testament
— A Procession to the Grave
— Committal
— A Threefold *Kyrie*
— The Lord's Prayer
— A Prayer of Commendation
— A Collect
— The Grace

Opening Sentences

The sentences of scripture that stand at the beginning of the service are the same as those used in the earlier rites (Jn 11.25-26; Job 19.25-27; 1 Tim 6.7 and Job 1.21). However in each text there are small changes of wording or of positioning which require some comment.

Jn 11.25-26
The wording used in the *BCP1662* concludes:

whosoever liveth and believeth in me shall never die.[6]

The 1549 service read:

whosoever liveth, and believeth in me, shall not die for ever.[7]

The difference between *never dying* and *not dying for ever* is subtle but clear. Both expressions could include a reference to the "second death" (Rev 2.11; cf. Matt 10.28), but the 1549 reading would more easily yield such an understanding. Whether this was in the minds of those who framed the liturgies cannot at this distance be satisfactorily resolved.

Job 19.25-27
The *BCP166*'s citation of the text includes the reference to the worms eating the flesh; a reference which 1549 adroitly turns.

---

[6] *BCP1662*: 388.

[7] W. Keeling, *Liturgiae Britannicae: or the several editions of the Book of Common Prayer of the Church of England, from its compilation to its last revision; together with the liturgy set forth for use of the Church of Scotland: arranged to shew their respective variations* (2nd edition), William Pickering, London, and J. Deighton, Cambridge, 1851: 329. Page references relating to the 1549 and 1552 rites are taken from Keeling's edition.

BCP1662

I know that my Redeemer liveth, and that he shall stand at the latter day upon the earth. And though after my skin worms destroy this body, yet in my flesh shall I see God: whom I shall see for myself, and mine eyes shall behold, and not another.[8]

1549

I know that my redeemer liveth, and that I shall rise out of the earth in the last day, and shall be covered again with my skin, and shall see God in my flesh; yea, and I myself shall behold him, not with other but with the same eyes.[9]

The 1549 text also turns the redeemer's stand upon the earth into the deceased's individual resurrection. This reflects the reading of the Vulgate; the *BCP1662* reveals the work of English translators.

1 Tim 6.7 and Job 1.21

1662 conflates these texts, while 1549 keeps them separate – although they are still intended to be used together.

The Reading of Scripture

As the funeral procession comes to its first stop in the church, a psalm or psalms may be read. Both Ps 39 and Ps 90 link the transience of human life with judgement for sin, and are used as penitential texts with a plea for mercy. There follows the reading of 1 Cor 15.20-58 – the passage in which St. Paul compares human resurrection with the seed which must die to bring a harvest, and contrasts the lesser glory of the earthly with the greater splendour of the heavenly.

The scriptures chosen speak of the shortness of life, of the darkness of sin (and, therefore, of death) and of the hope of the resurrection. Although the service makes no indication of hymnody or homily, these have generally been fitted into the order before the move to the graveside.

Hymns depend usually upon the availability of an organist and/or a choir, and may be omitted without much comment. The absence of a homily, however, cannot be so easily managed. Increasingly, what has been expected has been a potted biography of the deceased, rather than what the Reformers would have expected – a proclamation of the resurrection to judgement. In part, this is a result of the twentieth century revulsion against earlier lurid depictions of the last things – an aversion which arose from the horrors of mass warfare throughout the world and throughout the century. In part, it arises from the fact that many funerals are for those who, although they are not disqualified by the opening rubric, have with their families rejected institutionalised Christianity and who may not want the officiant to offer much more than a ritualised farewell. Moreover, recent surveys indicate that increasing numbers of churchgoers have no belief in life after death.[10] Such attitudes unnerve a good few ministers.

---

[8]   *BCP1662*: 388.

[9]   Keeling: 329. There is a variant reading: *these eyes* for *the same eyes*.

[10]   See the work of D. J. Davies, University of Durham.

Prayers of Committal

The committal and commendation effectively perform the central ritual action by which the body is laid to rest and the soul commended to God. At the graveside the words of commendation and committal are spoken, followed by prayers which include a version of *Deus, apud quem omnia morientia vivunt* and a Collect.

The committal begins with a citation of Job 14.1 ("Man that is born of a woman") and continues with the *Media Vita*. The mood is sombre and the note of judgement is dominant.[11]

> Yet O Lord God most holy, O Lord most mighty, O holy and most merciful saviour, deliver us not in the bitter pains of eternal death. . . . Judge eternal, suffer us not, at our last hour, for any pains of death, to fall from thee.

As the body is interred, this familiar prayer is said (followed by the words of Rev 14.13):

> Forasmuch as it hath pleased Almighty God of his great mercy to take unto himself the soul of our dear *brother* here departed, we therefore commit *his* body to the ground; earth to earth, ashes to ashes, dust to dust; in sure and certain hope of the Resurrection to eternal life, through our Lord Jesus Christ; who shall change our vile body, that it may be like unto his glorious body, according to the mighty working, whereby he is able to subdue all things to himself.

While the split between committal and commendation suggests a body-soul anthropology, this prayer shows that the resurrection of the body is also envisaged. There is a clear note of passage for the one who is dead, even if *BCP1662* no longer includes any prayer for the dead such as was found either in the earlier books or in the proposed revisions of 1928. While the note of judgement is clearly sounded, the use of

---

[11]   The *Media Vita* represents, in its appearance in funeral rites, the medieval concern with the darker themes of eschatology. The form found in *BCP1662* appears to reflect the translation of Miles Coverdale, the first verse of which Geoffrey Rowell reproduced:

In the myddest of our lyvynge
Death compaseth us rounde about:
Who sholde us now sucour brynge
by whose grace may we come out?
Even thou, Lorde Jesu, alone:
It doth our hartes sore greve truly
That we have offended thee.
O Lord God most holy
O Lord God most holy
O Lord God most myghtie
O holy and mercyfull Savioure,
Thou most worthy God eternall,
Suffre us not at our last hour
For any death from the to fall.
    Kirieleyson.

Rowell discusses *Media Vita* in depth in *The Liturgy of Christian Burial* (79-80).

Rev 14.13 and of the *Kyrie* express the Christian hope that death is the gateway to life eternal.

The Commendation

This section of the rites is based on *Deus, apud quem omnia morientia vivunt* and articulates this hope afresh, while the ensuing Collect reaffirms this, with its expressed assumption that the deceased has died in the faith of Christ.

The 1662 form of *Deus, apud quem omnia morientia vivunt* adopts the shorter form of the 1552 book rather than the extended version of 1549.[12] Even the 1552 version contains a phrase which *BCP1662* deletes. *BCP1662*, reproduced below, asks that "we, with all those that are departed in the true faith of thy holy Name, may have our perfect consummation and bliss", whereas 1552 sought that "we, with this our brother, and all other departed in the true faith of thy holy Name, may have our perfect consummation and bliss". The inclusion of the name of the deceased (whose funeral this now is) finds no place under the increasing influence of the Reformation. The excision indicates that the phrase was regarded as a prayer for the dead.

> *Priest.*
> Almighty God, with whom do live the spirits of them that depart hence in the Lord, and with whom the souls of the faithful, after they are delivered from the burden of the flesh, are in joy and felicity; We give thee hearty thanks, for that it hath pleased thee to deliver this our *brother* out of the miseries of this sinful world; beseeching thee, that it may please thee, of thy gracious goodness, shortly to accomplish the number of thine elect, and to hasten thy kingdom; that we, with all those that are departed in the true faith of thy holy Name, may have our perfect consummation and bliss, both in body and soul, in thy eternal and everlasting glory; through Jesus Christ our Lord. *Amen.*

While the *BCP1662* excises the direct reference to the deceased in the foregoing prayer, the Collect that follows permits those who mourn to express the hope that they may rest in Christ, "as our hope is that this our *brother* doth". The hope for the departed was, presumably, originally less a pious wish than the Pauline hope of faith (*elpis*), which might have fallen foul of being understood as petitionary for the dead. Whether this still holds true is less certain. We might now ask whether there is a shift in credal value between the hope expressed for "our brother" and that earlier referred to in the collect in which those who pray ask not to be sorry "as men without hope" – where the text clearly explicates that hope as Pauline *elpis*.

Summary

The burial service of *BCP1662* reveals a much simpler provision than the earliest rites of the Church of England. The liturgical change reflects the theological shift fostered in the ferment of Cromwell's Commonwealth. The old Catholic concerns with the faithful

---

[12] The prayer *Deus, apud quem omnia morientia vivunt* is derived from the Gelasian Sacramentary and appears in the English tradition in the Sarum rite. See H. A. Wilson (ed.), *The Gelasian Sacramentary: Liber Sacramentorum Romanae Ecclesiae*, OUP, 1894: 299, paragraph 752.

departed have been rejected, and any idea that the living can by their prayers obtain mercy for the dead has been rigorously expunged. The rite assumes that the deceased was a member of the Christian church in good standing (see the opening rubric), but is unwilling to do more than commit the dead to the mercy of God. That mercy is surely needed, since humankind is sinful and subject to the judgement of God (cf. Job 14.1 and *Media Vita*). While the hope of resurrection is not lost, the overall tone is one which declares the awfulness of the last things. The intention is as much to warn the living, and to use this instance of death as a reminder of the mortality of all, as it is to depict death as the gateway to life eternal.

Perhaps the exhortatory qualities of the rite had their place. Within three years of the *BCP1662*'s introduction, the Great Plague had arrived and was sweeping the South and Midlands of England, taking in its wake thousands earlier than they might otherwise have expected. In the midst of life, we are in death!

Such attention as is given to the bereaved in this rite is essentially parenetic. The death of another gives occasion for reflection upon our own mortality and the amendment of life accordingly.

This note of common mortality is very strong in *BCP1662*. In the twenty-first century, the text may appear impersonal. There is no mention of the deceased's name; reference is always to *"our brother"*. To modern ears and sensibilities, this is all too remote; we want to name the one who has died. Yet we are quite content with keeping death itself at arm's length. Cranmer's contemporaries were intimate with death and dying as we are not. We have simply transposed intimacy and remoteness.

The Christian hope of life in Christ, gained by trust in the merits of his passion, is a keynote of Cranmer's rite. The future predicated by *BCP1662* is not a vague hope that we may survive in some shadowy after-world or find ourselves reborn into the wheel of life. Drawing directly from 1 Cor 15, personal eschatology is seen as resurrection life in Christ. The Collect at the conclusion of the service concludes resoundingly with the words of Matt 25.34:

Come, ye blessed children of my Father, receive the kingdom prepared for you from the beginning of the world.[13]

When we ask what elements of a rite of passage this text displays, then we may note the strong sense of separation which the references to the finality of death evince. There is also a transitional state which refers both to the deceased and to the bereaved: for the dead, there is the immediate prospect of judgement; for the living, there is a call to an amendment of life. The sense of incorporation is really focussed upon the dead, and is expressed in the language of life in Christ and "receiving the kingdom".

BCP1662 offers only one service for a funeral. It is, therefore, unrealistic to expect a highly articulated rite of passage that more recent liturgies attempt to provide by means of a series of staged rites. Nonetheless, *BCP1662* assumes a physical procession from either the lychgate or the church door into church and thence to the graveside. In Cranmer's predominantly rural England, this was probably feasible for the vast majority

---

[13] Matt 25.34 does not include the word "children".

of funerals. In modern urban societies, the procession is often dislocated – even invisible.[14]

BCP1662 is the Anglican liturgical bedrock: all that has followed it has grown from it or reacted to it. Its importance is beyond question. Yet it is a text of its time – what else could it be? – and our day is different. On three occasions in the twentieth century, in 1928, 1965 and 1980, revisions were made by the Church of England. As the year 2001 dawned, a new set of liturgical books was in use under the title *Common Worship.*

Common Worship (2000)

Common Worship provides the kind of staged rites referred to above.[15] The following services are offered for use:

—   Ministry at the Time of Death
—   Before the Funeral
—   The Funeral (with a separate order for the funeral of a child)
—   After the Funeral

In addition, resources are supplied for use with the dying and at funeral and memorial services.

The brevity and simplicity of the single service found in *BCP1622* are replaced by a series of services with many options.[16] However, this diversity is not unique to *Common Worship*, it is shared by the recent funerary texts of many other Christian traditions. It arises by way of a response to the adverse criticism of *BCP1662* of its being impersonal and remote. There has been a desire to make the funeral personal and relevant. This comes at a time in Western Europe when the Christian Church experiences a huge decline in Sunday attendance and national influence. One of the few occasions when the churches are still expected to be automatically available is the funeral. Little wonder, then, that liturgies are cast in approachable and user-friendly styles!

MINISTRY AT THE TIME OF DEATH
We turn first to examine the resource provided for use with the dying. The structure of the rite is divided into two: the first two elements are for use with the dying person alone, the remainder is for use with others present.

—   Preparation
—   Reconciliation
—   Opening Prayer
—   The Word of God

---

[14]   However, in closely-knit communities, the funeral procession still persists. In Northern Ireland, in the East End of London, the difficulties of the urban environment are often overcome.
[15]   If we needed any proof that the ritual and liturgical significance of death is still of importance, we would have only to compare the provisions made in the 1662 *Book of Common Prayer* (some 25 pages if we include the Visitation of the Sick) with those of the 2000 service book *Common Worship* (nearly 180 pages).
[16]   The effect, at times, is almost that of a multiple-choice questionnaire!

— Prayers

— Laying on of Hands and Anointing

— Holy Communion

— Commendation

— Prayer when someone has just died

The preparatory material includes scripture sentences and the Lord's Prayer.[17]

Ministry with the dying continues with a penitential rite. As provided, this offers a general form of confession with a general absolution. If death is imminent, this is probably all that is practicable. However, there will be those (priests and people) who would wish to prepare for death with a more thorough examination of conscience and a more specific declaration of pardon.

A prayer for peace and faith is made, using an antiphonal setting of verses from Ps 130. Scripture is read and a brief credal statement may be said.[18] A litany follows seeking deliverance "from all evil and from eternal death", pardon for "all *N*'s sins", and the gifts of peace and faith. The *Agnus Dei* is said antiphonally.

The laying on of hands and the celebration of Holy Communion may follow. The laying on of hands and anointing (which are optional) are not such as suggested in Jas 5.14f. The notion of healing is far away; what is here proposed is chrismation for death.

The rite concludes with an act of commendation and a blessing. This begins with the Lord's Prayer. There follow three forms of words to be used with the dying person, two of which are variants of the *Proficiscere*. Two prayers of commendation are offered as alternatives: the first based on Rom 8.38-39, the second including the old form:

> Acknowledge, we pray, a sheep of your own fold,
> a lamb of your own flock
> a sinner of your own redeeming.

---

[17] The texts suggested are listed below in the order proposed by *Common Worship* at pages 217-218: Rom 8.35; Rom 14.8; Rom 14.9; 2 Cor 5.1; 1 Thess 4.17; 1 Jn 3.2; Ps 25.1; Ps 27.1; Ps 27.13-14; Ps 31.5; Ps 42.2; Matt 25.34; Lk 23.43; Jn 6.40; Jn 14.2; Jn 14.3; Jn 17.24; Acts 7.59; Lam 3.22-23.

[18] The specific texts proposed here are: Rom 8.35, 37-39; Pss 23; 139; Jn 6.35-40 (53-58).

Other texts are suggested in an extensive appendix (*CW*: 383-391) for use at any of the rites provided: Jn 6.35-40; Jn 11.17-27; Jn 14.1-6; Rom 8.31-39; 1 Cor 15.1-26, 35-38, 42-44a, 53-58; 1 Cor 15.20-58; 1 Thess 4.13-18; Rev 21.1-7. These are printed in full.

OT AND APOCRYPHA: Gen 42.29-38; 2 Sam 1.17, 23-27; 2 Sam 12.16-23; Job 19.23-27; Isa 53.1-10; Isa 61.1-3; Lam 3.22-26, 31-33; Dan 12.1-3(5-9); Wisd 2.22-3.5, 9; Wisd 4.8-11, 13-15; Ecclus 38.16-23.

PSALMS: Pss 6; 23; 25; 27; 32; 38.9-22; 42; 90; 116; 118.4-29; 121; 139

NT: Matt 25.31-46; Mk 10.13-16; Mk 15.33-39; 16.1-6; Lk 12.35-40; Lk 24.1-9(10-11); Jn 5.(19-20) 21-29; Jn 6.35-40 (53-58); Jn 11.17-27; Jn 14.1-6; Jn 19.38-42; Jn 20.1-11; Rom 6.3-8 (9-11); Rom 8.18-25 (26-30); Rom 8.31-39; Rom 14.7-12; 1 Cor 15.1-26, 35-38, 42-44a, 53-58; 1 Cor 15.20-58; 2 Cor 4.7-15; 2 Cor 4.16-5.10; Eph 3.14-19 (20-21); Phil 3.10-21; 1 Thess 4.13-18; 2 Tim 2.8-13; 1 Pet 1.3-9; 1 Jn 3.1-3; Rev 7.9-17; Rev 21.1-7; Rev 21.22-27; 22.3b-5.

A further list of readings suitable for the funeral of a child is also offered: Ps 84.1-4; Song of Solomon 2.10-13; Isa 49.15-16; Jer 1.4-8; Jer 31.15-17; Matt 18.1-5, 10; Jn 10.27-28; 1 Cor 13.1-13.

The prayer of St. Anselm ("Jesus, like a mother you gather your people to you") may be used at or just after death, and the rite concludes with a blessing.

Provision is also made within this section for prayers where someone has just died. The rubric suggests that a family member or a friend may lead the saying of these prayers which entrust the deceased to God, and seek the joy of heaven for the one who has died and the wisdom and peace of God for those who remain.

The range of texts offered indicates a desire to serve as wide a range of conditions as possible and an ecumenical longing to include the riches of the Christian Church worldwide and historical. It gives to this rite (and to those that follow) a depth and a variety that is vibrantly rich, offering pastoral sensitivity in the time of grief and sorrow with a vision of the heavenly hope.

BEFORE THE FUNERAL
Several services are offered for use before the funeral, providing for a range of situations:

— pastoral visitation (either on hearing news of the death or as part of the planning of the funeral service)
— a service for those who will not be able to be present at the funeral
— reception of the body into church
— a vigil
— a short preparation at home on the morning of the funeral

While each of these services carries its own pastoral response to death, it is to the reception rite and the vigil that I wish to turn the focus of attention, for they carry the ritual journey forward.

RECEPTION OF THE BODY INTO CHURCH
This rite proposes the sprinkling of the coffin, by which a candle may be placed. Although these signs are simply suggested, they indicate clearly the baptismal and paschal echoes that underpin the rite. The scriptures it proposes speak of the comfort to be found in Christ and of the glorious hope of the resurrection. Above all, the proposed opening prayer for use at the aspersion of the coffin declares the nature of the rite: a petition rooted in baptism, the sacrament of death and resurrection:

> Grant, Lord,
> that we who are baptized into the death
>   of your Son our Saviour Jesus Christ
> may continually put to death our evil desires
>   and be buried with him;
> and that through the grave and gate of death
> we may pass to our joyful resurrection;
> through his merits,

who died and was buried and rose again for us,
your Son Jesus Christ our Lord.
Amen.

A FUNERAL VIGIL
The vigil may be held in the church or any other suitable place. It begins by gathering those present with the hope of the Revelation – that we may be gathered at another place where there are no tears and where death is no longer known. With a selection of scriptures that provide assurance and comfort and refer to the faithfulness of God and the hope of heaven, the journeying note continues. The living and departed are summoned into God's presence by the risen Christ who goes before us.

Seasonal readings are provided for Easter and Advent, and special provision is made in the event of unexpected death and for the funeral of a child.[19]

In this rite, it is the concluding phase with its strong Trinitarian emphasis that summarises best that way to which death recalls us:

The Lord God almighty is our Father:
he loves us and tenderly cares for us.

The Lord Jesus Christ is our Saviour:
he has redeemed us and will defend us to the end.

The Lord, the Holy Spirit is among us:
he will lead us in God's holy way.

To God almighty, Father, Son and Holy Spirit,
be praise and glory today and for ever. Amen.

These two rites of reception and vigil establish clearly the intention of those who drafted the funeral rites in *Common Worship*. Death is our common lot; the death of another brings us all face to face with God – the God of our journey.

---

[19] Readings are provided to cover a variety of situations. Each offers the following: OT, Psalm, NT, Canticle and Gospel.

ASSURANCE AND COMFORT: Isa 61.1-3; Ps 139; 1 Pet 1.3-9; A Song of God's Children (based on Rom 8.2, 14, 15b-19); Jn 14.1-6.

THE FAITHFULNESS OF GOD: Isa 53.1-10; Ps 116.1-8 (9-17); Rom 8.31-39; A Song of the Justified (based on Rom 4.24-25; 5.1-5, 8, 9, 11); Jn 6.35-40 (53-58).

THE HOPE OF HEAVEN: Wisd 3.1-5, 9; Ps 25.1-9; Rom 8.18-25 (26-30); A Song of Faith (based on 1 Pet 1.3-5, 18-19, 21); Jn 14.1-6.

EASTER: Job 19.23-27; Ps 32; 2 Tim 2.8-13; A Song of the Redeemed (based on Rev 7.9, 10, 14b-17); Jn 11.17-27.

AN UNEXPECTED DEATH: Wisd 4.8-11, 13-15; Ps 6; 2 Cor 4.7-15; The Song of Simeon (the *Nunc Dimittis*); Lk 12.35-40.

A CHILD: 2 Sam 12.16-23; Ps 38.9-22; Wisd 4.8-11, 13-15; A Song of St. Anselm (from Anselm of Canterbury); Lk 12.35-40

THE FUNERAL

Provision is made for funeral rites to occur with or without a celebration of the Eucharist. The main structure of the Funeral Service follows the traditional form:

— The Gathering
— [Sentences]
— Introduction
— [Prayer]
— [Prayer of Penitence]
— The Collect
— Readings and Sermon
— Prayers
— Commendation and Farewell
— The Committal
— The Dismissal

Where the service occurs within the celebration of Holy Communion, the eucharistic section of the rite occurs between the prayers after the sermon and the commendation.

It is of interest that where a tribute is to be offered separately from the funeral sermon, the pastoral notes provided at the end of the service text suggest that it should occur in the Gathering phase of the rite:

> It is preferable not to interrupt the flow of the Reading(s) and sermon with a tribute of this kind.

The gathering begins with optional sentences of scripture.[20] There follows an introduction stating the purpose for which the congregation is met, and this may be followed by a prayer. A hymn may be sung, and where a tribute is to be made distinct from the sermon, its place is here. Prayers of penitence may be offered, which take the form of a general confession or of a threefold antiphonal *Kyrie*. A time for silent prayer is followed by the set Collect.[21]

> Merciful Father,
> hear our prayers and comfort us;

---

[20] Jn 11.25-26; Rom 8.38-39; 1 Thess 4.14, 17b-18; 1 Tim 6.7 and Job 1.21b; Lam 3.22-23; Matt 5.4; Jn 3.16.

A list of Supplementary Texts is offered. It includes some of the texts listed immediately above. However, for the sake of completeness I note them below.

PSALMS: Pss 16.10; 46.1; 130.1.

OT: Job 19.25-27; Eccl 5.15-16; Lam 3.22-23.

NT: Matt 5.4; Matt 25.34; Lk 23.43; Jn 3.16; Jn 6.40; Jn 6.54 (at the celebration of Holy Communion); Jn 11.25-26; Jn 14.2-3; Rom 8.38-39; 1 Cor 2.9-10a; 1 Cor 15.25-26; 2 Cor 1.3-4; 2 Cor 5.1; 1 Thess 4.14, 17b-18; 1 Tim 6.7 (and Job 1.21b).

[21] It is worth observing that in this gathering section of the rite only the introduction with its statement of purpose and the collect are required; the remaining elements are optional.

renew our trust in your Son,
whom you raised from the dead;
strengthen our faith
that all who have died in the love of Christ
will share in his resurrection;
who lives and reigns with you,
in the unity of the Holy Spirit,
one God, now and for ever.
Amen.

The readings and sermon follow. Readings may be selected from the lists noted earlier and Ps 23 (or another psalm or hymn) is used. A NT reading must be read; a reading from the OT or Apocrypha is optional. It is worth noting here that the rubric relating to the sermon is direct and to the point:

A sermon is preached.

The sermon is no longer optional, it is required. Explanatory notes to the service declare that the sermon "is to proclaim the gospel in the context of the death of this particular person". The clarity of this comment is both admirable and exemplary. The sermon is not a celebration of the life of the deceased; it is a celebration of Christ, risen from the dead. The gospel gives hope in the face of death; and it does so by proclaiming the resurrection of Christ.

The Commendation and Committal do not mark an absolute separation of body and soul. The Committal is obviously concerned with the body's return to the elements; but the Commendation, by avoiding soul-language, steers the anthropology away from body-soul dualism. Moreover, by using the language of transformation and resurrection in relation to the body, the Committal offers an integrative view of human personality – even if most mourners (and some officiants) do not notice it.

When the service includes a celebration of the Eucharist, the Peace is introduced with the words of Jn 14.27 and 14.1. The remainder of the rite follows the order found in *Common Worship: Services and Prayers for the Church of England.* The Propers resonate with the Easter and resurrection hope and the acclamation takes the form:

Praise to you, Lord Jesus:
dying you destroyed our death,
rising you restored our life:
Lord Jesus, come in glory.

The suggested words to be used at the administration are:

The bread of heaven in Christ Jesus.
The cup of life in Christ Jesus.

Those from the Protestant wing of the Church of England may be left wondering, "Who is the eucharist for? Is this a Requiem Mass?" Given that this text is authorised rather than commended, we must assume that a reassuring answer was given to those inclined to be suspicious.[22] Traditionally, Evangelicals would not have normally celebrated Holy Communion at a funeral service. However, the hard divisions of former days are less rigid than they used to be. Certainly, there is no provision within the authorised rite for "prayers for the dead". It is probable that Catholic clergy will draw upon such prayers. The rubrics and pastoral notes are silent; the matter is left to local custom and practice.

FUNERAL OF A CHILD

Additional resources are made available for use at the funeral of a child. These effectively form separate texts to be used with the structure laid out in the main Funeral Service. They are intended to meet the particular sadness associated with the death of a child. The introductory sentences (apart from Rom 8.38-39 and Rev 7.17) all refer to our childlike dependence upon God, and many of the proposed scripture readings have the same (or similar) resonance.[23]

The prayers call to mind Christ's own childhood and his care for children; they also dare to confront the anger as well as the grief of those who have lost a child, and seek in despair and brokenness the hope and confidence that the child is gathered safely into the love of God.

The parents are given an opportunity to say prayers themselves, giving thanks for what was given as well as seeking comfort in the loss of what has been taken away. Eight prayers are suggested from which a choice may be made, or other appropriate prayers said.

Prayers follow for the parents and for any surviving children. The second of the prayers for the remaining family is phrased to encourage memory that gives future strength.

When we are weary and in need of strength,
when we are lost and sick at heart,
we remember *him/her*.

---

[22] The 1928 and 1980 revisions had encountered considerable resistance from Evangelicals to the Catholic pressure for prayers for the dead. In 1928, the Evangelicals rallied sufficient support in Parliament to prevent the authorisation of the book. In 1980 and 2000, the General Synod adopted the solution of according prayers for the dead a commended rather than authorised status. Catholics were able to use the prayers as "optional extras" (though not, of course, optional to their theological position); Evangelicals were able to say the "full" service without compromising their sensitivities.

Damien Sicard (1978) argues that the Reformation suspicion of the Roman rites of death was misplaced. The old Roman use was simply to sing the *In Paradisum*, which linked biblical images together in the hope (*elpis*) that the dying Christian would be gathered into the community of the faithful in heaven. What the Reformers complained of were pre-Christian practices introduced into the Roman rite from Northern Europe. Sicard's magisterial discussion set the cat among the pigeons – but the pigeons do not seem to have noticed!

[23] Introductory sentences: Isa 66.13; Mk 10.14; 1 Jn 3.2.

Scripture readings: Ps 23; Ps 84.1-4; Song of Solomon 2.10-13; Isa 49.15-16; Jer 1.4-8; Jer 31.15-17; Matt 18.1-5, 10; Mk 10.13-16; Jn 6.37-40; Jn 10.27-28; Rom 8.18, 28, 35, 37-39; 1 Cor 13.1-13; Eph 3.14-19.

When we have a joy we long to share,
when we have decisions that are hard to make,
we remember *him/her*.

At the blowing of the wind and in the chill of winter,
at the opening of the buds and in the rebirth of spring,
we remember *him/her*.

At the blueness of the skies and in the warmth of summer,
at the rustling of the leaves and in the beauty of the autumn,
we remember *him/her*.

At the rising of the sun and at its setting,
we remember *him/her*.[24]

Where the funeral is that of a stillborn child, two prayers are proposed. The first includes the phrase: "Help them [the family] to find assurance that with you nothing is wasted or incomplete". The second asks that the parents' love for each other "may grow and deepen as a result of this experience".

The prayers address the pain and loss of what might have been; that is their strength. They may appear to be attempting too much in the short compass available. That is the perennial problem of funeral rites as we commonly experience them – a pastoral overload of the liturgical situation. To meet this difficulty demands a sea change in our bereavement practice. I suspect that the prayers may not always be able to bear the weight with which they are loaded.

What such a prayer also does, of course, is to raise the interesting question of how we define a human being. At what point during gestation do we accord funeral rites to an occurring death? To a stillborn child, yes. To an aborted foetus, our answers may well vary. For those who argue that the foetus is a human being, an aborted foetus (whether naturally or by external procedure) should logically be afforded a funeral. The Theological Note attaching to the resources tackles this kind of question. In doing so, it draws on advice from Oliver O'Donovan, Regius Professor of Moral and Pastoral Theology in the Oxford University. The Liturgical Commission chose in these circumstances not to take baptism as the touchstone of the "sure and certain hope" of the resurrection. We cannot baptise the dead nor can we baptise *in utero*. The important thing is to remember what baptism signifies: "the desire of the parents and the place of the child within the love of God". The note continues:

> To attribute faith to the dead infant is no more implausible than the assumption made in infant baptism itself.[25]

A final prayer of farewell names the child before God with the names chosen by the parents. This is extraordinarily important. Names are rarely chosen at random; there is

---

[24] The last stanza is reminiscent of the Kohima words used on Remembrance Sunday. This is unlikely to be known by the children, who are encouraged to say the whole.

[25] This (Baptist) commentator might add "and no less implausible either". On the face of it, the pass on infant baptism is effectively sold by this admission.

almost always a meaning or emotional attachment to the name chosen. Indeed, a name can be changed in our estimation by the person bearing it. Even names become unfashionable, or otherwise deemed inelegant, can become cherished simply by their attachment to the scrap of humanity that is our child, our sister, our brother, or our grandchild. For this reason, it may well be helpful to the speak the child's name at the earliest opportunity as well as at the last – and this may also be possible where the child was stillborn but a name had been chosen. If we truly believe that this stillborn child is a child of God, then her name, his name is important.

AFTER THE FUNERAL
Several provisions are made for use after the funeral: a service at home (either immediately after the funeral or at some later time); a rite for the burial of ashes; and a number of suggestions relating to memorial services.

AT HOME AFTER THE FUNERAL
This service is used to bless the home and to establish faith in Christ among those gathered. This it seeks to do with a prayer for peace at the door (drawn from the New Zealand rite – see below) and with readings[26] and psalms.[27]

Prayers follow, either set or perhaps more appropriately informal, with the suggestion that these are especially apposite where there is to be food after the funeral. The short service ends with a recital of Ps 121.

This service looks similar to the rite offered in the *New Zealand Prayer Book* for use at the home after a funeral. The New Zealand rite, with its declaratory words and actions, signals more clearly van Gennep's phase of incorporation. The service under discussion here draws the funeral rites to a close. While it points to the future, it lacks the ritual clarity of the New Zealand provision, which suggests the use of holy water in a quasi-baptismal exorcism, and which articulates the gathering and blessing of the family as it moves into a future where the one who has died is no longer present.

The intention of the service in *Common Worship* is similar, but lacks the conviction of the New Zealand rite. I suspect that, in large measure, this is because the English cultural background differs from the Maori setting. The New Zealand book adapted an existing tradition in its natural cultural milieu; the English service seems to have imitated what it saw as a good thing it could borrow.

THE BURIAL OF ASHES
The service begins with a preparatory greeting in which the minister contrasts the human condition ("dust and ashes") with the "heavenly dwelling place" that God has prepared for those who love him and invites those present to commit the deceased's remains to the earth. Scripture sentences are proposed for use, followed by a selection of readings. Two alternative formulae are offered for the committal of ashes into the

---

[26]   Jn 14.1-3 – the home that Christ prepares; Matt 11.28-30 – the rest offered by Christ whose burden is easy; and Phil 3.20-4.1 – the transformation of our earthly bodies into the form of his glorious body.

[27]   Ps 71.1-6, 17-18 – the promise of deliverance from youth to old age; Ps 126.5-6 – the reminder that God sends weeping to joy; and Ps 139.7 – the remembrance that the darkness (in this case of death and bereavement) is not darkness to God.

ground, and this is followed by the Lord's Prayer and other closing petitions. The rite concludes with a dismissal:

> May the infinite and glorious Trinity,
> the Father, the Son, and the Holy Spirit,
> direct our life in good works,
> and after the journey through this world
> grant us eternal rest with all the saints. **Amen.**

This can be a difficult rite to "stage-manage". It often occurs days, if not weeks, after the funeral; many of those who were present at the funeral are often unable to attend, and for those who are gathered the service frequently has an anticlimactic feeling. People usually describe themselves as already "getting on with their lives", and if they have had to travel any distance, the journey time seems excessive for the brief service. In such circumstances, the officiating minister may feel that there is a lack of ritual adequacy.

It would not be right to criticise this particular service on those grounds; those who prepared these resources have responded to an expressed need. Whether their solution proves satisfactory remains to be seen.

A MEMORIAL SERVICE

Two outlines are suggested for a memorial service – the second for use within a eucharistic celebration.

Within the British scene, memorial services have traditionally been accorded to "good and great". They have had more or less religious content according to the convictions of the person remembered, and they have been unashamedly celebrations of the deceased by his (nearly always his!) friends. Serried ranks of lawyers, actors, the military, civil servants or church dignitaries have joined to laud the departed with a list of his achievements. The tone is frequently cheerful, with stories designed to gild the lily and amuse the congregation – the perfect story, however, will jerk a tear as well as prompt a smile.

The Church of England, with its Cathedrals and great parish churches, frequently acts as hosts to such occasions. Those charged with devising the pastoral offices surrounding death have grasped an awkward nettle. If memorial services are to be held, should they be reserved for the good and the great? Do not "ordinary people" also wish to remember and celebrate the lives of those whom they have lost? If the event is held in church, can it be entirely devoid of any declaration of the Christian hope?

The outlines make it clear that there ought to be some authorised credal content and prayers should be said which should include a penitential element. Moreover, the deceased should be commended to God with authorised forms of words.

In making such provisions, *Common Worship* establishes important Christian markers for memorial services in Church, which in the memorial services for the "good and great" are not always all present. Indeed, on those occasions the credal and penitential elements may often be missing. Those who prepared the guidelines and gave a sample service have taken a courageous step. Whether the "good and great" take heed remains to be seen; but, as St. Paul remarks, the Church is not primarily made up of the mighty or nobly born (cf. 1 Cor 1.26). The memorial services proposed in *Common Worship* give the bereaved an occasion to be glad, but also a reminder to remember not only George or Mabel but also Christ, the firstborn from the dead (Col 1.18; cf. Rom 8.29).

RESOURCES

As its name implies this section provides additional resources for use with the various rites previously described:

— Prayers with Dying People
— Gathering Prayers
— Prayers of Penitence (*Kyries* and Absolutions)
— Collects for Funeral and Memorial Services
— Thanksgiving for the Life of the Departed
— Prayers for Those who Mourn
— Prayers for Readiness to Live in the Light of Eternity
— Litanies and Responsive Prayers
— Prayers of Entrusting and Commending
— Blessings and other Endings
— Prayers for Use after Psalms

Much of this material has been discussed in the commentary on the services and I propose to make no further detailed comment here.

Summary

Common Worship is suffused with the vision of heaven. Throughout its pages, the Church Militant is caught up into the Church Triumphant. The rites reviewed here share in that sense of journey. If the *Alternative Service Book* (1980) was criticised for being prosaic and rather flat, the same charge cannot be levelled here. A strong sense of the power of the image and the centrality of Christ, as the one who goes before, give to the funeral liturgies of *Common Worship* quite a different "feel".

The body-soul anthropology remains, but the language of the resurrection of the body is clear; the immortality of the soul scarcely survives (if at all). The heavenly vision and the sense of movement throughout these texts underline the idea of death as a gateway. There is provision for the backward look, but the overwhelming direction is forward.

A greater sense of passage, manifest both in the staged nature of the rite and a wider scope of provision make for many more text resources. Some find it almost too much; others still long for Cranmer. A liturgical book that lasts nearly three and a half centuries is unlikely in our times; but the texts found here recover and renew notes lost since before 1662. It is a most important contribution.

The Scottish Episcopal Church

Revised Funeral Rites 1987

The *Revised Funeral Rites 1987* are the result of careful consideration not only of the Anglican tradition, but also of the traditions of the wider Christian Church. Where material has been borrowed, thought has been taken as to its original context and purpose, and wherever possible these have been preserved. The rites also reflect a more homogenous theological position than exists in the Church of England. This, in turn, leads to a greater liturgical coherence.

The Introduction describes the rite as having:

> . . . the traditional structure of an office with psalmody, scripture reading and prayer. Where appropriate this can be adapted to become the liturgy of the Word preceding a celebration of Holy Communion.

In describing the function of the rite it continues:

> As well as committing the dead person into the keeping of God, within the context of the resurrection hope, there is a pastoral dimension to a funeral. Attention must be paid to the particular needs of the mourners at that death. Careful choice should be made from the alternative prayers provided. It may be right to discuss all the options explicitly with the bereaved family. On other occasions it may be the responsibility of the parish priest to make a sensitive selection, after listening carefully to the feelings expressed. Where the words provided do not meet the situation, other forms may be devised.

It is most important to observe that what is being offered is not one rite that must be used inflexibly whatever the pastoral circumstances, but a series of psalms, readings and prayers that can be adapted with the family to make in every case a unique funeral service.

PRAYERS WITH RELATIVES AT THE TIME OF BEREAVEMENT

In this rite, there occur four distinctive prayers. The first two commend the departed and the bereaved to the mercy of God, the third is used at the closing of the coffin, the fourth on leaving the house.[28] The third prayer is extraordinarily evocative in its use of language and the fourth is a calm and sensitive prayer of separation. I reproduce the third prayer without further comment:

> Father,
> your servant's eyes have closed
> in the final sleep of death,
> eyes that laughed, eyes that shed tears.

---

[28] This prayer is a condensed form of the prayer written for the French Catholic funeral rites in the early 1970s. Other material in *Revised Funeral Rites 1987* has been taken from the same source.

Let them wake to the full vision of your glory,
and our brother/sister see you face to face;
through Jesus Christ our Lord.
Amen.

THE RECEPTION OF THE COFFIN IN CHURCH BEFORE THE FUNERAL SERVICE
This is introduced by an opening sentence (Deut 33.27) followed by verses from Ps 42.
These are most apposite, echoing the Mozarabic rites where the psalter is articulated by
the congregation not for themselves, but in order to give voice to the cry of the dead:

My soul is thirsty for God, thirsty for the living God:
when shall I come and see his face?

O put your trust in God:
for I will praise him yet,
who is my deliverer and my God.

The reading from Jn 14.2f is followed by two prayers, the second of which is the old
Third Collect for Evening Prayer ("Lighten our darkness, Lord, we pray"). The first
prayer demonstrates how poetic imagery is able to gather into a few words a whole
range of emotion and ambience:

Father,
give peace to your servant,
whose body now rests in this place:
May the prayers of your whole Church uphold him/her
and support us in the face of death's mystery;
may the stillness of this house enter into us,
and our silence be the token of our trust. **Amen.**[29]

The linking of the evening stillness of the church with the stillness and silence of trust is
very powerful, carrying the resonance of Ps 46.10: "Be still, and know that I am God."
    This rite will not invariably take place in an evening, but it is likely to be the
prevailing practice. Moreover, the inclusion of the Third Collect from Evening Prayer
makes an evening context especially suitable.

THE SERVICE IN CHURCH
As was made clear in the Introduction, this service follows the normal pattern:
— Gathering[30]
— The Liturgy of the Word
— Commendation
— Committal

---

[29] *Revised Funeral Rites 1987*: 7.
[30] This categorisation of the opening part of the rite is used for this commentary; it does not appear in the text of the rite.

Gathering
The minister gathers the congregation with the words of Jn 11.25-26; other sentences may be added.[31] There follows a collect; two texts are offered, of which the first in particular gives emphasis to the element of passage in the rite:

> God our maker,
> your creative will gives life to all that is;
> your quickening power brings us to birth.
> Let your love sustain us to the end of our days
> and bring us through death to a new beginning;
> through Jesus Christ our Lord. **Amen.**

Other texts are provided in a section of additional collects.

The Liturgy of the Word
Psalms and readings are then sung or said, followed by a sermon.[32] The rubric for the sermon simply announces it; the permissive *A sermon may be preached* is not found here.

Prayers for the mourners and the prayer of faith should always be said. Additional prayers for particular circumstances are found in an appendix:

— thanksgiving for the life of the departed

— after a long life

— after a short life

— after a courageous death

— after a difficult death

— in sorrow, guilt and retreat

— pardon for the deceased

— in grief

The prayer texts of a confessional nature are of particular interest:

> *In sorrow, guilt and regret*
> Forgiving God,
> in the face of death we discover
> how many things are still undone,
> how much might have been done otherwise.
> Redeem our failure.
> Bind up the wounds of past mistakes.

---

[31] 1 Tim 6.7 and Job 1.21; Jn 3.16; 1 Cor 2.9; 1 Thess 4.14, 18; Lam 3.22-23; Matt 5.4.

[32] PSALMS: Pss 23; 90; 121; 130; 139.1-18.

OT: Isa 61.1-3; Wisd 3.1-9; 5.15-16; Wisd 4.8-15; Ecclus 38.16-23.

NT: Rom 6.3-8; 1 Cor 15.20-22, 51-58; 2 Cor 4.13-18; 1 Pet 1.3-9.

GOSPEL: Jn 6.37-40; Jn 14.1-6.

Transform our guilt to active love,
and by your forgiveness make us whole.
>Lord, in your mercy,
>**Hear our prayer.**

Pardon for the deceased
God our Redeemer,
you love all that you have made,
you are merciful beyond our deserving.
Pardon your servant's sins,
acknowledged or unperceived.
Help us also to forgive as we pray to be forgiven,
through him who on the cross
asked forgiveness for those who wounded him.
>Lord, in your mercy,
>**Hear our prayer.**

The confessional note at a funeral is important, since it is a reminder that the gateway to God is also the gateway to judgement. The Scottish Episcopal Church is not alone in sounding this note, but it is always noteworthy when it occurs.

Commendation

The deceased is commended to God with a short prayer to be followed by a hymn or an anthem: the kontakion and the *Proficiscere, Christiana anima* are suggested.[33]

Committal

Once again, it is the prayers that make the strong impression. There are two options for the Collect, and a Prayer for the Mourners, and a Prayer of Faith – all of which display a sense of appropriate liturgical expression allied to pastoral and theological awareness.

Given the attention which those who wrote these rites paid to the nature of grief and mourning, it is not surprising that the rubric at the end of this section reads:

The Prayer for the Mourners and the Prayer of Faith should always be said.[34]

If the Holy Communion is to be shared, the Liturgy of the Sacrament follows here.

Summary

The committee charged with the preparation of these rites took counsel from Dr Colin Murray Parkes who has for long been associated with the clinical study and care of the bereaved. The Liturgical Committee of the Scottish Episcopal Church chose their adviser well. Not the least of the reasons why their rites are so helpful is the underlying awareness of how bereavement grief needs to express itself both in the immediate

---

[33]   The kontakion referred to throughout this commentary is the Orthodox text "Give rest, O Christ, to your servant with your saints . . .", occurring in a variety of forms but always based on this ancient formula.

[34]   *Revised Funeral Rites 1987*: 10.

context of the funeral and in the continuing pastoral care that bereavement requires. The Christological and anthropological emphases of the texts are traditionally framed.

These 1987 rites led the way among Anglicans to an expressed articulation of the passage of the living and the dead.[35] The Anglican Church in New Zealand subsequently expanded this approach with specifically staged rites (as did the Church of England in its 2000 revision, *Common Worship*). However, unlike these later developments, the Scottish rites of 1987 managed to achieve their purpose in a small booklet of twenty-two pages that could be kept in an officiant's coat or cassock pocket. Such brevity has not commended itself to those drafting succeeding funeral liturgies.

---

[35] We ought perhaps to say "a recovery of an expressed articulation". The earliest rites of 1549 and 1552 had a strong note of the passage to be made by the dead. It was found in the prayers for the dead, which later became contentious as the Protestant Reformation increasingly influenced the Church of England. In 1662, that more Catholic note was silenced. It began to be heard again in the 1928 and 1987 revisions and is found in *Common Worship*; but, as noted in this commentary, it still remains among additional material for use rather than a central note of the Church of England's current liturgy.

The Church of the Province of New Zealand

A New Zealand Prayer Book /He Karakia Mihinare O Aotearoa (1989)

The prayer book published by the Church of the Province of New Zealand in 1989 is bilingual. By no means is this a token gesture to the Maori people. Indeed, an important part of the funeral rites is derived from Maori traditions. These are very significant in their introduction of sensitivities often missing from funeral rites in the British and North American traditions. The final rite, in particular, is immensely powerful.

In the variety of the rites that it offers, the *New Zealand Prayer Book* (*NZPB*) is similar to the Roman Catholic *Order of Christian Funerals*. The Funeral Service *per se* is no longer seen as an adequate response to death, and there is a much wider provision of rites to meet the unfolding process that marks death and bereavement. The pastoral task is structured in such a way that guidance is given to the Christian congregation in its care for the dying, the dead and the bereaved. *NZPB* reflects the growing awareness that the funeral service in isolation is rarely, if ever, an adequate response to death.. Nor do the rites offer an unchanging pattern of events that can be ministered to by the mechanical selection of a given set of words at each inflexible stage.

NZPB begins with a short pastoral note explaining how the services seek to meet the event of death. There is a clear recognition that, while Christian theology will want to proclaim Christ's victory over death, pastoral sensitivity will acknowledge the pain of loss which may be so intense that at first the only response possible seems to be denial. The essay sets out how the rites seek to minister to the threefold nature of rites of passage. Preparation for death and strengthening for life beyond bereavement are features of the rites that encircle the central funeral service.

PRAYER AT TIME OF DEATH

The pastoral notes that precede this ministry begin by observing the importance of preparing people for death. Where a eucharist is offered, the notes suggest that family and friends should be present to share in Holy Communion.

An opening greeting is suggested which will include a text (or texts) of scripture. The texts have been chosen to place human death in the context of the presence of God.[36]

This is followed by the *Nunc Dimittis*, which may be accompanied by the reading of a psalm.[37] The Lord's Prayer is then said. The prayer is available in three versions: the ELLC translation, the Maori setting, and the traditional English form ("Our Father which . . .").

---

[36]   Ps 23.4; Rom 14.8; 1 Pet 1.3.

[37]   The psalms from which selection may be made are: 23; 25; 91; 121.

<u>The Commendation</u>
The commendation referred to in this rite is parallel to the commendation of the person in the funeral itself. The dying person is commended to the care and mercy of God. Both the one who is dying and those who will shortly be bereaved are encouraged to place their trust and confidence in God. Included among the prayers is a form of the *Proficiscere*.

The rite concludes with a blessing, in which an introductory prayer precedes the blessing pronounced in either English or Maori:

> Our Lord Jesus Christ be with you to defend you,
> within you to keep you,
> before you to lead you,
> beside you to guard you,
> and above you to bless you.
> **Amen.**

> God be your comfort, your strength;
> God be your hope and support;
> God be your light and your way;
> and the blessing of God,
> Creator, Redeemer and Giver of life,
> remain with you now and for ever.
> **Amen.**

The psalms and the traditional form of the Lord's Prayer referred to earlier are then printed as additional material.

The importance of this rite lies in placing the dying person and her/his family among the communion of the faithful. It sets the coming separation in the context of the promise of incorporation into Christ.

PRAYER BEFORE A FUNERAL
The introductory rubric to this rite says that the prayers may take place at home, at church, at the *marae*, or wherever the body is to be viewed. A *marae* is a meeting-place or meeting-house where a tribe will assemble for formal debate. Every village has a *marae*, and visitors to the tribe or village will be welcomed at the *marae*. The *marae* is a significant place for the Maori people, and in all the funerary rites of *NZPB* there are suggestions that the *marae* is an appropriate site for liturgical action. Once again, the importance of Maori culture is displayed.

The rite begins with the traditional funeral text – Jn 11.25. However, the translation offered allows for the usual incongruity to be avoided, and yields a considerable pastoral advantage.[38] The text in *NZPB* reads:

---

[38] The incongruity arises since the text suggests that the believer will not die, and yet there she is – in the coffin. It may be argued that the objector has misunderstood the text; but in the context of a funeral, we need to make things plain without being prosaic.

Jesus said,
"I am the resurrection and the life;
even in death,
anyone who believes in me, will live".

The Greek text reads *ho pisteuōn eis eme kān apothanē zēsetai*. It is quite legitimate for the elided *kai* to have a concessive force; and in adopting such a translation, the text gains increased strength, as it now meets the objection about believers who die.

The rite develops to pray for peace and commends the departed to God. The *Nunc Dimittis* and the Lord's Prayer are said,[39] psalms and scripture are read,[40] and the rite concludes with the citation of Jude 24.

This little rite is so brief that some may doubt whether it is a rite. Yet it forms part of the ritual action of separation, and fully deserves to be seen in this light. It is best summarised by the versicle and response that follow the opening sentence of scripture:

God is with us;
God's love unites us,
God's purpose steadies us,
God's Spirit comforts us.
Blessed be God forever.

The presence of God as a uniting, purposive, steadying and comforting influence describes precisely the agenda at a Christian funeral. We bring the living and the departed into the love of God.[41]

THE FUNERAL SERVICE

Not the least of the strengths of the New Zealand rites are the introductory notes. In the case of the notes attaching to the Funeral Service itself, these are directly addressed to the congregation. They are of particular value in giving simple expression to Christian understandings of death. In this way, regular churchgoers are reminded of the faith, and those who are unused to Christian worship (or whose understanding of Christian belief may be slight or non-existent) are addressed honestly but hopefully about our dependence upon God in life and in death. The notes also summarise the forthcoming liturgical action, and provide guidance through the rite.

The Greeting

The service begins with an introductory statement about the rite. The statement falls into two parts: the first relates to the departed, the second to the bereaved. The pastoral and ritual agenda is clearly established from the outset:

We have come together
to remember before God the life of *N*,
to commend her/him to God's keeping,

---

[39] Whenever the Lord's Prayer is said, the three forms are available for use: ELLC, Maori, and traditional.
[40] Pss 27 and/or 139 and Rom 8.31b-39 are proposed.
[41] Cf. Rom 8.38-39, where St. Paul declares that nothing can separate us from the love of God in Christ Jesus.

to commit her/his body to be buried/cremated,
and to comfort those who mourn
with our sympathy and with our love;
in the hope we share
through the death and resurrection
of Jesus Christ.

The three duties to the dead outlined in this prayer form the main structure of the rite:

— remembrance

— commendation

— committal

As the service unfolds, these three phases follow in succession, but at this immediate point there is an invocation of the presence and blessing of God in the form of versicle and response.

The Love of God
In this section, one or more sentences of scripture may be said.[42] There follow a reminder that we need never be separated from God's love and a prayer invoking the comfort and reassurance of scripture and of the Holy Spirit. It is worth remarking that, with the exception of one sentence of scripture (Jn 14.1) and the final prayer, this opening section of the rite is bilingual.

The Remembrance
Attention now turns to the first duty to the dead, that of remembrance. The opening invitation is to silent thanksgiving for the life of the departed. After a silence a prayer is said, articulating the thanks of all, followed by a prayer speaking of death and resurrection and the hope of heaven. The second prayer provides an alternative where the funeral is of a child. The Lord's Prayer follows, and itself precedes the Ministry of the Word.

The Ministry of the Word
A selection of Psalms may be used, with the choice from Pss 23, 121, 130, and 139.1-11.[43] Choices for the scripture readings are set out in an appendix to the funeral liturgies.[44] Following a responsive prayer, a rubric declares: "A minister may speak to the people".

---

[42] Jn 11.25; Jn 14.1; Matt 11.28; Jn 3.16.

[43] The psalms are printed bilingually in the section headed "Alternative Commendation and Committal", which is otherwise the Maori language version of these phases of the service.

[44] The range is considerable:

OT AND APOCRYPHA: Prov 31 (selected verses); Eccl 3.1-14; Isa 25.6a, 7 -9; Isa 40.28-31; Lam 3.(17-21)22-26; 2 Esdr 2.42-48; Wisd 3.1-6 (7, 8), 9; Wisd 4.7-9 (10-12), 13-15.

PSALMS: Pss 23; 25; 27; 46; 103; 121; 130; 139.

EPISTLES AND REVELATION: Rom 6.1-11 (or, 3-4, 8-9 for a child); Rom 8.31b-39; 1 Cor 13; 1 Cor 15.12-19; 1 Cor 15.20-22, 35-38, 42-44, (53-58); 1 Cor 15.20-27a; 1 Cor 15.51-58; 2 Cor 1.3-5; 2 Cor 4.7-14; 2

The permissive form of the rubric seems to indicate that a sermon is not an invariable part of the Anglican funeral rite in New Zealand. In contrast, the *Order of Christian Funerals* is uncompromising on this issue. At the comparable point in *OCF*, the rubric says: "A brief homily is given after the gospel reading".[45]

The Prayers

Intercessions are then made for those who mourn. Two forms are offered. Both seek strength for all who mourn; both speak of God's mercy and compassion as the grounds for trust. The difference is in their structure. The first form finds its congregational participation in three prayers of response (each a sentence long) to an initial intercession by the minister. The second form is more in the nature of a brief litany with each petition eliciting the congregational response "Lord, hear our prayer".

Further prayers speaking of the victory of Christ over death are provided, and the accompanying rubric suggests that one of these may be used. Each prayer links the death and resurrection of Christ with the hope of resurrection to eternal life of the faithful. These prayers conclude with the text of Eph 3.21.

The Commendation

The second duty to the dead is now begun – that of commending her/him to God. One or both of Rom 8.38-39 and 1 Pet 1.3 may be said, either in Maori or English. There then follows an English language rite, which is followed by the English language version of the Committal. The Maori version is set out later. The commendation begins with a recital of the goodness of God, in which confidence the departed is commended

> to God's judgement and mercy,
> to God's forgiveness and love.

There then follows either a version of the *Proficiscere* – the commendation of the old Gelasian sacramentary – or the following:

> Gracious God,
> by your mighty power you gave us life,
> and in your love you have given us new life in Christ.
> We now entrust *N* to your keeping,
> in the faith of Jesus Christ
> who died and rose again,

Cor 4.13-5.10; Phil 3.3-21; Phil 3.20-4.1, 4-7; 1 Thess 4.13-14 (15-18) (also suitable for a child); 1 Pet 1.3-9; Rev 7.9-17 (also suitable for a child); Rev 21.1-7 (also suitable for a child).

GOSPELS: Matt 5.3-10; Mk 10.13-16; Lk 15.11-32; Lk 23.44-49; 24.1-7; Lk 24.13-19 (20-26), 27-35; Jn 5.19-29; Jn 6.36-40; Jn 6.46-58; Jn 10.1-15 (or 11-16); Jn 11.(17-20) 21-27; Jn 12.23-26; Jn 14.1-6.

[45] *OCF*: 109. Many contemporary Anglican funeral rites refer to proclamation in permissive form. This may reflect an Anglican diffidence about sermons, or it may acknowledge a variety in local customs. What it fails to do is to give an unequivocal invitation to the officiant to articulate with the family and friends a contemporary response of Christian faith to the fact of death. At a funeral, this marks a failure in the obligation to proclaim the word in season and out of season. The reading of scripture without explanation is not enough.

and now lives and reigns with you and the Holy Spirit
in glory for ever. **Amen.**

The text of the *Proficiscere* given in this rite offers a form of the opening stanza alone. The full text of the *Proficiscere* refers to the reception of the soul in heaven by angels and archangels, cherubim and seraphim, prophets and patriarchs, apostles and evangelists, and is accompanied by an extended litany. Originally, it was used as a prayer for the dying person, rather than for the dead. Certainly, where death is understood as the separation of the soul from the body, it makes far more sense to use the *Proficiscere* at the time of death rather than after death has occurred. It is a little late then to be telling the soul to go on its journey.

In the funeral rites of the Church of the Province of Southern Africa a form of the antiphon *In Paradisum* is used at the committal, which could equally well be used at this juncture:

> May the angels lead you into paradise;
> may the martyrs come to welcome you
> and take you into the holy city
> the new and eternal Jerusalem.
> May the choirs of angels welcome you.
> Where Lazarus is poor no longer
> may you have eternal rest.[46]

The Committal

The rite now enters upon the third duty to the dead – the committal to the elements. This may take place immediately or at a separate place where the service has been in church but where the cemetery or crematorium is elsewhere.

In the first instance, two alternative forms of committal are suggested: the first addresses the departed person directly while the second refers to the dead in the third person. The officiant may then cite Rev 14.13, after which the following reassurance is given:

> We have been parted from *N*,
> but none of us need ever be separated
> from the love of God.

The prayer that follows is a slightly amended version of the prayer that opens the funeral service in the Church of England's 1928 *Book of Common Prayer* and its *Alternative Service Book* (1980):

> Heavenly Father,
> you have given us a true faith and a sure hope
> in your Son Jesus Christ;
> help us to live as those who believe and trust
> in the communion of saints,

---

[46]   *An Anglican Prayer Book* (1989): 543.

> the forgiveness of sins,
> and the resurrection to eternal life.
> Strengthen this faith and hope in us
> as long as we live;
> so that we in turn
> may not be afraid to die.
> You are Lord of heaven and earth;
> your goodness never fails.
> Have mercy on your people who need your strength
> and bless us now and evermore.
> **Amen.**

The amendments to the form in the *Alternative Service Book 1980* require comment.

The first change is that the order of the second and third lines is inverted. While the meaning of the prayer is in no way altered, the effect of the change is nonetheless to weaken the prayer by obliterating the poetic structure which relied upon an inversion of the normal prose order. The *NZPB* adopts what the *Alternative Service Book* avoided, and the result is prosaic.

The second difference is to move the words "Strengthen this faith and hope in us" from their introductory connection with the reference to the Apostles' Creed to introduce a second half of the prayer. The addition to the clause of the words "as long as we live: so that we in turn may not be afraid to die" is clumsy in comparison with the sparse elegance of the 1928 language, which the *Alternative Service Book* modernised without loss.

The third alteration is in the nature of the addition of the last two sentences, "You are the Lord of heaven and earth, . . ." The sentiments expressed are strongly biblical and they articulate confident dependence upon God; but they weaken the prayer. The literary style is different from what has gone before, and the join is clearly visible. Equally, the petition expressed is quite different in content from the concern of the rest of the prayer, and so it loses force. It would have been better to have written a new prayer to meet the need to which the final sentences address themselves.

The changes have, without exception, enfeebled the original prayer, and it is a mystery as to why they were undertaken.

The Blessing of Peace

By contrast, the dismissal that follows is very clear in expression and intent. It echoes Rom 12.9 and invokes the blessing upon the congregation in the language of hope.

> Go forth into the world in peace,
> be strong and of good courage,
> hold fast that which is good.
> Love and serve the Lord with singleness of heart,
> rejoicing in the power of the Spirit;
> and the peace of the Lord
> be always with you.
> **Amen.**

Alternatively, the grace may be said, or the priest may give the blessing in another form.

A FORM OF COMMITTAL AT A GRAVESIDE OR CREMATORIUM

If the committal is at another place, an alternative form is provided. The texts of 2 Cor 1.3-4 and Deut 33.27 may be said, and further selections are offered under a separate section.[47]

There follow two forms of committal, as before. The first is addressed directly to the dead person – "we commit your body", and the second uses the indirect form "we commit *her/his* body". The provision of forms of commendation and committal that directly address the departed gives a strong expression to the credal faith in the communion of saints. Some might argue that direct address to the departed does not make sufficiently clear the need for separation, for letting the deceased go. However, that is expressed in commending and committing the departed to God and to the elements as the living acknowledge that they can no longer themselves care for those now dead, who must be surrendered to other hands and processes.

After further optional prayers the grace is said or a blessing pronounced. A Maori text is also provided.

A SERVICE FOR THE FUNERAL OF A CHILD

A separate service is provided for the funeral of a child. An opening reassurance to the parents is given with scripture sentences.[48] A prayer is said, alluding to Mk 10.13-16, and the scriptures are read. Ps 23 or another appropriate psalm may be said. There may follow an address and prayers. At the commendation, the words of committal adopt Rev 7.17 as an opening sentence. Final prayers and the Lord's Prayer precede the blessing:

> May Christ the Good Shepherd
> enfold you with love,
> fill you with peace,
> and lead you in hope,
> this day and all your days.
> **Amen.**

TE TIKANGA KARAKIA MO TE TAKAHI WHARE / PRAYERS IN A HOUSE AFTER DEATH

The introductory notes to this service explain how it operates as a post-liminal ritual act.[49] The bereaved family is incorporated into the new world in which the deceased is no longer part of the physical reality. The language and the ritual source of the service are Maori, and the English text is not a translation but a parallel. The commentary here is on the English text.

> *Returning to a house after the death of a family member can be a painful experience for a family. Friends may support them by accompanying them and sharing in a meal.*

---

[47] Job 19.25-26; Ps 25.5-9; Ps 46.1; Ps 103.8-18; Lam 3.22-23; Matt 5.4; Jn 14.1-6; Rom 14.7-9; 1 Cor 2.9; 1 Pet 1.3; Rev 7.17.

[48] Isa 40.11; Mk 10.14.

[49] Post-liminal, that is, to the death; the rite is, of course, *ad liminal* at the house.

In this service the Church marks the family's return home. It reflects the continuing care for their well-being as they take up their life again. In **Te Takahi Whare** *and the meal, the house is re-hallowed for the now smaller family. This is marked by a formal entry into the house.*

The service takes place at the earliest possible time after **The Funeral Service.** *Where possible, every room is visited, either by the minister alone or by the minister leading the bereaved family and friends . . .*

If it is the custom of the people concerned that the house should be sprinkled with water, the water should be sanctified before the service. (The form of sanctifying is given at the conclusion of this service.)

This service may be adapted as appropriate for use in other places.

The rite begins outside the house, and in the name of the Holy Trinity invokes the peace of the triune God. As priest and people enter the house, there is a quelling of the haunting memories and presences of the past:

Open, O God, the door of this house;
enter it and let your light shine here,
to drive away all darkness;
through Jesus Christ our Lord.
Amen.

It is God who opens the door on what is to happen.[50] When God opens the door of this house its future is opened, and the door to the past is shut.

As L. P. Hartley wrote in the prologue of his novel *The Go-Between*, "The past is a foreign country: they do things differently there". The intention of this rite is not to deny the past, but to allow it to be the past. As the darkness is driven away, the light of God (the light of salvation – cf. Ps 27.1) floods in. The Lord's Prayer is said by all and water may then be sprinkled:

We sprinkle this place
to wash away the effects of all evil,
whether of people, or of spiritual powers,
in the name of the Father,
and of the Son, and of the Holy Spirit.
Amen.

The water may be understood as a baptismal reference, and the prayer offered for the sanctifying of water reinforces that understanding. But with the reference to washing away the effects of evil, both personal and demonic, there is also a strong suggestion of exorcism which is increased when the text is taken in conjunction with the earlier call upon God to drive away the darkness.[51]

---

[50]   Although no reference is made, there is an echo of the Revelation to St.John on Patmos: "The words of the holy one, the true one, who has the key of David, who opens and no one shall shut . . ." (Rev 3.7).

[51]   Of course, these are not mutually exclusive understandings. Indeed, part of the meaning of Christian baptism is the driving away of evil. We are buried to sin and raised to newness of life.

There then follow prayers seeking comfort and peace for the mourners, which speak of the dead being at rest and of those who mourn being protected from the forces of evil. The rite concludes with the blessing, which uses the words of Heb 13.20-21.

Summary

In my judgement this rite, which incorporates the bereaved family into the future, is of such great significance that, even if there were no other reason for commending the funeral rites of the *NZPB*, it alone would be sufficient to demand the attention of liturgists who wish to create funeral rites in the future. Although there are orders for the committal of ashes and for the unveiling of a memorial stone, this rite of *Prayers in a House after Death* is a superb climax to funeral provisions that are, in my view, outstanding.

The New Zealand rites are rooted simultaneously in two traditions. A close theological attention to the Christian hope in which Christ leads us from death to life is allied to a strong understanding of indigenous cultures. The two meld to produce rites enabling those who mourn to walk with the dead into the presence of God, to leave the dead with God and to start life afresh – the living and the dead. This ought to be the goal of all Christian funerary liturgy: "the sure and certain hope" of the resurrection.

The Anglican Church of Australia

A Prayer Book for Australia (1995)

In 1995, the Anglican Church of Australia published *A Prayer Book for Australia*, to be used alongside the 1662 *Book of Common Prayer* and *An Australian Prayer Book* of 1978.

A Prayer Book for Australia (*PBAus*) provides, in its pastoral offices, material for ministry with the dying and a range of services for use at funerals. The funerary texts cover the following circumstances:

— Before the Service
— A Funeral Service for use in a church building, the funeral chapel or at the home
— The Holy Communion on the Day of a Funeral
— At the Graveside or Crematorium
— The Interment of Ashes
— A Funeral Service for a Child
— A Funeral Service for an Infant who had died near the time of birth

MINISTRY WITH THE DYING
The texts and resources provided for use in ministry with the dying are arranged under the following headings:

— Preparation
— An Act of Faith
— The Ministry of the Word
— Confession and Absolution
— Anointing
— Prayers
— Commendations
— Blessings

Preparation
The service begins with an opening greeting and scripture sentences.[52] A threefold *Kyrie* may be said followed by the Lord's Prayer. It is worth recording at the outset of comments on *PBAus* that the Anglican Church of Australia uses the ELLC text alone for the Lord's Prayer in this book.

---

[52]   Lam 3.22-23; Ps 46.1; Jn 3.16.

An Act of Faith
A short credal formulary is proposed:

> Holy God,
> Father, Son, and Holy Spirit,
> I trust you,
> I believe in you,
> I love you.
> Jesus, remember me when you come into your kingdom.
> Lord, I believe: help my unbelief.
> Lord Jesus Christ,
> Son of God,
> have mercy on me, a sinner.
> Father, into your hands I commend my spirit.
>
> **In darkness and in light,**
> **in trouble and in joy,**
> **help us, O God, to trust your love,**
> **to seek your purpose,**
> **and to praise your name;**
> **through Jesus Christ our Lord. Amen.**

As with all the material in this rite, these texts are optional and maybe included or omitted, as the situation requires. An Act of Faith of this kind for use at a Christian's death calls to mind the Islamic practice of reciting in the ears of a dying person the appropriate Qur'anic *suras* and the affirmation "There is no God but Allah and Mohammed is his Prophet". Confession of one's sins and of the Holy Name are the best final preparation for death.

The Ministry of the Word
Either Ps 23 or Ps 71.1-6 may be read; these may be followed by other suitable readings of scripture. Proposed are Rom 8.38-39 and Jn 14.1-3.

Confession and Absolution
Where the dying person wishes to make a particular confession of sin, it is suggested that material be used from the rite for Reconciliation of a Penitent. Alternative material is offered in this section, which concludes with a form of absolution.[53]

Anointing
The dying person may be anointed, and a prayer at completion of the anointing draws a parallel between the anointing outwardly with oil and inwardly with the Holy Spirit. The final form of short litany with the response **Shine on your servant with the light of your love** follows in four petitionary clauses:

> In you, O Lord, have I put my trust:
> deliver me in your righteousness.

---

[53]   The material in this section was adapted from the Church of England's *Alternative Service Book 1980*.

Incline your ear to me:
make haste to deliver me.
Be my strong rock, and house of defence:
be my guide and lead me for your name's sake.
I will be glad and rejoice in your mercy:
for you have redeemed me, O Lord God of truth.

Prayers

Two prayer texts are proposed and a litany for use near the time of death. These are drawn and adapted from the Canadian *Book of Alternative Services*.

Commendations

Three forms of commendation are suggested: a form of the *Proficiscere*, the Russian kontakion "Give rest, O Christ, to your servants with your saints" (attributed here to ECUSA's 1977 *Book of Common Prayer*) and this text drawing on Rom 8.38-39:

Gracious God,
nothing in death or life,
nothing in the world as it is,
nothing in the world as it shall be,
nothing in all creation
can separate us from your love.
Jesus commended his spirit into your hands at his last hour.
Into those same hands we now commend your servant N,
that dying to the world, and cleansed from sin,
death may be for *him/her* the gate to life
and to eternal fellowship with you;
through the same Jesus Christ, our Lord. **Amen.**

Blessings

The rite concludes with a blessing and a short anthem of praise. Four forms of blessing are provided, based successively on Col 1.12, the *Proficiscere*, Phil 4.7 and Num 6.24-26. The anthem draws its inspiration from the opening verses of Ps 103.

BEFORE THE FUNERAL SERVICE

Two short groups of material are provided for the reception of the body and the placing of Christian symbols.

Reception of the Body

Where the body is received separately from the funeral rite proper, it is "with confidence in God, the giver of life, who raised the Lord Jesus from the dead" and scripture sentences are used drawn from the main funeral rite. A short prayer is said, a pall may be used to cover the coffin, and flowers "or other similar natural objects" may be placed on or near the coffin, as may other symbols of the person's life.

As this section is set out, it does not bear the marks of a distinctive separate rite, but of an introductory preamble. There are not, therefore, those additional provisions found in the rites of other Churches who do have separate rites for the reception of a body into church.

Placing of Christian Symbols

Similarly, the placing of Christian symbols forms part of the funeral service proper and may occur either at the beginning of that rite or at some other stage during it. Four suggested symbols are itemised:

— a lighted [Easter] candle, with words echoing 2 Tim 1.10 ("you brought life and immortality to light");

— water, with reference to baptism;

— a copy of the scriptures, the source of the deceased's nourishment in faith;

— a cross, recalling Christ's bearing of our sins.

A FUNERAL SERVICE FOR USE IN A CHURCH BUILDING, THE FUNERAL CHAPEL OR AT THE HOME

An opening pastoral note is addressed to the congregation in which the universal sense of the mystery of death and its being marked with appropriate rituals is noted. The Christian's belief in God as the giver of life and in Christ the victor over death is declared and the note concludes with a summary of the purpose of a Christian funeral:

> We gather in the presence of God,
> and remember the person who has died.
> We listen and respond to the Word of God,
> and proclaim the death and resurrection of Christ.
> We give thanks for the life now ended,
> and pray for those in need.
> We leave the deceased in God's care,
> and we continue life's journey.

The service contains the following elements:

— Gathering in God's Name
— The Ministry of the Word
— The Prayers
— The Farewell
— The Committal
— The Blessing and Dismissal

Gathering in God's Name

The Minister greets and gathers the congregation, stating the purpose of their meeting as thanking God for the deceased's life, mourning and honouring the deceased, laying the body to rest and supporting one another in grief. The certainty of our own death and judgement is acknowledged and, confessing Christ's resurrection, the congregation is invited to turn in faith and hope to God.

The words of Jn 11.25 are said or sung and other scriptures may also be read,[54] and a congregational prayer for compassion for one another, the calm of God's peace, the kindling of hope and the gift of joy in the face of grief, may be said. A tribute from a family member or friend may be given here, and the family and congregation may place flowers or other symbols on or near the coffin.[55]

The gathering phase of the rite concludes with a psalm.[56]

The Ministry of the Word

At least one passage of scripture is read.[57] No passage from the Old Testament (other than the Psalter) is proposed. While it may be argued that the specifically Christian texts about death are to be found in the New Testament, this silence about the Hebrew scriptures is remarkable.

The reading of scripture is followed by a sermon and a hymn – an extract from the *Te Deum* (ELLC text) and the anthem *Christ our Passover has been sacrificed for us* are proposed, though others may be used.

The Prayers

This section of the rite offers prayers under a range of headings.

We begin with thanksgiving. Two prayers are proposed; either or both may be used, or other appropriate prayers may be said. The first of the printed prayers suggests things for which thanks may be given. These include the deceased's

— family life and friends;

— contribution to the community;

— commitment to work;

— leisure activities and other interests;

— personal qualities;

— strength in adversity;

— faith, love and hope;

— ministries in the Church.

In a prayer of thanksgiving a penitential note may not be appropriate, but its absence elsewhere in the non-eucharistic form of rite leaves the feeling that congregations may lose sight of this darker note in the generally eulogistic and optimistic tone of the

---

[54] Opening sentences proposed are: Lam 3.22-23; Eccl 5.15-16; Ps 46.1; Ps 130.1; Jn 3.16; 1 Cor 2.9; 1 Cor 15.25-26; Rom 8.38-39.

[55] There is no specific advice about the nature of the symbols that may be placed at or near the coffin. Whether custom and practice discourage the kind of secular symbols prohibited by other church traditions is not clear from the liturgical book.

[56] Pss 23, 90 and 121 are set out in full. Other suitable psalms are suggested: 46; 71; 130 (at the funeral of a child); 139.1-11 (at the funeral of an infant).

[57] Rom 6.3-9; 1 Cor 15.50b-58; Jn 14.1-6 are set out in full.

Other suitable passages are proposed: Rom 8.31-38; 1 Cor 13; 1 Cor 15; 2 Cor 4.16-5.10; Phil 3.10-16, 20-21; 1 Thess 4.13-18; Rev 21.1-7.

Matt 5.1-12a; Jn 6 35-40; Jn 11.17-27; Jn 20.11-18.

service.[58] The second printed prayer recalls the baptism and eucharistic practice of the deceased.

Prayers are then made for those who mourn. The first text proposed is the well known "God of all mercy, giver of all comfort"; the second is taken from the Uniting Church of Australia's 1988 book *Uniting in Worship*.[59]

Additional prayers may be offered or a litany may be used. This latter option is particularly recommended where the service is eucharistic.

The litany begins by rehearsing the coming of Christ to die for us and his resurrection from the dead. It moves in its second stanza to a penitential note. Thereafter it seeks strength for amendment of life, faith for those who mourn and mercy on the dying. The final petition is that we, with all the faithful, may

> be brought to a joyful resurrection
> and the fulfilment of your eternal kingdom

Where the service is not eucharistic, the Lord's Prayer is said (ELLC text).

The Farewell
A non-eucharistic service proceeds to its close with prayers that the faith of the deceased may call the congregation to renew its trust in God's love. The minister then invites those present to entrust the one who has died to the mercy of God. The final prayer of commendation is said congregationally.

The Committal
The penultimate section of the rite allows for committal from church as well as at the graveside or crematorium and follows a traditional form.

The Blessing and Dismissal
The service concludes with the grace or the Aaronic blessing and the simple "Go in peace in the name of Christ. **Amen.**" As the body is carried out, a hymn or anthem may be sung. Two anthems are proposed: a form of the kontakion, and the *Nunc Dimittis* (ELLC text).

THE HOLY COMMUNION ON THE DAY OF A FUNERAL
Where the service includes the celebration of the Eucharist, the eucharistic rite follows the ministry of the word and the prayers and begins with the peace. There follow the Great Thanksgiving, the Breaking of Bread and the Communion, and the Postcommunion.

The Great Thanksgiving
The eucharistic prayer follows the general form of the thanksgiving used by the Anglican Church of Australia. The preface is found below:

---

[58] At the place of committal a final prayer does seek that those present may "use aright the time left to us. while we have opportunity, lead us to repent of our sins and to do what we have left undone."

[59] The Commentary deals with this prayer in its own place in the Uniting Church's funeral rites.

Blessed are you, gracious God,
creator of heaven and earth,
giver of life, and conqueror of death.
By his death on the cross,
your Son Jesus Christ
offered the one true sacrifice for sin,
breaking the power of evil
and putting death to flight.

With all your saints
we give you thanks and praise.

Through his resurrection from the dead
you have given us a new birth into a living hope,
into an inheritance which is imperishable,
undefiled, and unfading,

With all your saints
we give you thanks and praise.

The joy of resurrection fills the universe,
and so we join with angels and archangels
with [N and] all your faithful people,
evermore praising you and saying . . .

A proper memorial acclamation is also provided:

Renew us by your Holy Spirit,
unite us in the body of your Son
and bring us with [N and] all your faithful people
into the joy of your eternal kingdom;
with whom, in the unity of the Holy Spirit,
through Jesus Christ our Lord,
we offer our prayer and praise:

**Blessing and honour and glory and power
are yours for ever and ever. Amen.**

In the eucharistic form of the Funeral Service, the Lord's Prayer (ELLC text) is said here.

The Breaking of Bread and the Communion
This follows the normal pattern of the Anglican Church of Australia.

After Communion
The celebrant says the postcommunion prayer:

Lord of life and death,
we thank you that in your great love
you have given us this foretaste of the heavenly banquet
prepared for all your saints.

Grant that this sacrament of Christ's death may be to us
a comfort in affliction,
a firm assurance of his resurrection,
and a pledge of our inheritance in that kingdom
where death and sorrow are no more,
but all things are made new. **Amen.**

The service resumes at the Farewell.

AT THE GRAVESIDE OR CREMATORIUM
As the body is brought to the place of committal, a hymn may be sung or other music used and the minister prepares the congregation, greeting them with the grace and peace of the Lord. Scripture sentences are spoken,[60] and the body is committed to the elements.

The Committal
Two texts are printed for the beginning of the committal: a form of *Media Vita* and Ps 103.8, 13-17. Either or both may be used. The minister then faces the coffin and commits the body to the elements with words previously noted.

The Prayers
Prayers begin with the Lord's Prayer (ELLC text), the minister offers prayer for grace to use the time left to us for repentance and amendment of life and entreats that God may be our refuge and strength, enabling us to go forward to meet the risen Christ.

The service ends with blessings (drawn from Jude 24-25 and 2 Cor 13.14), the prayer

May God in his infinite love and mercy
bring the whole Church,
living and departed in the Lord Jesus,
to a joyful resurrection
and the fulfilment of his eternal kingdom. **Amen.**

and a final dismissal in the peace of Christ.

THE INTERMENT OF ASHES
This short rite provides for the final disposal of cremated remains in a place of rest. The rubrics are quite clear that what is intended is interment, and not scattering. The service falls into three sections:

— Gathering
— The Interment
— The Prayers

---

[60] Rom 14.8-9; 1 Pet 1.3-4; 1 Thess 4.14; 1 Tim 6.7; Job 1.21.

Gathering

The minister greets those present with the customary versicle and response and an opening sentence.[61] A prayer may follow, giving thanks to God's giver of life for the life of the departed and asking God to

> Preserve among us the good of *his/her* example,
> and keep us in the way of truth,
> until we come to your eternal kingdom

The Interment

The ashes are interred "in a prepared place", as the minister utters a short prayer, claiming the love of God who has created us as the potter fashions the clay. A short acclamation of thanksgiving may be said by all and the minister reads 1 Cor 15.51-53.

The Prayers

The Lord's Prayer (ELLC text) is said, after which the minister continues with a prayer asking that

> we, with all who have believed in you,
> may be united in the full knowledge of your love
> and the unclouded vision of your glory

Additional prayers may be offered, and the service concludes with the grace (2 Cor 13.14) or the blessing (Jude 24-25).

This service is unremarkable other than that it does offer specific provision for what is often required, but for which there is not always precise instruction.

A FUNERAL SERVICE FOR A CHILD

The shape of this rite is identical to that provided for the funeral of an adult. Commentary will, therefore, take note of differences in provision, which highlight use for a child's funeral. What should be noted, both with this service and with that provided for the funeral of an infant, is that language has been kept simple to accommodate the fact that more children are likely to be present on such occasions than at a "normal" funeral.

— Gathering in God's Name
— The Ministry of the Word
— The Prayers
— The Farewell
— The Blessing and Dismissal
— At the Graveside or Crematorium
    — Preparation
    — The Committal

---

[61] Jn 11.25-26; Rom 6.9-10; Rom 8.38-39; 1 Pet 1.3-4.

Gathering in God's Name
The minister's opening greeting directs the congregation to the deep sense of loss occasioned by the death of a child and continues:

> We share this sadness with *his/her* family,
> and seek to support them in their grief.
> Jesus taught that the Kingdom of God belongs to children.
> Therefore in faith and trust we turn to him.

Opening scriptures may be said.[62]
There then follows a rubric suggesting that "if appropriate, the Sermon may follow at this point". Why the sermon should be separated from the ministry of the word, and placed before the formal reading of scripture is not clear to this commentator.[63]

Prayers may be said, and two texts are proposed; the first refers to Mk 10.13-16 and parallel passages and seeks comfort in grief, and the second looks for consolation and healing. A third congregational text seeks trust in God.

Opportunity may be given to friends and family to speak of the child who has died and for the placing of flowers and other symbols of the child's life on the coffin. This may be followed by silence or by music.

This section of the service concludes with responsive psalmody.[64]

The Ministry of the Word
The ministry of the word begins with the reading of scripture.[65] Whereas in the form of service for the funeral of an adult Old Testament readings were not printed in the body of the service text, here they are.

The sermon, if not already preached, follows at this point.

The Prayers
Prayers are offered for the family and all those who mourn. The minister then leads the congregation in thanksgiving for the child's life; particular mention may be made of:

— the way s/he grew and developed

— the way in which s/he reached out to others

— the way in which s/he discovered the world around her/him

— her/his love of school and hobbies

— her/his friendships

---

[62]   Isa 40 11; 1 Jn 3.2; Rev 7.17.

[63]   If a eulogy of the child is intended, that is another matter – though it is thence but a short step to the kind of sentimental panegyric that suggests that childhood is angelic. The angelic view of childhood is superficially supported by those texts that report Jesus as describing the kingdom of God belonging to the childlike. This leads to a misconstrual of Jesus' purpose in these utterances, which surely were not intended to suggest that children or the childlike deserved salvation because of their inherent goodness, but that God wills it because of their inherent vulnerability.

[64]   Pss 23; 130.1-2, 5-6; 103.8, 11-14, 17. The verses of Ps 103 are cast in the second person singular form.

[65]   Isa 11.6-9; selected verses from Lam 3; Rev 21.1-7; Matt 18.1-5; Mk 10.13-16. Other suitable passages suggested are: Rom 8.31-38; Eph 3.14-19 (printed in the Funeral for an Infant); 1 Pet 13-9; Lk 8.43-56.

— her/his courage in suffering

— those who have cared for N

Petition is further made that what was good in the child's example of enjoyment, skill and commitment might be kept alive among us.[66]

Further thanksgivings may be made and these prayers are gathered into the Lord's Prayer (ELLC text).

The Farewell

Two opening prayers are proposed. The first includes the formula "a lamb of your own flock, a child of your own creating". The second is drawn from the *Order of Christian Funerals:* "Tender shepherd of the flock".

The committal may be included at this point, unless it is to happen at another place or at some other time.

The Blessing and Dismissal

The congregation is dismissed in the peace of Christ and a hymn may be sung or other music played as the coffin is borne out.

At the Graveside or Crematorium

The mourners are gathered with the reading of scripture,[67] and the committal follows the normal form. The body is committed to the elements. The Lord's Prayer is said and the minister commends the prayers of those who mourn. Those present are dismissed in the peace of Christ.

A FUNERAL SERVICE FOR AN INFANT WHO HAD DIED NEAR THE TIME OF BIRTH
What is provided for here is not a rite, but a resource for flexible use. The pastoral introduction concludes:

> Parts of it may be used after the burial or cremation, as well as before. Prayers and readings from this service may be used in church, in hospital, or in the home, irrespective of arrangements for burial or cremation.

> Words only are provided: they need to be filled out with silence, touch, actions and gestures.

Resources are made available for the following elements:

---

[66] While this note of thanksgiving is praiseworthy in its tone and intention, it has become a list of commendable forms of behaviour, leading to the inference that the child was deserving of our love and God's love. I wonder about the child whose behaviour was less admirable, who hated school and his/her parents, sneered at teachers and other friendly role models, and was less easy to like. The problem with lists is that, if not all the categories fit, we may be left with little to say. Moreover, we may imply that love can be won or earned by being compliant. Love is not an accounting mechanism – least of all the love of God.

We must, of course, commend all those who have died to God. This, indeed, is the point of a funeral: entrusting of the dead to God, rather than advocating their worth. We all stand in need of God's mercy. Lord Hailsham was asked once whether he feared death. He answered that he did not; what he feared was judgement. He knew whereof he spoke, for he had been head of the English and Welsh judiciary for a long period as Lord Chancellor. "I shall plead guilty," he said, "and throw myself on the mercy of the court."

[67] Proposed texts: 1 Pet 1.3; Rev 7.17; Ps 46.1.

—   The Gathering of the Community
—   The Ministry of the Word
—   The Prayers
—   The Farewell

The Gathering of the Community
The customary versicle and response couplet opens the service, and the minister continues with these words of introduction:

> We gather today in the face of terrible loss.
> We are overwhelmed by the mystery of life and death
>   that we have experienced in N.
> We come together as family and friends
>   to support each other by our love and prayers.
> We grieve over the ending of N's life so near its beginning.
> Jesus loves all little children.
> He died and rose again to bring them and us to fullness of life.
> And so we celebrate God's never-ending love for us,
>   even in the face of death, disappointment and dashed hopes.

Opening sentences of scripture may be read. The section concludes with a congregational prayer.

> **Loving and living God, you are the source of all life.**
> **You make nothing in vain,**
>   **and love all that you have made.**
> **Thank you for sharing with us the power to give life.**
> **Thank you for sending N into our lives.**
> **Give us grace to entrust *her/him* to you,**
>   **knowing *s/he* is safe and secure in your care. Amen.**

The Ministry of the Word
Passages of scripture particularly appropriate to the circumstances have been chosen.[68] A sermon may be preached here or elsewhere in the service; music may be played.

Generally, this commentary has argued that sermons should not be optional. An urgent plea is often made that there should be no sermon in the circumstances of perinatal death. Those who espouse such a view argue that a sermon will seem trite. I understand the pastoral force of that objection; yet to say nothing – not even to articulate that deep groaning which accompanies such a loss – may be even worse. The fact that the sermon might be trite ought to be summons to make it not so. Anything said in the face of death can be trite, yet "words against death" are required. We should prepare with all the greater care to make sure that our ministry ministers the gospel rather than easy platitudes about time being the great healer. The great healer is God,

---

[68]   Ps 139.13, 15-16; Ps 42.1-3, 11; Isa 49.1, 15-16; Eph 3.14-19; Rom 8 (selected verses); Mk 10.13-16.

and the great cure is the cross where the Father sees his son die. God is among the bereaved, and his word against death is our hope. This, at least, is not trite.

The Prayers

Eleven prayer texts are proposed together with a litany. An initial rubric reminds those who lead the prayers to use the names of the infant, mother and father as appropriate.

Prayers (a) and (b) give thanks for life; (c) is specifically for a baby who has died at or before birth; (d) and (e) are petitions for the mother; (f) for the father; (g), (h) and (i) are for the parents jointly; (j) is for all those who mourn; (k) gives thanks for caregivers.

Prayer (d) for the mother makes reference to Mary who "stood by when you were dying" and continues:

> Be near to this mother, *N*.
> Be to her a strong and loving friend.
> Give healing for her hurt,
> and hope in place of desperation
> for you alone can show us how to triumph over death.

The reference to Mary is apposite since she saw her son die, but may be thought a little contrived in this instance since Jesus lived to adulthood.

Prayer (f) for the father equally mixes apparent congruity with difference. The opening sentence names Jesus as "man of sorrows", and, certainly, the father of a dead infant is a sorrowful figure. Yet Jesus' sorrows are quite different in kind and in effect. There is, moreover, a further difficulty, which may arise as the prayer is said. In the final sentence, strength is sought that the father may stand by his partner and share "his" deepest feelings. Why should he share *his* feelings? Why not hers? At a second reading one sees that what is being sought is that the father should not suppress his own feelings (least of all with his partner who may otherwise think that he is unfeeling). However, second readings do not happen in the context of the funeral. This prayer will need careful voicing, if the effect given is not opposite to that intended.

> Man of sorrows, Jesus of Nazareth,
> make your presence known to N in his time of grief.
> In place of emptiness let him know your love.
> In place of confusion let him know your peace.
> In place of despair let him find hope and strength in you.
> Give N strength to stand by his partner,
> to share his deepest feelings,
> to follow your example of strong caring,
> and to receive your comfort.

Each of these prayers aims at a pastoral alignment of the bereaved with central characters of grief in the gospel story, and each prayer is a strong and powerful intercession. Yet each leaves questions that, if they occur to the mourners, may not easily be resolved.

Prayer (g) for the parents jointly is altogether more successful. Taking the form of a short litany, its four sentences are brief and to the point. Each concludes with the versicle and response: Lord in your mercy, **hear our prayer**.

> God of life and love,
> we bring before you N and N, now bereft of their child.
> You know the preparations they made, the hopes they bore,
> the love and joy they shared these past months.
> We stand here with them, sharing something of their emptiness,
> and we believe you are with us.
> Comfort and sustain them in their grief and pain,
> that they may be able to support one another,
> and go forward in their journey together.

Prayer (k) for caregivers remembers medical helpers, those who have prayed, and family members and friends:

> God of all comfort,
> thank you for those who have cared in recent days:
> Through them we have felt something of your love.
> We bless you for their skill, compassion and time,
> and ask you to bless and sustain them.
> Thank you for all they mean to us.

A prayer that thanks God in this simple way achieves two important things. It expresses the thanks that so many in this position feel for those who have shared the burden with them; this is right and good. It also begins to look beyond the immediate situation as it seeks that blessing for others; this is a great gift. The prayer does not attempt to be clever; it expresses the heart. It is a model of its kind.

The litany picks up this outward vision as it prays for all parents whose children have died, for all caregivers, for all who are anxious through a pregnancy. The litany continues to embrace all siblings and grandparents, and all support groups. It looks for a world that understands and cares for those mourning perinatal death. It prays for those experiencing infertility and concludes by remembering those present who hold on "to promises unfulfilled". Like prayer (k) this is a fine prayer, simply crafted and warmly expressive of the heart's depths.

The prayers conclude with the Lord's Prayer (ELLC text).

The Farewell
The standard words of committal are preceded by a short prayer referring to Mk 10.13-16 and using the "sheep of your fold, lamb of your flock" formula. There follows a prayer for trust "in darkness and in light, in trouble and in joy".

Those present are dismissed with the Aaronic blessing.

ADDITIONAL PRAYERS
A separate provision is made of twenty-one additional prayers for use with any of the foregoing rites. They are grouped under a range of headings:

—   thanksgiving for the victory of Christ (3)

—   prayers of thanksgiving and commemoration (4)

—   prayers for those who mourn (3)

—   for a married person (1)

—   after release from suffering (1)

—   suitable for a child who dies before being baptised (1)

—   after a sudden death (1)

—   after a suicide (2)

—   prayers of struggle (5)

The range of provision is wide and helpful; that is its strength. As always with lists, it cannot be comprehensive; that is its weakness.[69] Of the making of lists, there is no end!

Summary

The Anglican Church of Australia has produced extensive funerary rites and resources. In common with many contemporary texts, they are characterised by a pastoral concern for the bereaved. This ought not to obscure the central Christian hope. The Australian prayers are full of reference to the death and resurrection of Jesus, and the pastoral note relating to the sermon is explicit.

The Sermon should contain at least some of the following:

(a)   proclamation of the Christian hope – Christ Crucified and risen;

(b)   acknowledgement of the reality of suffering, and that God in Christ has embraced it;

(c)   sensitive concern for the bereaved;

(d)   thanksgiving to God for the life of the deceased; and

(e)   some reminder of our own coming death and judgement.

The agenda is unarguable, and for the most part the liturgical texts meet it. If there is a hesitation, it is about point (e). The note of judgement was sounded so forcefully in the 1662 *Book of Common Prayer*, that our contemporary liturgies seem sometimes almost apologetic in tone.

The reasons are understandable. The horrors of war in the twentieth century have made us hesitant about some of the lurid language of judgement. A concern to declare the love of God in Christ Jesus and to celebrate his victory over death has gained a greater emphasis. A right and godly reluctance to condemn others, in the knowledge that we are all sinners, has fostered an anxiety not to offend.

The pastoral concern currently predominates, and *A Prayer Book for Australia* expresses the pastoral note well.

---

[69]   In my own work, I have produced similar lists of prayers. From the Australian provision I see things that I have missed; I also see things that they might have included.

The Anglican Church of Canada

The Book of Alternative Services (1985)

The provisions in the *Book of Alternative Services* (*BAS*) offer a preparatory *Ministry at the Time of Death* in addition to three forms of Funeral Service.

MINISTRY AT THE TIME OF DEATH
In effect, this is the initial phase of the task of separation within the funeral rites. The predominant notes are two: petition that God be merciful to the deceased, and the letting go of the deceased by the family and friends. In this, it shares the emphasis of other resources for ministry to the dying and their families and friends that we have examined.[70]

The structure of the liturgical resources provided for ministry at the time of death is as follows:

— Prayers with a Person who is Dying
— Prayers with Family and Friends
— Prayers at Death

Prayers with a Person who is Dying
An opening rubric suggests, if appropriate, the slow, phrase-by-phrase, repetition of the prayers, so that the dying may make their own participation. Otherwise, they should be said in the dying person's name.

The prayers begin with the Lord's Prayer and the *Gloria Patri*. ELLC text and Modified Traditional forms are offered in each case. There follows a simple commendation of the one who is dying into God's care:

Father, Son, and Holy Spirit, help me.
Father, I place myself in your hands.
Holy God, I believe in you.
I trust you.
I love you.

Any others present may then lay their hands on the dying person in silent prayer. The minister may then say:

God of mercy,
look with love on *N*,
and receive *him/her* into your heavenly kingdom.

---

[70] There is no great liturgical difference to be found in the Canadian rite, although it is worth noting that the language used is gender-inclusive, unlike the parallel ECUSA texts in the 1979 *Book of Common Prayer*. The Canadian rites were published six years after those of the Episcopal Church in the United States of America. That period established the new language in which the masculine specifically does not include the feminine, but in which both must be spelled out in distinction and complementarity.

Bless *him/her*
and let *him/her* live with you for ever.
We ask this grace through Christ the Lord.
Amen.

In this clear act of faith, the beginnings of separation and transition are rehearsed.

Prayers with Family and Friends

This phase begins with the reading of scripture sentences.[71] There follows a litany with the response "Have mercy on your servant". The dying person is commended to the triune God, and God's mercy is invoked as the incarnation, passion, burial, resurrection and ascension of Christ and the bestowal of the Spirit are recalled. Deliverance and pardon are sought and petition is made that the dying person may be brought to the blessing and joy of the kingdom. The litany concludes with the versicles of the *Agnus Dei* interspersed with the same response, "Have mercy on your servant".

The prayers conclude with a commendation "that death may be for *him/her* the gate to life and to eternal fellowship with you".

Prayers at Death

At death the kontakion may be said, or a form of the *Proficiscere*.

THE FUNERAL LITURGY

The introductory essay, which precedes the liturgical texts, is an excellent summary of the anthropological, biblical, liturgical, pastoral and ritual constituents that lie behind the structure of a funeral.[72] It repays careful reading and offers to officiating ministers a wise and helpful guide to the task upon which they engage in the Christian funeral. Of particular importance are the reminders of the variety of ways in which human beings in general, and Christians in particular, have thought about death and the warning that the funeral is not the property of the clergy or of the undertaker but of the family and friends of the deceased.

The three rites that follow are patterns provided for various possible situations, which the essay in its conclusion lists and annotates:

(a)   a funeral composed of three events separated by two processions. Prayers are provided for use in the home or in an undertaker's premises; a liturgy is provided for use in church; a committal is provided for use at the grave or other appropriate place.

(b)   a funeral composed of two events: a liturgy in a chapel and a committal at the grave.

(c)   a funeral which takes place entirely in a home or other suitable place. (This form would usually be observed in special circumstances, e.g., when a committal must be deferred because of inclement weather or the distance of the grave.)

---

[71]   Pss 23; 91; 121; Jn 6.37-40; Jn 14.1-6, 23, 27 are proposed for use.
[72]   *BAS*: 565-569.

These various forms of services are provided as broad outlines for different kinds of circumstances and not as rigid alternatives. For instance, although Form I is intended for use in a church ceremony (whether the eucharist is to be celebrated or not), sometimes Form II may be better suited to a funeral in church. Similarly, prayers and readings with family and friends some time before the principal funeral service are not forbidden when Form II is used, although it may be decided not to read all the opening sentences on each occasion and to substitute one of the additional prayers for the opening prayer at one of the services.

Form I

This tri-partite rite provides for prayers in the home or elsewhere, a funeral rite for use in church and the committal.

Prayers in the home are intended to prepare the close mourners as they gather before proceeding to church. Opening scriptures form the greeting.[73] There follows a reading of scripture drawn from a list of suggested suitable passages.[74] A short non-biblical source may be read instead of one of the scripture passages before the gospel.

The readings are followed by prayers, concluding with the Lord's Prayer (ELLC text or Modified Traditional). The part of the rite ends with the words of Deut 33.27.

The Funeral Service in Church (which may be eucharistic) adopts the following structure:

— Greeting and Gathering[75]
— The Proclamation of the Word
— The Prayers of the People
— [Eucharist]
— The Commendation

Greeting and Gathering

The congregation gathers and is greeted with the grace. There follows a hymn, canticle or anthem or a composite formula containing elements of *Media Vita*, the *Trisagion* (as a refrain which may be sung), and the *Libera Me*. Silent prayer may follow, and the collect is said:

> O God, the maker and redeemer of all,
> grant us, with your servant *N*
> and all the faithful departed,

---

[73] Jn 11.25-26; Jn 14.1-3; Rom 8.38-39; Ps 23; Ps 130 are all printed in full. Other suggested psalms are: 90; 121; 122; 126; 132; 134.

[74] OT: Job 19.1, 21-27; Isa 25.6-9; Isa 61.1-3; Lam 3.17-26, 31-33; Dan 12.1-3; Wisd 3.1-6 (7-9).

PSALMS: Pss 23; 25; 42; 51: 90; 121; 122; 126; 130; 134; 139.

NT: Rom 6.3-9; Rom 8.14-19 (34-35, 37-39); Rom 14.7-9; 1 Cor 15.20-28 (35-44a); 1 Cor 15.51-57; 2 Cor 4.7-18; 2 Cor 5.1-9; Phil 3.20-21; 1 Thess 4.13-18; 2 Tim 2.8-12a; 1 Pet 1.3-9; 1 Jn 3.1-2; 1 Jn 4.7-18a; Rev 21.1-7.

GOSPEL: Matt 5.1-12a; Matt 11.25-30; Mk 15.33-39; 16.1-7; Lk 24.13-16 (17-27) 28-35; Jn 5.24-27; Jn 6.37-40; Jn 10.11-16; Jn 11.17-27; Jn 14.1-6; Jn 20.1-9.

[75] This caption is the present commentator's; none is provided in *BAS* for the opening section of the rite.

the sure benefits of your Son's saving passion
and glorious resurrection;
that in the last day,
when you gather up all things into Christ,
we may with them enjoy the fullness of your promises;
through Jesus Christ our Lord,
who lives and reigns with you in the unity of the Holy Spirit,
God for ever and ever. **Amen.**

The Proclamation of the Word
Two or three passages of scripture are read. A passage from the Gospel is always read at a celebration of the Eucharist. There may follow a congregational recitation of the Apostles' Creed (ICET text).

The Prayers of the People
The prayers that follow are led either by a deacon or by a lay member of the community (who may be a close mourner). Each petition evokes the congregational response "Hear us, Lord". Seven petitions seek in turn:

—   light and peace for the Church in heaven and on earth;

—   resurrection to newness of life for the baptised;

—   the guidance of the Spirit for the living;

—   pardon and peace for the faithful;

—   consolation for those who mourn;

—   courage and faith for the bereaved; and

—   grace to entrust the deceased to the mercy of God.

[Eucharist]
Where celebrated the eucharistic order is that normally followed by the Anglican Church of Canada. The Great Thanksgiving contains a short proper for the dead.

. . . we give you thanks and praise,
through Jesus Christ our Lord,
whose victorious rising from the dead
has given to us the hope of resurrection
and the promise of eternal life.

The postcommunion prayer may take the following form:

Almighty God, we thank you
that in your great love you have fed us
with the spiritual food and drink
of the body and blood of your Son Jesus Christ,
and have given us a foretaste
of your heavenly banquet.

Grant that this sacrament may be to us
a comfort in affliction,
and the pledge of our inheritance
in that kingdom where there is no death,
neither sorrow nor crying,
but fullness of joy with all your saints;
through Jesus Christ our Saviour. **Amen.**

The Commendation

The kontakion may be used to begin the commendation, and may be followed with the prayer "Acknowledge, we pray, a sheep of your own fold". The people are then dismissed and the coffin is borne out of church. A suitable hymn, canticle or anthem may be sung. A rubric suggests as particularly appropriate: the *Benedictus*, the *Nunc Dimittis*, or the anthem *Christ our Passover*.

The Committal follows at the place of disposal. It begins with scripture sentences.[76] The deceased is then commended to God "in sure and certain hope of the resurrection" and the body is committed to its resting place. Prayers may then be said. Where there has been a time lapse between the funeral service and the committal, the Lord's Prayer may be said. The rite concludes with a responsive form of the *Requiem aeternam*, followed by the prayer,

May *his/her* soul,
and the souls of all the departed,
through the mercy of God, rest in peace.

The congregation replies with a simple "Amen" rather than with the traditional response "and rise in glory."

The officiant then dismisses the mourners with the prayer of Heb 13.20-21.

Form II

This rite is bi-partite, providing for a service in church and a committal. It uses the same passages of scripture as Form I and has a similar structure. It exists as an alternative form, but it can draw upon material from Form I as appropriate. It requires, therefore, no further comment.

Form III

This is a form for extraordinary use. Indeed, the provision consists solely of a number of suggestions and notes. One note observes that

It is suitable for use in a home or hall when a church building is too far away or unusable because of bad weather, and when the committal must be deferred because of weather or the distance of the grave.

Given the climatic extremes of a Canadian winter and the geographical remoteness of much of Canada, one quite understands and appreciates the circumstances that would give rise to use of Form III.

---

[76] Proposed for use are: Jn 6.37; Rom 8.11; Ps 16.9; Ps 16.11.

Interment of Ashes

Where ashes are to be interred, a short service is proposed. The officiant may greet those present with words of scripture.[77] The remainder of the rite is the same as the Committal rite noted above.

Additional Prayers

Several prayers texts are offered for use as the officiant or celebrant chooses. The first of these is a version of *Deus, apud quem omnia morientia vivunt*. Also included is a form of the prayer "we pray for those we love but see no longer . . .". Perhaps most interesting is the text which makes strong and explicit reference to the communion of saints:

> O God, the king of saints, we praise and glorify your holy name for all your servants who have finished their course in your faith and fear: for the blessed Virgin Mary; for the holy patriarchs, prophets, apostles, and martyrs; and for all your other righteous servants, known to us and unknown; and we pray that, encouraged by their examples, aided by their prayers, and strengthened by their fellowship, we also may be partakers of the inheritance of the saints in light; through the merits of your Son Jesus Christ our Lord. **Amen.**

The prayers generally seek rest for the departed and comfort for the bereaved. In the final, longer, text there occur two paragraphs worthy of particular comment:[78]

> We ask you that *he/she* may go on living in *his/her children, his/her* family and *his/her* friends; in their hearts and minds, in their courage and their consciences.

> We pray for ourselves, who are severely tested by this death, that we do not try to minimise this loss, or seek refuge from it in words alone, and also that we do not brood over it so that it overwhelms us and isolates us from others.

On the face of it, the first of these is the sort of thing that anyone of any faith (or none) might be able to say: the life of the deceased goes on in our remembering. Whether this is enough for Christian faith is open to considerable question. The second petition is stronger, affording a direct confrontation with the dark reality of bereavement grief and its power to entrap mourners so that they fail to emerge into "newness of life". It is, in one sense, "a word against death". However, it is somewhat didactic and serves almost as a reminder to the congregation rather than a petition to God. Nonetheless, the prayer concludes, "We ask this in the name of the risen Lord", and its proponents may feel that this guards sufficiently against the comment made here.

Three additional prayer texts are also suggested for use at the funeral of a child. The first of these alludes to Mk 10.13-16 (and the parallel synoptic passages), and petitions that all may be brought to the heavenly kingdom. The second is made for the parents, that they may not be overwhelmed in their loss but find confidence in the goodness and

---

[77] Job 19.25-27; Rev 14.13.

[78] The prayer is adapted from "For a Dead Person" taken from *Your Word is Near*, Huub Oosterhuis (1968)

strength of God. The third asks that the family may find their hope "in your infinite mercy".

Summary

The general observation ought to be made that the Christian hope of resurrection is fully enunciated throughout these rites. Equally, there is a clear recognition of the darkness of death and the solemnity of judgement. The transitional nature of death is clearly expressed as well as the separation it entails. However, while there are prayers of general intention that the deceased may be granted the joys of all the faithful departed and that the bereaved may be given comfort and strength in the days that follow, there is less clearly expressed the particular need of incorporation.

This is in many ways the most difficult part of the rite of passage to articulate in funeral liturgy. In large measure, this is because it is usually far too early to be speaking of the future at the time of the funeral. Nonetheless, the task needs to be undertaken at a later stage of bereavement, and in common with many others, the Canadian rites do not provide clear proposals as to how the ministry of the Church in this third phase of rites of passage may be liturgically expressed.[79]

---

[79] The Additional Prayers make some general references to the need for solace and hope in the time of bereavement, but not much more. They also include prayers for use at the funeral of a child.

The Episcopal Church in the United States of America

Funerary texts for use in the Episcopal Church in the United States of America (ECUSA) are found in two books: the *Book of Common Prayer* and the more recent *Enriching our Worship*. The material in each book reflects a broadly Catholic stance in its liturgical expression.

The *Book of Common Prayer* (*BCP1979*) offers texts for ministration at the time of death and two forms of burial service. *Enriching Our Worship 2 – Ministry with the Sick or Dying: Burial of a Child* (*EOW2*) contains two forms of a litany at the time of death; these fill out the provisions of *BCP1979* for use at the time of death, and a service for use at the funeral of a child.

The Book of Common Prayer (1979)

MINISTRATION AT THE TIME OF DEATH

Three main provisions are made: a litany to be said at death, prayers for a family vigil before the funeral, and a brief form for the reception of the body into church.

Litany at the Time of Death

The Episcopal Church in the United States of America makes it clear at the outset that praying for the soul of the departed is an important part of the rite. The Litany begins with an antiphonal invocation of the Trinity, with the response, "Have mercy on your servant".

The litany then moves to a threefold petition seeking for the deceased deliverance from evil, sin and tribulation by Christ's incarnation, cross and passion, death and burial, and resurrection and ascension, and by the coming of the Spirit. The congregation makes these petitions its own with the response "Good Lord, deliver *him*" made at each of the three stages. Together with the four petitions which follow and which seek the release of the dying from their sins, the intent is immediately clear; and whatever the Protestant reservations may be, the rites for the vigil and the reception continue the theme of praying for the departed.

Prayers for a Vigil

In the Vigil's opening invitation to prayer the following sentence occurs:

> Let us pray, then, for our brother (sister) *N.*, that *he* may rest from *his* labors, and enter into the light of God's eternal sabbath rest.

If there is no thought that the prayers will achieve something in God to whom the prayers are addressed, there is not much point in praying – unless the intention is simply to soothe the feelings of the mourners. That this is not the case is shown in the rite of Reception, where intercession for the departed is continued, and where a separate prayer is made for those who mourn.

Further prayers are offered that God will receive the one who has died, wash him in the font of everlasting life and clothe him in a heavenly wedding garment as he hears the words "Come, you blessed of my Father" (Matt 25.34). The short section of prayers ends with words from *In Paradisum* and a version *of Deus, apud quem omnia morientia vivunt.*

Reception of the Body
A short order for the reception of a body into church is provided. An initial greeting at the church door is followed by two prayer texts. A psalm or anthem may precede prayers drawn from the material provided for the Vigil.

The resources provided for use in ministry at the time of death, for a vigil and for reception of the body into church are brief and suggestive rather than comprehensively full. It is not surprising, therefore, that in the service texts to be found in *Enriching our Worship* there were further suggestions that both revised the 1979 provisions and expanded upon them.

THE BURIAL OF THE DEAD
Two burial rites are offered in *BCP1979*; Rite One uses traditional archaic language, while Rite Two uses modern language forms.

The Burial of the Dead: Rite One
As with the funeral rites of many other traditions, there are vestiges of the processions of earlier Christian funerals. In the introductory notes, the celebrant is instructed to meet the body and "go before it into the church or towards the grave". There is also a note to remind the minister that the proper liturgical community is the local congregation, and that the funeral is an occasion for its presence:

> Baptized Christians are properly buried from the church. The service should be held at a time when the congregation has opportunity to be present.

The rite takes the following order:
— Opening Sentences
— Collect
— Old Testament[80]
— Psalm or Canticle[81]
— New Testament[82]
— Psalm, Canticle or Hymn[83]
— Gospel
— [Sermon]

---

[80] Isa 25.6-9; Isa 61.1-3; Lam 3.22-26, 31-33; Wisd 3.1-5, 9; Job 19.21-27a.
[81] The psalms proposed, from which a selection may be made, are: Pss 42.1-7; 46; 90.1-12; 121; 130; 139.1-11.
[82] Rom 8.14-19, 34-35, 37-39; 1 Cor 15.20-26, 35-38, 42-44, 53-58; 2 Cor 4.16-5.9; 1 Jn 3.1-2; Rev 7.9-17; Rev 21.2-7.
[83] Pss 23; 27; 106.1-5; 116.

- [Creed]
- [Communion]
- Commendation
- Committal
- Dismissal

A prayer for the consecration of the grave and other additional prayer texts are also offered.

Collect

Two Collects are provided – one for use at the burial of an adult, the other for use at the burial of a child. Each follows a fairly conventional form and requires no particular comment.

Gospel

It is interesting to note that all the proposed texts for the gospel reading are taken from the Fourth Gospel.[84]

[Sermon]

ECUSA continues, in this service book, in the Anglican tradition that regards a sermon as optional. I have referred elsewhere to this use and make no further comment.

[Communion]

Where there is to be a celebration of the Eucharist, the prayer texts are provided to serve as the Prayers of the People. Each prayer text is a single sentence and the sequence moves from the elect as the mystical body of Christ to the final hope of the resurrection. Only two of the intervening prayers refer specifically to the one who has died; one seeks that those who are bereaved may entrust him/her to God's mercy, and the other asks that the deceased "may go from strength to strength in the life of perfect service in thy heavenly kingdom". The remaining petitions are pastorally directed to those who mourn.

Commendation

The twofold farewell to the departed is made with a commendation of the soul to God and a committal of the body to the elements. Where there has been a Eucharist, the Proper Preface of the Commemoration of the Dead is said in place of the postcommunion prayer:

> Almighty God, we thank thee that in thy great love thou hast fed us with the spiritual food and drink of the Body and Blood of thy Son Jesus Christ, and hast given unto us a foretaste of thy heavenly banquet. Grant that this Sacrament may be unto us a comfort in affliction, and a pledge of our inheritance in that kingdom where there is no death, neither sorrow nor crying, but the fullness of joy with all thy saints; through Jesus Christ our Savior. **Amen.**

---

[84]   Jn 5.24-27; Jn 6.37-40; Jn 10.11-16; Jn 11.21-27; Jn 14.1-6.

If the committal is to take place other than at the church, the commendation proceeds with the kontakion "Give rest, O Christ, to thy servant(s) with thy saints . . ." and the prayer "Acknowledge, we humbly beseech thee, a sheep of thine own fold . . ." As the body is taken from the church, a hymn or anthem may be sung or said. Two anthems are proposed, "Christ is risen from the dead, trampling down death by death, and giving life to those in the tomb" or a version of *In Paradisum*.

Committal

The committal begins with a form of the anthem *Media Vita* or verses from Jn 6.37, Rom 8.11 and Ps 16.9, 11. At the point where the body is committed to the elements, the officiant begins "In sure and certain hope of the resurrection to eternal life through our Lord Jesus Christ" and concludes with the Aaronic blessing. The Lord's Prayer is said; the celebrant may use the prayer "O Almighty God, God of the spirits of all flesh, who by a voice from heaven didst proclaim: Blessed are those who die in the Lord . . ."

There may also follow the versicle and response

Rest eternal grant to *him*, O Lord:
And let light perpetual shine upon *him*.

and

May *his* soul, and the souls of all the departed,
through the mercy of God, rest in peace. Amen.

Not offered is the response **"and rise in glory"**.

Dismissal

The mourners are dismissed with the words of Jude 24-25.

Where the burial is in a place not previously consecrated, a prayer is provided for the consecration of the grave. Nine additional prayers for use during the rite are proposed, but need no particular comment. The final prayer is for those who mourn, while the first eight prayers all set death within the context of the Paschal Mystery.

The Burial of the Dead: Rite Two

The rite is an expansion of Rite One in modern language. It is therefore necessary only to comment on the additional material.

Opening Sentences

Additional opening sentences take up Rom 14.8 and Rev 14.13 and a form of the anthem *Media Vita*.

Collect

Two additional collects are suggested, providing a choice of three for use at the burial of an adult. The first roots human death in the hope of the resurrection. The second expresses the mood of mourning, while referring to death as "the gate of eternal life".

Similarly at the burial of a child, Rite Two offers an additional prayer for the parents:

Most merciful God, whose wisdom is beyond our understanding, deal graciously with *NN.* in *their* grief. Surround *them* with your love, that *they* may not be overwhelmed by *their* loss, but have confidence in your goodness, and strength to meet the days to come; through Jesus Christ our Lord. **Amen.**

[The Creed]

The Apostles' Creed is printed in the ICET text of 1975.

[Communion]

For the Prayers of the People, a litany is proposed as an alternative to the provision made in Rite One. Using the response, **Hear us Lord**, the petitions rehearse the raising of Lazarus and Jesus' promise to the repentant dying thief; referring to the deceased's baptism and attendance at the Eucharist, they seek his/her fellowship with the saints at the table of the heavenly kingdom. They conclude with a petition for the comfort of those who mourn.

The Litany assumes the Christian faith and practice of the one who has died. Since it occurs in what is in effect a Requiem Mass, such an assumption is not unreasonable. It is hardly likely that such a funeral rite would be offered (or, indeed, sought) for one who had no Christian formation.

Enriching our Worship 2 (2000)

THE BURIAL OF A CHILD

In *Enriching our Worship 2* (*EOW2*), a separate rite is offered for use after the death of a child.

The pastoral note at the beginning of the service has a paragraph additional to those provided in the *BCP1979* burial services. It deals specifically with the death of a child.

> When children die, it is usually long before their expected span of life. Often they die very suddenly and sometimes violently, whether as victims of abuse, gunfire, or drunken drivers, adding to the trauma of their survivors. The surprise and horror at the death of the child call for a liturgical framework that addresses these different expectations and circumstances.

Changed circumstances and expectations have led us to adapt our responses to infant mortality. One hundred and fifty years ago, when infant mortality was very high, no separate liturgical texts were drafted. The death of the child would have been sad, but not so traumatic in its unexpectedness. Of course, some children would have died in tragic circumstances (many in industrial accidents); others would have died from diseases that are now preventable by immunisation; yet others would have died before reaching their first birthday. Perinatal death was far more common. All this is simply to note that our reaction to the death of a child is heightened by two factors: its comparative rarity, and our contemporary understanding of childhood in developmental terms. For people of our day, the death of a child is seen as a waste of potential, as a theft of what might have been.[85]

The service takes the following structure:

— Gather in the Name of God
— The Lessons
— The Sermon
— The Prayers of the People

The commendation and committal follow.

Gather in the Name of God

The opening sentences are said, or sung as an anthem.[86] The officiant constitutes the assembly by referring to the purpose of their meeting and calling those present to prayer. A choice of opening prayer is offered: each acknowledges the loss of a child; the first seeks our reunion "in your Paradise", while the second more directly seeks comfort for those who mourn.

The Lessons

At least one scripture passage is read, with the note that at the Eucharist the reading of scripture must conclude with the Gospel.[87]

The Sermon

In this rite, at least, the sermon seems to be assumed. It may be followed by the Creed; the 1975 ICET text is reproduced.

The Prayers of the People

The prayers take the form of a litany with the response "O God, have mercy". In succession the parents, brothers and sisters (who are named) and all the family and friends of the dead child are remembered before God. For them is sought support in grief, patience and gentleness "with ourselves", and faith that we will be reunited at the heavenly banquet. The petition for gentleness is very important; there is almost always the feeling at the death of a child that something more might have been done to prevent

---

[85]   This particularly so in developed countries, where the incidence of infant mortality is very low.

[86]   Isa 40.11; Deut 33.27; Isa 66.13a; Hos 11.1a, 3-4; Lam 1.16a; 5.19; Matt 19.14; Rev 7.17.

[87]   The OT readings here are of special note: 2 Sam 12.16-23 (the death of David's child); Isa 65.17-20, 23-25 (I am about to create new heavens and a new earth); Isa 66.7-14 (as a mother comforts her child, so will I comfort you); Jer 31.15-17 (Rachel weeping for her children).
The other readings are listed below.

NT: Rom 8.31-39 (Who will separate us from the love of Christ?); 4.13-14, 18 (we do not want you to be uninformed about those who have died); 1 Jn 3.1-2 (see what love the Father has given us). The NT reading may be followed by a psalm – 121; 139.7-12; 142.1-6.

GOSPEL: Matt 5.1-10 (blessed are those who mourn); Matt 18.1-5, 10-14 (this child is the greatest in the kingdom); Mk 10.13-16 (let the little children come to me) – see also Matt 19.13-15; Lk 18.15-17; Jn 10.11-16 (I am the good Shepherd).

It is worth noting that each of the proposed passages is identified by a text from the reading with the exception of Matt 18 – where a gloss has been introduced.

the tragedy. This feeling of reproach does not always accord with reality – and even where it does, we still need patience and gentleness.

The final petition in the litany asks:

> Finally, our God, help us to become co-creators of the world in which children are happy, healthy, loved and do not know want or hunger, we pray.

There follows a Collect:

> Compassionate God, your ways are beyond our understanding, and your love for those whom you create is greater by far than ours; comfort all who grieve for this child N. Give them the faith to endure the wilderness of bereavement and bring them in the fullness of time to share with N. the light and joy of your eternal presence; through Jesus Christ our Lord. **Amen.**

Where the Eucharist is to be celebrated, the Proper Preface found in *BCP 1977* is used – but in modern language.

The Commendation opens with a version of the kontakion. The minister then commends the deceased to the mercy of God, and addresses the child:

> N., our companion in faith and fellow child of Christ, we entrust you to God.

This is followed by a form of the *Proficiscere*. Alternatively, a commendation with the prayer "Acknowledge a sheep of your own fold" may be used.

The Committal begins with an anthem drawn from either Rev 7.15-17 or Rev 21.3b-4, 7. The coffin is committed to the elements with the formula "in sure and certain hope of the resurrection" and the Aaronic blessing. Then the scripture may be said or sung

> Jesus said to his friends, "You have pain now; but I will see you again, and your hearts will rejoice, and no one will take your joy from you." (Jn 16.22)

This is followed by alternative prayers expressing the bitter grief of losing a child. The first prayer seeks the presence of God "as we struggle to understand the mystery of life and death". The second is simpler in form seeking the light of God's love and peace "in the name of Mary's child, Jesus the risen one". The Lord's Prayer follows, and is given in two parallel forms – with the modern language version to the left (an indication, however subtle, of its preferred status). What is also to be noted is that ECUSA adopts the ELLC text unamended.[88]

Those present are dismissed with the blessing taken from Heb 13.20-21 and a final sentence from 1 Thess 4.13-14.

Additional prayers for use in special circumstances are provided for:

— the death of an infant

— a miscarriage

— a stillbirth or a child who dies soon after birth

---

[88]   The adoption of the ELLC text is significant. In common with all other churches in the Anglican Communion (apart from the Church of England), ECUSA has adopted this ecumenically agreed text without amendment.

- a mother whose child has died near birth
- a child who dies by violence (three options)
- one who has been killed
- those who mourn (four options)
- a child dead by suicide (two options)

Summary

The ECUSA rites are good examples of traditional funeral liturgy, which hint at the nature of rites of passage without making the structure as explicit as the Anglican texts of Scotland and New Zealand do.

With the publication of *EOW2*, the issue of gender in liturgical language has been tackled in relation to talk about human beings. The impression of ECUSA, as in some ways standing in quite a conservative Catholic tradition, is reinforced by the source texts that the rites use, as well as by the language used to describe God (which has remained predominantly masculine). This provokes comment simply because of the very lively contemporary debate on this issue in the United States.

What is equally clear is that much of the language in the prayer texts for those who mourn has drawn (consciously or otherwise) from the work of Elizabeth Kübler-Ross on the stages and phenomena of bereavement grief. Kübler-Ross's influence has been as great in that field as van Gennep's has been on rites of passage. In funeral rites, her work is chiefly revealed in the concentration of ministry for the mourners, and ECUSA is a clear example of this.

The Church of the Province of Southern Africa

An Anglican Prayer Book (1989)

The funerary texts of the Church of the Anglican Province of Southern Africa were published in 1989.[89] The Preface to the rites sets out with exemplary clarity the nature and task of the Christian funeral,[90] describing it as a

> celebration of the incarnation, death, resurrection and ascension of Jesus and the giving of the Holy Spirit which together constitute what has been called the Paschal Mystery of Christ.

It continues by referring to the incorporation of Christians into the Paschal Mystery by baptism, and describes the joy and solemnity that a Christian funeral occasions. The notes of judgement and salvation are sounded and the preface concludes:

> . . . many elements combine in the Christian liturgy for death. Always there should be held together the opposites of joy and sorrow, mercy and judgement, the reality of sin and the vision of heaven.

The present commentator says, "Amen!"

Provided are resources and orders for use before a funeral,[91] the funerals of adults and of children (with separate committal rites), a memorial service, the interment of ashes and the dedication and unveiling of a tombstone. A final appendix of prayers is included for use at any of these services. General rubrics at the beginning of the section offer collects for the funerals of adults and children, guidance on liturgical colours,[92] and general tables of scripture texts for use at any service. Where specific readings or psalms are proposed in the body of the text, a rubric always observes that others may be chosen from the list in the general rubrics.[93]

---

[89] Hereinafter referred to as *PBSA* (Prayer Book of Southern Africa).

[90] *PBSA*: 525-527.

[91] An order for ministry to the dying is also provided. It follows conventional lines and is not included for comment here, other than to note that it uses the *Proficiscere* in perhaps its most appropriate place – at the point of death.

[92] White, purple or black. Since this exhausts all the possibilities and no preference is stated, the rubric simply functions as a reminder rather than as guidance.

[93] OT: Isa 35.1-2, 8-10; Isa 63.7-9 and (for a child) 2 Kgs 4.18-26 (Is it well with the child?).

PSALMS: Pss 27; 42.1-7; 103; 121; 130; 139.1-8; 147.1-7. The following psalms are suggested for use during a procession from the home or church: 116; 121; 123; 126; 132; 134; 139.1-18.

NT: Rom 8.31-39; 2 Cor 4.7-18; Phil 3.7-21; 1 Thess 4.13-18; 2 Tim 1.8-12; 1 Pet 1.3-9; 2 Pet 1.1-11; Rev 7.9-17; Rev 21.1-7: Rev 21.22-22.5 and (for a child) Eph 3.14-19.

GOSPEL: Matt 5.3-10; Lk 23.33, 39-43; Jn 5.24-29: Jn 6.37-40; Jn 14.1-6; Jn 20.1-18 and (for a child) Matt 11.25-30; Jn 11.17-27.

A SERVICE FOR USE BEFORE THE FUNERAL

In effect what is provided are resources for a gathering rite at the home or other place of meeting before going on to the funeral. They may also be used for the reception of a body into church.

The shape of the rite is very simple:

— Opening sentences
— Psalmody
— Reading of Scripture[94]
— Prayers
— Credal antiphons

The opening sentences suggested are Lam 3.22-23; Jn 3.16; and Matt 11.28. A number of psalms may be said from the list in the general rubrics, but Ps 42.1-7 is printed in full in the body of the text. The credal antiphons are shaped like biddings with an antiphonal formula at the end of each bidding: This is our faith/**Lord, increase our faith.** The bidding successively refers to Rom 8.38-39; Jn 11.35; Eph 1.17; and Jn 3.16. The final antiphonal formula concludes the rite:

This is the faith of the Church
This is our faith. Amen. Alleluia.

THE FUNERAL OF AN ADULT

The service follows a traditional order:

— Opening Sentences[95]
— Psalmody[96]
— Reading of Scripture
— Sermon
— Prayers
— Committal

The opening sentences are followed by the prayer "Heavenly Father, in your Son Jesus Christ you have give us a sure hope" and this precedes the psalmody (which according to the rubric is said). Scripture is read; a rubric notes that more than one passage may be used. The reading of scripture may be followed by a sermon.

Although the rubric does not require a sermon, it does require that where one is preached it should be "in exposition of the Scripture reading".[97] The preface comments that a tribute should be honest and have the purpose "of moving those present to thank God for what he has accomplished by his grace in and through the person concerned".

---

[94] From the list of proposed readings printed in the general rubrics.
[95] Jn 11.25-26; Job 19.25, 27; Ps 143.2; Rom 8.38-39; Ps 25.7; 1 Tim 6.7 and Job 1.21; 1 Cor 13.12; Rom 14.7-8; Deut 33.27; Jn 14.2; 1 Cor 2.9; 1 Thess 4.14, 18.
[96] Pss 23; 90; 130.
[97] *PBSA*: 539.

Thus a clear distinction is drawn between a tribute and a sermon in their content – though not their purpose, which should be the praise of God.

A sixfold *Kyrie* is said followed by the Lord's Prayer and intercessions drawn from the appendix of prayer texts provided at the end of the section of *PBSA* entitled "Funeral Services".[98]

The funeral service concludes with prayers for the one who has died, for the bereaved and for the congregation. The Grace is said, or a priest may give a blessing.

A final rubric notes:

> If the body is to be cremated, the committal may follow here.

This suggests that cremation usually occurs at a distance and may not necessarily be attended by those present at the funeral service.

The committal offers a prayer for use where the body is to be buried in otherwise unconsecrated ground. It is well known, but is reproduced here:

> Almighty God, your Son Jesus Christ by his burial sanctified the grave to be a bed of hope to your people: bless this grave that it may be a resting place, peaceful and secure, for the body of your servant *N*; for the sake of him who died and was raised and is alive for evermore. **Amen.**

The committal begins with the words of Job 14.1-2, the *Media Vita* and the *Trisagion.* Alternative words from Ps 103 may be used. Two committal formulae are offered for use followed by the words of Rev 14.13. Prayers may be said, followed by the words of Ps 16.11 and Jude 24-25 and the Grace.

The anthem *In Paradisum,* the kontakion and the *Nunc Dimittis* are printed in full. Any or all of these may be sung or said.[99]

THE FUNERAL OF A CHILD

The shape of the funeral service for a child is the same as that for an adult. This commentary will proceed by noting the difference in provisions at the various stages.

The opening sentences offer texts considered appropriate for the circumstances and omit those less fitting.[100] Similarly, the provisions for psalmody and the reading of scripture are amended.[101]

The prayers refer to Jesus taking "little children into your arms" and blessing them and (in a second prayer) the compassion described by scripture for "Jairus and his wife" and the widow of Nain. Perhaps somewhat unfortunately, this second prayer observes that the children in these cases were restored to life. Although this is transmuted into the hope of resurrection to eternal life, one cannot help but feel that this may not really be what the parents want. A final prayer refers to God's ways as beyond our understanding,

[98] *PBSA:* 563-568.
[99] Although these are printed at the conclusion of the committal rite, the rubric suggests that they (or a hymn) may be used as the coffin is taken out of church.
[100] Retained from the adult service are: Jn 11.25-26; Job 1.21; Deut 33.27. Added are: Rom 5.8; Lk 18.16; Matt 5.8; Matt 18.10; Isa 40.11.
[101] Omitted are Pss 90 and 130; included is Ps 121. Baruch 4.19, 20b, 22-23a and Mk 10.13-16 are proposed as pertinent readings for the funeral of a child.

and seeks the comfort and faith that grieving parents need. There is no doubt that we ought to pray for the parents in this way, but the reference to "God's ways" is somewhat difficult. Can we attribute infant death to God's ways in this unglossed fashion? The phrase surely raises more questions than it seeks to resolve. The prayer stands well without such a reference and might have been better without it.[102]

At the committal the opening sentences retain Job 14.1-2, but the *Media Vita* and *Trisagion* are omitted. In their place are suggested 2 Sam 12.22-23 (David's lament after the death of Bathsheba's child) and Jer 31.1-17 (Rachel's lament in Ramah).

The committal scripture proposed is Rev 7.15-17 and after the Grace, the *In Paradisum* and the kontakion are included for use.

MEMORIAL SERVICE

The opening rubric clearly directs that the memorial service is additional (not alternative) to the funeral. The funeral is rooted in the Paschal Mystery in a way that the memorial service is not.

The service takes the following shape:

— Opening Sentences

— *Kyrie*

— Lord's Prayer[103]

— Psalmody[104]

— Reading of Scripture

— Sermon

— Prayers

— Blessing

There is little to note in detail. The rubric relating to the sermon once again notes that the sermon should be in exposition of the scripture. Any eulogy or tribute is to follow immediately after the opening sentences and to precede the *Kyries*.

The special prayer texts provided are general in tone, and refer successively to:

— "those who have gone before us";

— the comfort offered to Mary and Martha and the hope to be found in Christ "the Resurrection and the Life";

— Christ as the "first-born from the dead" in whom we find forgiveness of sins (cf. Col 1.15-20).

---

[102] It might have been drafted with a single amendment (indicated here by italics): "Lord God, *this death is* beyond our understanding, *yet* your love for those whom you created is greater by far than ours; comfort these parents whose hearts are full of grief for the child they have lost. Give them the faith to endure the darkness of bereavement and bring them in the fulness of time to share with *N* the light and joy of your eternal presence; through Jesus Christ our Lord. **Amen.**"

[103] The ELLC text of the Lord's Prayer is printed.

[104] Pss 16 and 34.

A final ascription of glory to the Holy Trinity[105] precedes the concluding Grace or blessing.

The service here is somewhat different from the British understanding of a memorial service, which resembles rather more a celebration than a reflection. It is, perhaps closer in tone to a thanksgiving service. However, it is noticeable that the eulogy or tribute, which is often the central feature of memorial and thanksgiving services elsewhere, remains here clearly subservient to the exposition of scripture and indeed is placed among the prefatory elements of the service. Whether this provision (published in 1989 and presumably drafted a few years earlier) meets the demands of today is unclear – we might even say doubtful. However, what the South African memorial service makes clear is the continuing centrality of Christ to the observance of rites for the dead. This is a considerable achievement.

INTERMENT OF ASHES
Provision is made in PBSA for the interment of ashes.[106] The sentences and prayers used are parallel to those used at a grave burial, and the shape of the rite is essentially the same.

THE DEDICATION AND UNVEILING OF A TOMBSTONE
Where a tombstone has been erected, it might be thought that this was the end of the matter. The monumental mason's work is completed; the superintendent or sexton has set the stone in place. What more need be done? The Church of South Africa sees the possibility of marking this with a "joyous" rite, which, in the words of the opening rubric, "stress[es] the Christian hope of the resurrection and the communion of saints". The rite does not require the presence of a priest; a lay minister may conduct it.

The greeting takes the form of the Easter acclamation:

> The Lord is risen
> **He is risen indeed, alleluia.**

The opening prayer refers to the communion of saints and our baptism into the death and resurrection of Jesus. Scripture is read,[107] and a short expository sermon may follow.

The tombstone is unveiled and the Lord's Prayer said. Other prayers follow and the stone is dedicated with a prayer for the blessing of God. Further prayers (based on Rom 8 and 1 Cor 15) are made and the *Requiem aeternam* couplet is said antiphonally. The rite concludes with the blessing:

---

[105] The ascription of glory is based largely on Eph 1.3-14 with its references to our being accepted in the Beloved and the loosing of our sins by the blood of the Son.

[106] Many Christian traditions (though not all) do not allow for the scattering of ashes. This is regarded as derogatory of the unity of the person, which should be preserved in the disposal of remains. The desire to preserve this integrity means that where body parts are subsequently recovered there should be a clear site where what has been separated may be reunited. Those who do not object to the scattering of ashes do not necessarily hold the human person in any less regard. Their desire is frequently to distinguish between the "reality" of the dead and their mortal remains. Whether this implies a dualism, which is not present in the burial of ashes, is debatable.

[107] Gen 28.10-22 (the pillar at Bethel); Gen 35.16-20 (the pillar at Rachel's tomb); Rom 8.31-39; 1 Cor 15.20-26.

May the God of peace make perfect and holy; and may you all be kept safe and blameless, spirit, soul and body, for the coming of our Lord Jesus Christ. God has called you and he will not fail you.

Summary

The rites of the Church of Southern Africa for use at and around the time of death are expressive of the Paschal Mystery and of the journey that the dead and those who mourn must each undertake. The anthropology is the body-soul pattern (with the further refinement of spirit, soul and body). What is impressive throughout is the dignity and restraint of language, which expresses not only the natural sorrow that death evokes but the Christian hope of the resurrection. One cannot avoid the centrality of Christ in these rites, and in the final rite – the dedication of a tombstone – that note abides. God, revealed in Christ, is faithful "and he will not fail you".

The Anglican Church of Kenya

The funerary texts of the Anglican Church of Kenya were found in 2002 in the new liturgical book, *Our Modern Services*. This book follows (chronologically) the Kanamai Statement – about which something should be said first.

The Kanamai Statement (1993)

This statement was drafted following meetings at Kanamai in 1993 of forty-three representatives to the International Anglican Liturgical Consultation (IALC) who gathered to delineate principles for the African inculturation of Anglican Liturgy.
The statement was divided into five sections, the last of which dealt with death and burial liturgy and began with these words:

> The African Christian's attitude to death is inevitably shaped both by African tradition and Christian belief. Some tradition beliefs can be, and have been, incorporated into Christian use; others must be subjected to criticism based on the gospel and the tradition of the Church.

Several issues were identified: the marital status of the deceased; distinctions between men, women and children; attitudes to suicides and criminals; rites relating to burial, mourning and remembrance; property distribution; and the naming of children after the deceased.
Traditional African understandings about the causes of death were contrasted with the Christian understanding that, however death occurs, it is God who holds and withholds life. It is God who raised Christ from the dead and in that resurrection the ministry of comfort is grounded. Judgement belongs to God alone, and therefore it is not part of the Church's task to refuse its prayers even to those who have taken their own lives. They are commended to the mercy of God with the prayer that "they may be granted the forgiveness which Jesus came to bring".[108]
In a series of general notes, pastoral and liturgical guidance is given to cover local circumstances (see footnote).[109] Sample prayers for use were produced for funerals

---

[108] *Anglican Liturgical Inculturation in Africa: The Kanamai Statement 'African Culture and Anglican Liturgy'* (Bramcote: Alcuin/GROW 28, page 47).

[109] The general notes read as follows:
1. The family of the deceased should have the various possibilities for the funeral liturgy explained and be allowed to choose what is most appropriate.
2. The practice in certain African societies, as in some Eastern churches, is to anoint the body with oil prior to burial. This sign of love may appropriately be done for Christians.
3. Funerals may be celebrated at any lawful time. On Sundays, however, priority is given to the worship of the church.
4. The funeral rite need not take place within a church building, but may be conducted wherever is convenient, whether indoors or outdoors.

following a sudden death, the death of a child, the death of a single man or woman, the death of a suicide and the death of both parents.[110]

It is important to remember that in most traditional African cultures burial usually occurs very soon after death. Family and friends gather around the one who is dying and minister to him. At the point of death, wailing begins and burial is undertaken as soon as possible.[111] The climate requires it. For this reason, the burial may have occurred before a priest or other authorised church person can arrive. In twenty-first-century Africa, it may be that some members of the family may not have been able to arrive either. The geographical scattering that urbanisation engenders has not left the countries of Africa untouched, and those living far from home may not have been able to get back in time for the burial. The Christian rite has, therefore, to accommodate a variety of possibilities, and may indeed often follow the burial of the deceased.

The importance of the Kanamai Statement lies in its international character (emerging as it did from the IALC) and in the traditional cultural norms it seeks to address. Kenyan Anglicans had ample time to reflect upon it as they prepared their new service book.

Our Modern Services (2002)

The new service book of the Anglican Church of Kenya offers two full service texts for funerals and an alternative outline. The services assume burial as the means of disposal. The first service is effectively the normal provision; the second is drafted specifically for the burial of a suicide; the alternative outline order is offered for those with a Christian heritage who die before baptism.

BURIAL SERVICE
This rite takes the following order:

— Procession to the place of service

— Opening sentences

— Greeting and statement of purpose

— Litany and psalmody

— Eulogy

---

5. Any traditional customs concerning the burial which are appropriate for a Christian may be followed. The use of a coffin is not compulsory. Where the place of burial is not consecrated or set apart for Christian burial, a prayer of blessing should be said over the grave before interment.
6. It is appropriate to provide prayers for different types of people covering differences in age, status in community, and cause of death.
7. A memorial service held some time after the funeral is important for African societies. Provision for such a service according to local custom is appropriate for Christians.

[110] These prayer texts have not been reproduced here, since they are examples of what might be used rather than texts drawn from services in use. They may, however, be found on page 48 of the Alcuin/GROW edition of the Kanamai Statement.

[111] In a concluding note to the Kanamai Statement's section on death, the following observation is made: "The liturgy traditionally has not provided for wailing and mourning . . . ; *these are needed*" (p. 48: stress mine). See also the account given by Bishop Keith Russell of death rites in Northern Uganda (*Men without God?*: 55-58).

—   Reading of scripture
—   Sermon
—   Prayers of intercession
—   Anthem
—   Procession to the grave
—   Scripture sentences
—   Consecration of the grave
—   Committal
—   Blessing and dismissal

Introductory notes indicate that the service is not to be used for the unbaptised, the excommunicated, or those who have committed suicide. For the first and last of the groups, other provisions are made available.

The notes also observe that the service should proceed without interruption, that any eulogy or tribute "should be well organized and strictly controlled", that the service should take no longer than two hours and that "a simple and inexpensive burial is advised: burial ceremonies should not overtake the resources of the bereaved". There are some Western situations where any or all of these injunctions could usefully be rehearsed!

Where the service begins with a procession with the body to the place of burial, scripture sentences are to be said.[112] When all are gathered, the minister declares the purpose of the service: the burial of the body and the remembrance of the hope of the resurrection for those who have died in Christ. The congregation then join in the prayer, "Heavenly Father, in your Son Jesus Christ, you have given us a true faith and a sure hope". There follow, in the form of a litany, the words of Eccl 3.2-8 ("For everything there is a season") and a psalm.[113]

Before the reading of scripture, any eulogy or tributes may be given and a hymn is sung. This ordering preserves the integrity of the proclamation of the word in the reading of scripture and the preaching. It is required that only one passage of scripture be read. A selection of passages is proposed and, while all but one are drawn from the NT, it is possible that the only scripture read in the service is the OT text. Two gospel passages are included in the selection, but neither is printed out in full.[114] A hymn precedes the sermon (which is not optional). After the sermon there may be an offertory.

Prayers of intercession are made with the opening invitation to thank God for the life of the one who has died and remember what that person has meant to those present. Various intercessions follow, these cover in turn:

---

[112]   The following texts are proposed for use: Isa 40.7; Matt 5.4; Ps 116.15; 2 Tim 2.11-13; Jn 3.16; Heb 2.14; Rev 3.21; Ps 48.14; Rev 2.10.
        A hymn is sung, either during the procession or at the start of the service.
[113]   Ps 23 and Ps 121 are printed in full. Suggested alternatives are: Pss 16.1-11; 49.7-15; 73.21-28; 139.1-18.
[114]   Isa 25.6-9; 1 Thess 4.14-18; Rev 20.11-15; Rev 21.1-4 are printed in full. Suggested alternatives are: Jn 6.35-40; Jn 14.1-13; Rom 4.1-17; Rom 5; Rom 6.5-14; Rom 8.31-39; 1 Cor 15.20-28.

—   the shortness of life and the need to live accordingly;

—   the grief of the family;

—   a remembrance of the faithful departed and the hope of the resurrection;

—   the need for divine compassion in time of sorrow;

—   resolution to live in the light of the cross and resurrection on the journey to "the land where there will be no death and no sorrow".

The final intercession is the well-known prayer, "O Lord support us all the day long." Generally, the tone of the prayers is earnestly Evangelical. There is no suggestion of prayer for the dead in the Catholic sense and the references to journeying indicate the living rather than the dead.

As the congregation prepares to process to the grave, the minister says either *In Paradisum* or the kontakion "Give rest, O Christ, to your servant with the saints". In the case of the kontakion, the congregation join in the final threefold Alleluia.

The procession to the grave is made as the congregation sing hymns or choruses interspersed with scripture sentences.[115] The minister may then consecrate the grave:

> Lord Jesus Christ, through your own time in the grave, you made the graves of all believers sacred. May the body of *N* lie peacefully in the earth, and may he participate in your resurrection, through the power of the Holy Spirit. Amen.

The body is lowered into the grave and there is silence. The committal begins with a threefold *Kyrie* and the words of Rev 14.13. The committal prayer takes the traditional twofold form, though 'spirit' here replaces 'soul':

> Therefore, trusting in God's abundant provision of grace and in his gift of righteousness through the one person Jesus Christ, we give the spirit of our *brother* here departed, into the everlasting arms of God to take *him* to himself, while we commit his body to the ground.

The minister casts soil over the body with the formula "earth to earth, ashes to ashes, dust to dust" and continues with words drawn from Phil 3.21 and 2.9.

The minister continues with the words of Rev 7.15-17 and invites the congregation to join in the Lord's Prayer.[116]

The grave is then filled. This is a most important part of the rite. Nobody leaves until the grave has been filled. It marks most clearly the finality of the separation of the living and the dead.[117] A cross may be erected over the grave and the final words of blessing

---

[115]   One or more of the following may be used: Jn 11.25; Job 1.21; Dan 12.2-3; Job 19.25-27; 2 Tim 1.9b-10; 1 Tim 6.7; Rev 3.5; Jn 5.28; Jn 14.2-3.

[116]   The Lord's Prayer is printed in the form adopted by the Church of England in the *ASB* and in *Common Worship*.

[117]   The same tradition continues among the Black Churches beyond Africa. Normally, it is the men who undertake the task. I encountered the same in the funeral of a Chinese woman at which I officiated. There, the husband did not come to the graveside but returned home after the service in the chapel. The sons undertook the filling in of the grave (assisted by the mechanical diggers of the cemetery authorities).

and dismissal are pronounced, using either the Aaronic formula or the words of Eph 3.20-21 or of Phil 4.7.

The Grace is said and the people depart.

Additional prayers for use in various circumstances may be included at the point of the intercession. Forms are provided for the death of a young child, accidental death, violent death, death after a wasting sickness, or death in old age. The prayers are in places quite didactic, and their clear purpose is to express the concerns of those gathered. A few extracts will give a sense of the general tone:

> *After an accident*
> . . . Hear us, Lord, as we pray that you would instil in all drivers a sense of responsibility over the people they carry . . .

> *After violent death*
> . . . We are tearful and bitter at what Cain can still do to his brother Abel . . .

> *In old age*
> . . . Grant by the same grace that our lives will be safely secured and guarded against the rolling billows of our life's tumultuous pilgrimage . . .

Summary

The text and shape of this Kenyan burial service is marked by strong and repeated references to the death and resurrection of Christ. It does not clearly bear signs of ritual inculturation, although some of the language and allusions in the prayer do mark the African milieu. The evident Evangelical tone of the rite suggests that perhaps the need to express the counter-cultural nature of the Gospel has prevailed over a more incarnational and inclusivist stance. It is worth noting that no separate rite is provided for the funeral of a child. This may reflect a higher incidence of infant mortality than is experienced in the so-called developed countries.

However, in the rite that follows the more tolerant African understanding accorded to suicide clearly emerges.

BURIAL OF ONE WHO HAS COMMITTED SUICIDE
The shape of the service is similar to that of the main burial service.

The opening sentences vary,[118] as do the suggested passages of scripture – where there is a clear instruction that there shall be a reading from both the OT and the NT.[119] The proposed passages each express something of the hardness or bitterness of life, while those from the NT and from Lamentations go on to declare that God is yet to be trusted. These texts have been carefully chosen to articulate something of the awfulness that may drive a person to suicide.

Two prayers of intercession have been drafted which directly related to the circumstance of death. The second expresses something of the heaviness of life "as we

---

[118]   Jn 14.1; Jn 14.27; Jn 16.33; Heb 4.14-16; 2 Cor 4.8-9.
[119]   Job 3.1-26; Jer 20.15-18; Lam 3.19-26; Lk 12.22-34; 2 Cor 1.8-9.

trudge along life's pilgrimage". The first attempts to live in the mind of the one who has died. It begins almost as though the Coroner (or magistrate) were introducing a verdict:

> Loving Father, we thank you for *N*. It is saddening that he had to take his own life for reasons that may never be clearly understood by any of us. We can only imagine the anguish he experienced as he pondered the meaninglessness of staying alive. You alone understand the hearts and minds of people and the motives therein. We may have failed *N* when he needed us most; forgive us, Lord. Relieve us from the pain and hurt we feel his action has caused us and help us to release him to eternity. Through Jesus Christ our Lord. Amen.

It is interesting to compare the rather homiletic nature of this prayer compared with the text proposed in the Kanamai report:

> Lord Jesus Christ, you knew the agony of the garden and the loneliness of the cross, but remained in the love of your Father. We commend N to your mercy and claiming no judgement for ourselves commit him/her to you, the righteous judge of all, now and for ever. Amen.

The Kanamai text does not attempt any direct psychological imagining; rather, it draws attention to the agony of Jesus and leaves the deceased there. While the Kenya text is clearly motivated by the highest pastoral concern, the Kanamai prayer seems to have taken a more effective route to the same end. In moving directly to the Gethsemane narrative it meets the human predicament with a saving word.

Further intercession is made in the Kenyan order for those who mourn and the procession to the grave begins.[120] A committal prayer seeks a blessing on the grave and continues:

> And because it is only you, Loving Father, who truly understand us inwardly, let your will be done on the spirit of N, as we commit his body to the soil . . .

The grave is filled and the service concludes with a blessing using the words of Jude 24-25. The Grace is in the same form as used for the main burial service.

Summary

The sympathetic tone of the service may be scandalous to those who regard suicide as serious sin. Given the strong Evangelical tone of the main burial service, one might have expected a more guarded note. However, one detects that Christian theology has here accommodated itself to meet African attitudes. The rite suggests a clear understanding that God does not abandon those who take their own life, and for this commentator that indicates a welcome pastoral sensitivity.

---

[120] The suggested processional sentences retain Jn 11.25-27; Jn 5.28. Introduced are Lam 3.22-23; 3.31-33.

ALTERNATIVE BURIAL SERVICE

An outline order is provided for the funeral of those with a Christian heritage who die before they are baptised or for those of other faiths who at the time of death were interested in joining the Christian faith. It may also be used where the deceased's religious identity cannot be easily discovered. A final pastoral note adds that the service is to be conducted at the graveside.

These instructions remind the reader that the Kenyan (unlike the English) Anglican does not assume Christian faith or accord Christian rites to those who die in the parish. Christian faith is a public issue and is clearly identifiable. This funeral does not take place in church. A clear distinction is drawn and maintained.

The order of the rite is broadly that of the main burial service and differs principally in the sentences and scripture readings proposed.[121]

Summary

The burial service found in the Kenyan service book displays an overwhelming pastoral care for those who mourn, a clear body-soul anthropology and a strong Evangelical proclamation of the cross and resurrection of Christ. The importance attached by Africans to filling in the grave shows clearly the kind of separation rite van Gennep discerned in the studies he recorded in his work on rites of passage.

The services also evince the less condemnatory attitude to suicide that seems to be part of many African societies and at the same time a clear distinction between those who profess Christian faith and those who do not. In these ways the Anglican Church of Kenya provides examples of how the gospel may receive or resist inculturation.

---

[121]   Opening Sentences: Pss 100.5; 102.17; 103.8, 10; Matt 7.21; Jn 10.16; Mk 10.14; Matt 18.10.
Scripture Readings: Eccl 3.1-11; 12.1-7; Pss 90; 130; Jn 10.11-16; Rom 8.35-39.

Marthoma Syrian Church

Order of Services (1988)

The Marthoma Syrian Church is a reformed church of the West Syrian tradition in communion with the Anglican Communion. Its occasional services were published in an authorised English-language edition in 1988.[122]

The funeral service is in three parts with a strong processional thread running through the whole:

— The Service at Home
— The Service in Church
— The Procession and Committal

This commentary will use the Indian names for the various prayers and anthems. For the ease of the reader, the explanation of these terms given in the service book is set out here.

Ekba	A short one-verse anthem.
Ethra	A prayer used when incense is put into the censer.
Hoothama	A closing prayer (literally, 'a seal').
Kolo/Qolo	A short anthem of several verses, sometimes modelled on the Psalms.
Kukaya/ Madroshso	Technical terms for various songs, canticles and chants. The names reflect different music and metre in the original Syriac.
Promion	An introductory prayer, introduced by a dialogue.
Sedra	A long prayer in prose or verse, usually dealing with the main subject of the service.

THE SERVICE AT HOME

This section of the rite takes the following shape:

— Opening Prayer

— Psalmody and Chant

— Promion, Sedra and Ethra

— Chant and Supplication of Mar Jacob

— Reading of Scripture and Sixfold *Kyrie*

---

[122] In a short preface to *Order of Services*, Metropolitan Alexander wrote: "Many requests have been received from different places for an authentic English version of the Order of Services of the Marthoma Church . . . We are happy that we can now publish an authentic version in English of the different services, as we have received the help of an expert in Liturgy, Rev. Dr. John Fenwick of the Anglican Church in England. He was helped by the Rev. Peter Hawkins . . ." Metropolitan Alexander commended the book on 1 June 1988.

— Lord's Prayer
— Blessing

Opening Prayer
The opening prayer gives thanks for redemption through Christ, and seeks that God will hear the prayers and petitions made during the funeral. It concludes by seeking for those gathered in their turn "a blessed and peaceful departure".

Psalmody and Chant
An anthem follows, comprised of various texts from the psalms and concludes with the *Gloria Patri*.[123] The chant that follows is printed in Malayalam. Alternatively, there may be chanted verses addressed to the "Lord the Messiah", which seek deliverance in the judgement and resurrection to eternal life that those singing on earth may stand before the heavenly king. The chant ends with the antiphonal response in either Greek or English:

> *Stōmen kalōs*:
> **Kyrie eleison.**
>
> Let us stand and attend:
> **Lord, have mercy.**

The call to "attend" is crucial in Orthodox liturgy. Time and again the Deacon will call the congregation to "attend" to the words of scripture or to some other particularly important part of the liturgy.

Promion, Sedra and Ethra
A brief antiphonal exchange, inviting the congregation to pray for help and mercy and to offer "praise, adoration, worship, thanksgiving and glory", prefaces the Promion, which addresses praise, honour and worship to Christ the source of all life and the hope of the dead.

The Sedra invokes God as the creator of all things "out of nothing" who has given humanity its royal dignity.[124] It rehearses the Genesis account of the fall, yet adds that God "did not cast mankind away as fallen" but secured our redemption by the death of Jesus "the great physician for all mankind". It seeks that at the judgement, when "he will reward the good and bad according to their deeds", the one

> . . . who has been baptised in your name, who has taken part in your divine sacraments and trusted in the Crucifixion of your only Son, will not be abandoned in the deep pit, will not suffer pain in the unquenchable fire, but will rejoice in the light of your countenance . . .

---

[123] Pss 49.1-2; 39.6; 90.3; 103.10, 14-17; 115.17-18. These are the numbers as given in the service book. However, while the first four psalms follow the Hebraic numbering, the final psalm is given its liturgical (LXX) numbering.

[124] The *Order of Services* does not use inclusive language; wherever possible, this Commentary will continue to do so.

The prayer seeks consolation and comfort for all who mourn – especially for the family – and solicits "the peace that is above all anxiety". It asks that they may be brought to saintly perfection and join Job in saying that the Lord gives and the Lord takes away. It concludes by asking that those present may be made ready for their own death, when they may find "an exalted position before your throne".

The Ethra summarises the Promion and Sedra in the following words:

> O God, Father of our Lord Jesus Christ, you are life and resurrection and have assured us that those who believe in you will live even though they died, and you have promised that no one who believes in you shall die: we magnify your holy name for all your servants who have departed this life in faith and trust in you. Lord, enable us by following their noble example to be made worthy of your heavenly kingdom and to render glory, worship and honour to you and to your Son and the Holy Spirit, now and for ever. Amen.

The priest continues by encouraging those present to remember

> ... where we are today and where we shall be tomorrow. Today we converse in houses, tomorrow we shall be quiet in our graves ...

He concludes with a further reminder of the transience of our life and the imperishability of God.

Chant and Supplication of Mar Jacob
A chant in Malayalam may be sung, or an English text proclaiming to the dead the imminence of the resurrection and exhorting them not to grieve for the "destruction of your body". The English-language chant continues by rehearsing Christ's descent to the dead and seeking that

> ... when you come to raise the children of Adam on the last day, graciously raise your servants who have believed in you.

The petition of the chant is then rehearsed in a supplication of Mar Jacob.

Reading of Scripture and Sixfold *Kyrie*
Two readings of scripture are proposed at this stage of the rite. The passage from the OT is determined by the gender of the deceased; the Epistle is common.[125] A sixfold *Kyrie* is said or sung antiphonally and is followed by versicles and responses seeking the blessing of God and the answering of prayer.

Lord's Prayer
Priest and congregation together pray the Lord's Prayer, using the ICET version.

Blessing
This stage of the rite concludes with the blessing formula of Phil 4.7 and the body is taken to church.

---

[125] OT: Gen 50.1-13 (for a man); Gen 23.1-20 (for a woman)
EPISTLE: 1 Cor 15.12-19

THE SERVICE IN CHURCH

The section of the rite takes the following shape:

— *Gloria Patri* and Opening Prayer
— Psalm and Ekba
— Promion and Sedra
— Kukaya
— Ethra
— Kolos
— Madroshso
— Petition of Mar Jacob
— Epistle
— Gospel
— Litany with *Kyries*

Gloria Patri and Opening Prayer

The opening prayer addresses Christ as "the immortal One who died in the flesh to redeem us mortals from the death of sin". The descent to the dead is seen as the harrowing of Hell by which Adam is set free, and the resurrection of Christ is the guarantee of our resurrection. A stronger evocation of the Easter triduum and its relation to our human death could scarcely be made.[126]

Psalm and Ekba

The opening verses of Ps 103 are sung and there follows the Ekba:

> . . . the sun and moon and stars fade away at the command of their Creator, the world moves towards its end. Tombs burst open. The dead in them rise up and go forth prepared to receive their reward in the just, true and unerring judgement.

The language is apocalyptic, but also echoes something of the Matthaean account of the phenomena accompanying the crucifixion in which the passion of Christ cannot be confined to the local, but transcends time and space and even death itself.

There follows the summons to the congregation to pay heed:

Stōmen kalōs:
Kyrie eleison.

Let us stand and attend:
Lord, have mercy.

---

[126] See the discussion of this in Volume I.

Promion and Sedra

The Promion and Sedra vary according to the gender of the deceased. I reproduce them in parallel for the sake of comparison.

For a man

Promion

To the Lord Jesus Christ, who is the Sun of righteousness, in whose light the heavenly beings tremble, at the manifestation of whose glory the angels marvel, who visits those in their graves with the rays of his radiance, who is the true light that lightens the darkness with his wondrous splendour, who raises the dead with his powerful voice, who wakes those who are asleep with the beckoning of his divine will, the living and life-giving God, who is the Judge of the living and the dead – to him be glory, honour and worship, now at the funeral of his servant and all the days of our life. Amen.

Sedra

O Christ, our Lord, the power and wisdom of the eternal Father, you create and give life to all creation. You are the God of the saints and the righteous, and the true resurrection of those who sleep in the dust. You have brought us into being out of nothing by the holy will of the Father and the Holy Spirit. You joined us to your divine and blessed state. We have fallen into destruction and decay by the enticement of Satan. By your mercy you became man in all respects except sin to redeem us.

For a woman

To the Lord Jesus Christ, who is the hope of those who have lost hope, who raises up those who are buried in the earth and those asleep in the dark caverns of Hades, who renews and adorns those who have perished in death, who gives hope and comfort to those who have fallen under sin, death and destruction – to him be honour, glory and worship at the funeral of his servant and all the days of our life. Amen.

O God, who are the Lord of everything, the Creator of souls and bodies, who formed mankind and give time for repentance to the living, who bring death and raise death, who lower into Hades and rescue from it: mighty, merciful and compassionate Lord, accept our prayers and petitions that we make at the funeral of this your daughter.

Lord of lords, we believe that this your servant will reach the haven of peace, join all the saintly and holy women who have kept

You have wiped out the power of death by your resurrection. You have given us the gift of new life and the blessed resurrection.

O gracious and merciful Lord, accept these prayers which we your people offer with broken hearts and contrite spirits at the funeral of this your servant, who departed [*sic*] from this transitory life. Lord, we trust that in the last day when body and soul are united once more, he will be saved from darkness, he will shine with your light, he will rejoice in the joy of all your saints, he will abide in the blessed dwelling places and enjoy eternal life in your presence.

Our true High Priest, we hope that he will know you fully and rejoice and will rise up from the bondage of hell and dust, will be delivered from the fiery furnace and will rejoice at the feast in your Kingdom, with his face radiating the glory of your countenance.

O gracious God and merciful Lord, comfort now us who are in sorrow and lamentation and strengthen us to lead sober lives in the path of righteousness. Keep us sinless in this world. Protect us under the shadow of the wings of your grace, and draw us closer to

your commandments,[127] who enjoy the dwelling places set apart for all your saints, and will rejoice with all the angels.

Merciful and gracious Lord, we hope[128] that this your servant will abide in ineffable light, in the dwelling places of the saints, in the joyful mansions of light where there is no sorrow, pain or groaning, and in the home of comfort and eternal life to hear the voice of renewed praise and spiritual joy.

O Lord of compassion, forgive all our sins committed knowingly or unknowingly, because there is forgiveness of sins and great redemption in your presence.

Equip us, O Lord, to be ready to start our journey and to receive by [*sic*] your grace when it pleases you to call us. May we sing praises to your love of mankind in our life here, enter into the glorious mansions of eternal happiness, become worthy of the heavenly bridal chamber of inexpressible joy and sing praises to you, and to your Father and the Holy Spirit, with all saints. Amen.

---

[127] In the earthly congregation, men and women stand apart. The hope that the deceased women will join the saintly and holy women in heaven is doubtless an echo of this arrangement. One wonders about Gal 3.27!

[128] In both forms of the Sedra 'hope' is used where 'trust' might have sounded a firmer note. 'Hope' here sounds rather feeble. Whether the English translation consultants picked this up is uncertain, but it leaves the prayer feeling less confident than the context (or the prevailing theology) demands. The problem arises elsewhere in the texts.

How much the English consultants were able (or felt able) to contribute to the translating process in not clear. Throughout the texts, there are what one might consider weak word selections which give the resulting translation a slightly awkward feel. This may be simply the inevitable result of translating from a more familiar to a more remote language. Given the richness of the images, this commentator longs for less frail language.

the dwelling places where there is
no sorrow or pain. Make us
worthy, O Lord, to meet you with
joyful faces and to praise you with
all the righteous and the saints in
your eternal Kingdom. And to you,
with the Father and the Holy Spirit
we ascribe praise and thanksgiving, now and for ever. Amen.

What each form of the Sedra displays is a clear understanding of the journey to be
undertaken by the dead. For the Christian, death is the gateway to the peace and joy of
heaven. And what is affirmed for the one who has died is sought for those who remain.
The consolation of the bereaved is in the hope (*elpis*) now granted to (and realised by)
the departed.

Kukaya
A Malayalam canticle is followed by an English text extolling Christ as the hope of
sinners.

Ethra
The prayer at incensing describes Christ as "the sweet fragrance and perfume of the
Father", who enlightens in heaven and those in the tomb and asks that those present
may, trusting in him, know the resurrection and remission of sins and on the Last Day
be found among the sheep at his right hand (cf. Matt 25.31-46).

Kolos
Four Kolos are proposed; the second and third appear in Malayalam and English forms.
    The first Kolo is typically Orthodox in its allusions and citing here will give a good
sense of what the Church in the West misses.

> O warrior, who by your death killed the dragon who brought death to the
> children of Adam, grant us white robes when you come with your holy
> angels.

> The King who raises the dead comes with majesty from on high! The dead
> from the tombs will rise up together and praise you, who give them life.

> We praise and worship Jesus the triumphant King who came to us in his love
> and redeemed us by his cross, and is to come again to raise the children of
> Adam and array them with white robes of glory.

The sense of heaven is urgent and explicit and rests upon the warrior-king, who in the
Western tradition is *Christus Victor*. The combination of comparatively modern English
with the ancient imagery of the Orthodox tradition is extremely arresting to ears not
accustomed to it.
    The remaining English-language Kolo texts continue to sound the notes both of
impending judgement and of the victory won by Christ, who welcomes the faithful to
share in his triumph. The centrality of Christ in the rite is never obscured; throughout,

the living are called in their grief for the one who has died to lift their gaze to the victory joys of heaven accorded by Christ to his saints.

Madroshso
The canticle immediately following the Kolo gives praise to Christ whose death destroys death. The bitterness of death is confronted and its universality acknowledged. The naturalness of death is declared and the powerlessness of friends to help confirmed. However, there is more; the canticle concludes:

> O Lord, all tongues praise you, because by you the dead live, they rise up and sing as they inherit the Kingdom.

Petition of Mar Jacob
The English text invokes the Lord to hear and continues:

> Death is a teacher and preacher to those who shun injustice and seek righteousness.[129] Death cries out, do not rely on your life for it is beyond your control.

> Death preaches to all generations and teaches all people. Death spreads from Adam to all generations. It leads tribes and families to destruction. There is no one who escapes from the yoke of death, nor from its authority, for it binds all people alike and sends them to the grave.

> Answer unto us, O Lord. Answer unto us, O Lord. Bless us and turn the hearts of men to repentance.

Epistle
Three passages are proposed to preface the Epistle; one or more may be read.[130] The Epistle passage itself is 1 Thess 4.13-18 and is read by the Deacon.

Gospel
The Deacon calls the congregation to stand and listen in silence and reverence to the reading of the Gospel, which is announced as proclaiming life and salvation to the world, evoking the congregational response:

> Blessed is he that has come and will come again. Praise to the Father who sent him for our salvation. May his blessing be ever upon us.

The Gospel passage to be read varies according to the gender of the deceased.[131]

Litany with *Kyries*
The petitions of the Litany are interspersed with congregational responses of *Kyrie eleison*; the final response is threefold. The petitions address Christ as the ruler of death

---

[129] I have written 'seek'. The text has 'sees' which does not really make sense. I hope that my attempted reconstruction does the original text no violence.
[130] Ezek 37.1-10; 2 Pet 3.8-13; 1 Cor 15.35-49.
[131] Jn 5.19-29 (for a man); Matt 25.1-13 (for a woman).

and separation, the resurrection and the life and saviour and seek the promises of Christ thus portrayed.

Here the rite moves to its final stage in a procession to the place of committal.

THE PROCESSION AND COMMITTAL
The section of the rite takes the following shape:

— Processional Chant
— Placing of the Coffin in the Grave
— Ekba
— The Praise of the Angels
— The Nicene Creed
— Hoothama and Blessing

Processional Chant
The service book offers two versions of the processional chant – Malayalam and English language. The second form draws (though not exclusively) on scripture texts traditionally associated with funerals.[132]

Placing of the Coffin in the Grave
Before the coffin has been placed in the grave, sand is placed in it. A version of the formula "Dust to dust, ashes to ashes" is said, or a Malayalam chant is sung.

Ekba
If the Ekba has not been read in church after the Litany, it may follow here. It speaks of the horror of Hades and of the tombs of the mighty and asks why, if all human life ends in death, do rich and powerful hoard gold or the wise take pride in their wisdom or the beautiful exult in their beauty. The youth of the young ends as surely as the power of the powerful:

> O David, the divine musician, come with your harp and sing to us that man
> is a short-lived being and that his days pass as vapour and wither as the

---

[132] Jn 11.25-26; 1 Jn 2.17; Job 14.1; Job 5.7 and Eccl 7.1; 1 Tim 6.7; Eccl 12.7 and Job 1.21; Eccl 7.29 and Num 23.10; Eccl 2.22 and 1.4; Eccl 3.1-2; Eccl 11.8; Ps 6.5 and 30.9b; Ps 39.6; Eccl 12.13.
   The remaining sentences are as follows:
— how piteous is this sight. It is painful to consider death. Why does mankind experience death like this?
— By the fruit that Adam ate in Eden, destruction befell mankind. By disobeying the commandments, man encountered sadness, disease and death.
— We send him to dust with honour. In sadness we bury him with love. Friends and relatives all cry out as he becomes a prey to dust and worm.
— Behold how Jesus died for you on the Cross. He triumphed over death and crushed the head of the Evil One. He delivered us and gave hope to all believers.
— Jesus ascended to heaven and intercedes for you before the Father. He will come soon; there is no delay. He will remove your sorrow and give you happiness.
— Jesus, full of compassion, we thirst for your coming again. Keep us without sin in this world and give joy to the bereaved.
— Lord, in your coming give us joy and salvation. Give us grace to rejoice before you and sing Hallelujah.

flowers of the field. Therefore, O God who raise the dead, we praise you.
Let us cry aloud and say: Praise to you, Lord of all.
Hallelujah, hallelujah, hallelujah.
Praise to you, O God.

In this anthem, the horror of death and the glorious hope of the resurrection are equally addressed. There is neither hopelessness in the face of death, nor a glib gladness in the thought of life beyond death. The equipoise is absolute.

The Praise of the Angels
The *Gloria in Excelsis* is sung. Thus the congregation joins the hymn of heaven.

The Nicene Creed
The Deacon makes the traditional summons:

Wisdom cries aloud. Let us stand in reverence and affirm together.

and the Nicene Creed (with no *filioque* clause) is recited, with the opening clause introduced by the priest and taken up by the congregation at the words "maker of heaven and earth . . ."
The Deacon then asks once again for attention.

Barek Mor. Stōmen kalōs:
Kyrie eleison.

Bless, O Lord. Let us stand and attend:
Lord, have mercy.

Hoothama and Blessing
These two texts conclude the rite and should be cited in full as showing how the rite is summarised and the future opened in these formulae:

Hoothama
May the holy Cross of the Son of God which is a mighty fortress to the faithful, a terror to the demons, and glory to the angels, protect us night and day from the anger of the wicked, from the envy of the demons and unbelievers, from powers that may do us harm, from unkind masters, from all our enemies, visible and invisible, from the snares of the Devil, from all evil thoughts that hurt soul and body, and from all the power of sin. May the Lord deliver and restore us and keep us all the days of our life. **Amen.**

Blessing
You are blessed by the Lord who created heaven and earth. May the Lord God bless and sanctify you all who have attended this divine service with us.[133] May God, the Father, the Son and the Holy Spirit, hear and accept before the throne of grace our weak and inadequate prayers. **Amen.**

---

[133] The Sign of the Cross is made here.

Summary

I have quoted extensively from the Marthoma texts because I imagine that they will be less familiar than the Western texts to most readers. What is very clear is that, while the Marthoma Church is a church in communion with the Anglican Communion, its liturgy springs vigorously from its Orthodox roots. Not the least of the immediately noticeable differences from the Western tradition is the frequent direct address to the dead. In the Mozarabic rites, the Church of the West spoke the words of the dead. In the widespread contemporary borrowing of the kontakion, modern Western traditions resume that practice. However, it is very difficult to imagine many churches in the West speaking to the dead as the Marthoma text does:

> Do not grieve for the destruction of your body. The one who created and clothed you will raise your body and reward the righteous according to their deeds.

Perhaps those of our contemporaries who use mediums to contact the dead would find such direct address pastorally helpful!

Throughout the rite there is a strong sense of the Easter event. It forms the whole and explains the whole. Death is real (expressed as separation of soul from body), is dark and sorrowful. This is clearly articulated. At the same time the death and resurrection of Christ are the powerful expression of hope leading to the joyful hymns of heaven and the communion of saints in glory.

CHAPTER 5

Churches of the Reformation

Introduction

Included under this heading are Christian traditions owing something to the Reformation, yet responding differently to it. The Lutherans trace their roots directly to the debates initiated by Martin Luther. Baptists, with their origins a century or so later, describe themselves as part of "the radical Reformation". Methodists spring from the spiritual regeneration sought by Wesley and Whitfield. Some of these traditions have more or less formal connections with the State. The Church of Scotland is "by law established" in Scotland. Others from the Independent and Anabaptist streams reject any link with the State. They are diverse, but are gathered here in this general (and arbitrary) grouping.

Lutheran

The Lutheran Book of Worship (1978)

In this book the Lutheran Church in North America provides a core order of service for a funeral. The order is very simple and allows the officiant the freedom to make choices with the family as to readings and hymns. It may also be adapted for use at memorial services.

— At the Entrance to the Church
— Procession
— The Liturgy of the Word
— [Holy Communion]
— Commendation
— Committal

An opening pastoral note makes explicit the exclusively Christian nature of the rite:

> The ceremonies or tributes of social or fraternal societies have no place within the service of the Church.

Although the instruction is terse almost to the point of being abrupt, it does have the merit of freeing the minister from extended discussion about what is permitted and what is not. The note says it all in fewer than twenty words.

At the Entrance to the Church
The minister greets the coffin and the pallbearers at the entrance to the church as they arrive with the family.[1] God is blessed as the Father of Jesus and the source of all mercy and comfort. A pall may be placed on the coffin with baptismal words drawn from Rom 6.3-5.

Procession
The minister then leads the coffin and the close mourners into church. As the procession makes its way to the front of the church a psalm, scripture sentence or hymn may be sung.

The Liturgy of the Word
The minister greets the congregation and leads those present in prayer. One of five texts may be used (the fifth is proposed for use at the funeral of a child and makes allusion to Mk 10.13-16).

Scripture is read. If two passages are used, a gradual psalm, hymn or anthem may be sung. There follows a gospel acclamation, and the congregation stands for the Gospel, which is followed by a sermon.

---

[1] The rubrics refer to "the ministers". Where in this section of the commentary reference is made to "the minister", the possibility of more than one officiant should be understood.

A hymn is sung and the congregation says the Apostles' Creed. The 1975 ICET text is used. There follow prayers, which may use the texts printed or take another form. The printed texts offer a series of petitions to each of which the congregation replies, "Hear us, Lord". The petitions refer successively to:

— the church as one communion in the mystical body of Christ;

— the resurrection of Christ, and our share in it, to newness of life;

— our continuing earthly pilgrimage and our need of the Holy Spirit;

— our need of cleansing from sin;

— the mourners' need of consolation;

— the need of the bereaved for strength in days ahead;

— our faith in the communion of saints in the midst of uncertainty;

— the deceased, that he/she may be received by God with mercy.

[Holy Communion]

When the service includes Holy Communion, the eucharistic rite begins here with the Peace and continues to the postcommunion canticle (*Nunc Dimittis*) and prayer. Where there is no celebration of Holy Communion, the service continues with the Lord's Prayer.[2]

Commendation

The minister stands by the coffin and prays:

> Into your hands, O merciful Savior, we commend your servant *name*. Acknowledge, we humbly beseech you, a sheep of your own fold, a lamb of your own flock, a sinner of your own redeeming. Receive *him/her* into the arms of your mercy, into the blessed rest of everlasting peace, and into the glorious company of the saints in light.

As the procession leaves the church, the *Nunc Dimittis* may be sung if it has not been used in the celebration of Holy Communion.

Committal

The minister precedes the coffin to the place of disposal. As the coffin is borne to its place, scripture sentences may be sung or said.[3] This prayer may then follow:

> Almighty God, by the death and burial of Jesus, your anointed, you have destroyed death and sanctified the graves of all your saints. Keep our *brother/sister*, whose *body* we now lay to rest, in the company of all your saints and, at the last, raise *him/her* up to share with all your faithful people the endless joy and peace won through the glorious resurrection of Christ our

---

[2] No form of the Lord's Prayer is printed. Where a modern language version is to be used, it will presumably be the ICET text – or would have been at the time that the *Lutheran Book of Worship* was published.

[3] Ps 118.5, 8-9, 13, 15-17, 19-20; Job 19.25-26; Rom 14.7-8; Jn 11.25-26a.

Lord, who lives and reigns with you and the Holy Spirit, one God, now and forever.

Scripture may be read; three passages are proposed of which one may be used.[4] The coffin is then made ready for disposal and the deceased is commended to God as the body is committed to "the ground/the deep/the elements/its resting place". The committal sentence may conclude with the Aaronic blessing.

The Lord's Prayer may then be said. A concluding prayer invokes Christ as the one who draws the sting of death and leads the way beyond death. There follow the *Requiem aeternam* and the dismissal formula from Heb 13.20-21.

Summary

The Lutheran rite here described is very brief. Its great strength is the reminder of our common mortality and our common hope in Christ. The continual note of the communion of saints is (as is most proper) redolent of Martin Luther's theological tradition, and the controlling emphasis on the work of God in Christ is vividly powerful.

However, like other churches, the Lutherans saw the need for a revision yet more powerfully expressing the Paschal Mystery. In 2002, the resultant work was published in Volume 4 of a series entitled *Renewing Worship*.

Renewing Worship: Volume 4 – Life Passages (2002)

The central note of the Paschal Mystery is sounded in the introductory note:

> The church's most deeply held conviction is the paschal mystery: Christ's saving passage through death to resurrected life as the new creation, the same passage into which Christ calls the baptized to follow. God's people gather round Christ in word and sacrament every Lord's Day to celebrate that passage through death to life and that call to follow. So, too, when the church gathers to mark the end of life, the paschal mystery in which the baptized live is the source of worship, the heartbeat of mutual consolation, and the hope of healing.[5]

Three staged rites are offered in *Renewing Worship* for use at funerals:
— Comforting the Bereaved
— Funeral Liturgy
— Committal

Stage 1: Comforting the Bereaved
This brief rite may be used either at the place of death or at the deceased's home. It may equally take place at a funeral establishment. Its purpose, before the funeral proper, is to allow friends and family to say an initial farewell and to commend the one who has died to God's mercy and keeping. The rite takes the following shape:

---

[4] Jn 12.23-26; 1 Cor 15.51-57; Phil 3.20-21a.
[5] *Renewing Worship*, at page 58.

—   Gathering
—   Word
—   Prayer

GATHERING
The leader greets those gathered, outlines the purpose of the rite and invokes the presence of God, using either a threefold *Kyrie* or the *Trisagion*. Prayers are said which seek strength to entrust the one who has died to God, and entreat the comfort of the Holy Spirit.[6]

WORD
The reading of scripture follows; selected passages are suggested as guidelines.[7] This may be followed by words of comfort spoken by the leader or a time of reflection by the group.

PRAYER
Prayers are said, and a range of prayer texts is offered. These recall the baptism of the one who has died, entreating God to grant her a place in the communion of saints, commend the bereaved to the compassion of God and seek the gifts of faith and love for those gathered. Prayers conclude with the Lord's Prayer and a blessing which additionally prays that God may "defend us from all evil, and bring us to everlasting life".

Stage 2: Funeral Liturgy
Here we find the central funeral rite whose setting is the church. The main shape of the rite is as follows:

—   Gathering
—   Word
—   [Meal]
—   Commendation
—   Sending

GATHERING
The officiant welcomes the congregation in the name of the risen Christ and states the purpose of the rite.

---

[6]   Also included are a form of the prayer "that casting all their sorrow on you, they may know the consolation of your love" and a prayer for use following the death of a child which cites the familiar text of Jesus taking children into his arms and blessing them.

[7]   OT: Isa 49.13b-16a; Isa 54.10.
      PSALMS: Pss 121; 130.
      NT: Rom 6.3-9; 2 Cor 4.16-5.1.
      GOSPEL: Jn 10.27-29; Jn 14.27.

Greeting

The minister then meets the coffin and the bereaved at the entrance of the church and the congregation turns to face the funeral procession. The minister greets the whole assembly with the words of the Grace or with the following words:

> The blessed and holy Trinity, one God,
> who gives life, salvation,
> and resurrection,
> be with you all.

Remembrance of Baptism

The rite continues by recalling the baptism of the one who has died.[8] A pall may be placed on the coffin (which may also be sprinkled), as our creation from the dust, the saving death of Christ and the comfort and hope of the Spirit are invoked.

The procession then enters the church as a psalm, hymn or anthem is sung.

Prayer of the Day

A prayer is said which is effectively a proper of the dead.[9] Reminiscences and eulogies, if so desired, may follow. In this way the sermon is linked securely to the reading of scripture and the proclamation of the Paschal Mystery.

WORD

The reading of scripture is found in two or three passages;[10] when communion is celebrated the final reading is from the gospels. The sermon should be followed by a reflective silence.

After the singing of a hymn, the Apostles' Creed may be said.[11] The use of the Apostle's Creed with its reference to Christ's descent to the dead is particularly apt,

---

[8]   The prayers use the words of Gal 3.27 and Rom 6.2-5.

[9]   Two prayers are printed in the main service text. Three further texts are found in the Supplemental Material found at the conclusion of the three staged rites. These latter prayers include one for use at the funeral of a child.

[10]   The readings are part of the "proclamation" of the word. Scripture is proclaimed, just as is the sermon or homily. This strong liturgical use of scripture contrasts with the widespread Free Church practice in which the congregation follows the reading in their own copies of the bible. Scripture in worship is not simply a study text. It is the primary focus of the proclamation of the word.
Suggested passages are listed as follows:

OT: Job 19.23-27a; Eccl 3.1-15; Isaiah 25.6-9; Isa 40.1-11, 28-31; Isa 43.1-3a, 18-19, 25; Isa 55.1-3, 6-13; Isa 61.1-3; Jer 31.8-13; Lam 3.22-26, 31-33. At the funeral of a child: Isa 40.1, 6-11; Isa 43.1-3a, 5-7; Isa 65.17-20, 23-25; Isa 66.10-14.

PSALMS: Pss 42.1-7; 46.1-7; 121; 143. At the funeral of a child: Pss 23; 42.1-7; 121; 142.1-6.

NT: Rom 5.1-11; Rom 8.31-35, 37-39; 1 Cor 15.12-26; 2 Cor 4.7-18; 1 Thess 4.13-14, 18; Heb 12.1-2; 1 Pet 1.3-9; Rev 7.9-17; Rev 21.2-7; Rev 22.1-5. At the funeral of a child: Rom 8.31-35, 37-39; 1 Thess 4.13-14, 18; 1 Jn 3.1-2.

GOSPEL: Matt 5.1-10; Matt 11.25-30; Mk 16.1-7; Lk 24.1-9, 36-43; Jn 1.1-5, 9-14; Jn 6.37-40; Jn 10.11-16; Jn 11.21-27; Jn 14.1-6; Jn 14.25-27. At the funeral of a child: Matt 5.1-10; Matt 18.1-5, 10-14; Mk 10.13-16; John 10.11-16.

[11]   The ELLC text is printed in full. A pastoral note suggests that the creed and the preceding hymn may be omitted where the deceased was not baptised or where the congregation is not predominantly Christian.

keeping the focus on the nature of Christ's death for us. It prepares the way for the intercessions, which are introduced by an invitation to pray to Christ, "the resurrection and the life".

Intercessions

The prayers that follow recall the death of Lazarus, the compassion Jesus showed to Martha and Mary, his grief at the tomb and his word of resurrection; they continue by reference to the promise of paradise to the repentant thief. The baptism which washes us and the table which nourishes us are claimed as promises for the one who has died of communion with the saints at the banquet of heaven. The intercessions conclude with a rehearsal of the work of Christ in destroying death and opening the kingdom to all believers and claim the promise of Rom 8.38-39.

Where there is not to be Holy Communion, the Lord's Prayer is said and the rite moves on to the Commendation and Sending.

[MEAL]

At a celebration of the Eucharist, the liturgy continues with the greeting of peace and the customary Eucharistic order with a proper preface for the great prayer of thanksgiving.[12] The post-communion prayer calls to mind the messianic table and includes an echo of the kontakion:

> Almighty God, we thank you that in your great love
> you have given us a foretaste of your heavenly banquet,
> Grant that this sacrament may be to us a comfort in affliction
> and a pledge of our inheritance of life eternal
> where there is no death, neither sorrowing nor crying,
> but the fullness of joy with all your saints;
> through your Son Jesus Christ our Lord.
> **Amen.**

COMMENDATION

Where reminiscences and other thanksgiving of the life of the one who has died have not been included earlier, they may occur here. The officiant then invites those present to commend to God the one who has died. Two prayer texts are offered: "a sheep of your own fold, a lamb of your own flock"; and a petition to receive into paradise (with a reference to Rev 21.4) one who was baptised.

This section of the rite concludes with a farewell, which may be sung, based either on the canticle *Nunc Dimittis* or the anthem *In Paradisum*.

SENDING

The funeral service in church ends with an act of sending in these words:

> Let us go forth in peace.
> **In the name of Christ. Amen.**

---

[12]   Two forms of eucharistic prayer are printed among the Supplemental Materials.

Where the committal is to be at another time, a blessing may also be pronounced.

Stage 3: Committal
In the final stage of the rites, we move to the committal. This takes the same generic shape as the earlier stages:

— Gathering

— Word

— Committal

— Sending

GATHERING
As the coffin is taken in procession to the place of interment,[13] sentences of scripture may be said.[14] The minister then greets those present with the words "Grace and peace from our Savior Jesus Christ be with you all" and invites them to pray. While an alternative text is offered in the appendix of supplemental materials, the prayer printed in the main service order gives special emphasis to the central Christological emphasis:

> Holy God, holy and powerful,
> by the death and burial of Jesus your anointed,
> you have destroyed the power of death
> and made holy the resting places of all your people.
> Keep our sister/brother name, whose body/ashes we now lay to rest,
> in the company of all your saints.
> And at the last, O God, raise her/him up to share with all the faithful
> the endless joy and peace won through the glorious resurrection
> of Christ our Lord,
> who lives and reigns with you and the Holy Spirit, one God,
> now and forever.
> **Amen.**

WORD
Scripture is read before the committal of the body or ashes to their resting place. Suitable passages are suggested.[15]

COMMITTAL
Committal is made "in sure and certain hope" and may be followed by a form of *Requiem aeternam* couplet.

SENDING
The final act of the funeral rites begins with a litany:

---

[13] The service text has "interment" without reference to cremation, although the prayer of committal does provide for the interment of ashes.

[14] Suggested are: Job 19.25; Ps 23; Ps 42.1-7; Ps 121; Rom 14.8; Rev 21.1-4; Jn 11.25-26a. For use at the funeral of a child: Is 40.1-11; Hos 11.1, 3-4; Rev 7.17; Matt 19.14.

[15] 1 Cor 15.51-57; Phil 3.20-21; Jn 12.23-26. At the funeral of a child: Rev 7.15-17; Rev 21.3b-4, 7.

Jesus, saviour of the world,
be gracious to us.

By your incarnation and nativity,
be gracious to us.

By your prayers and tears,
be gracious to us.

By your grief and anguish,
be gracious to us.

By your cross and suffering,
be gracious to us.

By your atoning death,
be gracious to us.

By your rest in the grave,
be gracious to us.

By your triumphant resurrection,
be gracious to us.

By your presence with your people,
be gracious to us.

By the promise of your coming at the end of the ages,
be gracious to us.

The minister says the prayer "O Lord, support us all the day long" and those present may say the Lord's Prayer together. The assembly is blessed and dismissed either with a simple form or with the words of Heb 13.20.

Supplemental Materials
Reference has already been made to the resources provided either as alternatives or as supplements to what is found in the main service texts. For the most part these comprise prayer texts (opening, eucharistic and intercessory), acclamations, commendations and the like.

Resources for the Commendation of a Stillborn Child
No separate service is offered for a child's funeral,[16] but resources are provided for commendation following a stillbirth. These address the special heartbreak of such circumstances. Particular attention has been given throughout the funeral rites to the name of the deceased. In this rite, it is very important that where a name has been chosen it should be used. A prayer text for the mother asking for support and protection in Christ is printed as well as a wider prayer for all those who mourn this stillbirth.[17]

---

[16] Provision is made by means of special texts and prayers within the common funeral rite – rightly, in my view.

[17] Scripture passages suggested for such an occasion are listed: Deut 33.27a; Isa 40.27-31; Ps 139.1-15; Rom 8.26-27; 1 Jn 3.1-2.

Summary

If the 1978 *Lutheran Book of Worship* was terse, the 2002 texts are much wider and richer in scope. A similar comment can be made about the Christological centre. The rites in *Renewing Worship* explore in much greater detail what the earlier service strongly affirmed.

There is a strong assumption in the drafting of the rite that the funeral is for the baptised. In my view, that is a correct line to adopt .Of course, more or less frequently, ministers will be asked to officiate at the funeral of those who had no Christian allegiance – or, at least, none discernible to any but God. However, the norm of a Christian funeral rite ought surely to be the funeral of a Christian. If we have to make adjustments, it ought not to be to adapt for those who do have faith!

If the Christological emphasis is clearly rooted in the Paschal Mystery (as it is), the anthropological assumption is evident. Maybe this reflects the continuing variance among believers between those who adopt a unitary view and those who espouse the body-soul line. Committal is clearly of the body, but commendation is of the person rather than the soul. One wonders whether a deliberate ambiguity has been allowed to stand.

The shape of the rites follows the paradigm of gathering and sending.[18] This accords with the Christological nature of worship in which the assembly is gathered around Christ and sent out by him into the world. The missiological note reminds us that we bear witness to Christ and to our sure and certain hope both as we gather and as we go out. There is no uncertain trumpet in these Lutheran rites!

---

[18] The bipolar axis of the liturgical assembly (gathering and sending) was described in the report *Towards Koinonia in Worship* produced by the World Council of Churches' Faith and Order Consultation, which met in Ditchingham, England, in August 1994.

The Baptist Union of Great Britain

Patterns and Prayers for Christian Worship (1990)

In its preparation of a book for those who lead worship in Baptist churches, the committee entrusted with the task consciously strove not to produce set liturgies or orders of service. It argued that set prayers and orders were inimical to the nature of Baptist worship,[19] which was seen to be characterised by freedom and flexibility. Accordingly, there is no funeral liturgy as such. There are two main suggestions given as to how a funeral service may proceed and several prayers are provided. However, the failure to articulate clearly a theology of death and bereavement results in services without ritual.[20]

The preface to the two patterns provided declares at the outset that "Pastoral concerns should always be uppermost". It follows that in each of the service patterns that follows reference to the dead is never what I would call of a primary variety but always of a secondary nature.[21]

FIRST PATTERN

This form proposes a "funeral service with committal followed later by a service of thanksgiving". The initial welcome declares that the service is designed to say farewell, to give thanks and to commit the deceased and ourselves to God, and invites the mourners to listen to the promises of Scripture.

Selected scriptural sentences are then offered. All are traditional words used at funerals. Noteworthy as an opening sentence is 1 Pet 1.3-4 – although this is also found quite widely as a reading (usually in the pericope to verse 9). While this text seems at first sight a strange opening for a funeral, it has the great merit of tying human death into the death of Christ and into the hope of the resurrection of the dead. It is clearly intended as a text for use at the funerals of those who professed Christian faith.

The opening prayer is the *ASB* version of the prayer introduced in the 1928 *Book of Common Prayer*. While the prayer itself is a strong articulation of Christian faith, it is strange to find its clear reference to the concluding lines of the Apostles' Creed in the funeral service of a Christian tradition not given to saying the creeds in weekly worship.

---

[19]   The compilers recognised that the lack of written texts does not thereby imply lack of order. Even my Quaker neighbours comment that at Meeting the same people say much the same thing at much the same juncture week by week. Even if orders are not written down, they generally emerge by custom and practice. Further, the adoption by Baptists of the styles of the "soft charismatics" did not reflect the prevailing historical tradition known among Baptists. *Patterns and Prayers for Christian Worship* is a halfway house between those who claim the Spirit of liberty and those who claim the Spirit of order. While the creation of a book of patterns and prayers might be thought of as more likely to come from those committed to a liturgical stance, the book's general tone is more sympathetic to those of the contrary view.

[20]   For most British Baptists, this is a strong recommendation; for the present writer, it is not!

[21]   Primary reference to the dead implies articulating *for* the dead their cry to the Lord; secondary reference is talk *about* the dead.

ation: Baptist Union of Great Britain* 125

For the Anglican communicant this prayer links the Church on earth at the altar with the church expectant and triumphant with the Lord. The one who has received Christ in the Eucharist (where the Creed is repeated) is now received by Christ. For most Baptists this resonance is probably entirely lost.[22]

Reading from scripture is followed by a "brief address". I am relieved to see that my own tradition does not regard this as optional; I wish they had avoided the word "address", which allows the tribute to supplant the sermon.

Prayers of Thanksgiving for Victory in Christ and of Remembrance and Thanksgiving are followed by what is called the act of committal. In fact, commendation and committal are offered in alternative prayers. It would be unsafe to conclude that this was because the distinction between the commendation of the soul and the committal of the body had been consciously rejected since in the second pattern there is an apparent distinction made. However, when this was pointed out to a member of the committee who prepared the book, he had not consciously been aware of the two approaches.

The service ends with the *Nunc Dimittis* and a prayer from the *ASB*.[23] If the *Nunc Dimittis* were intended to be applied to the deceased, it would mark an interesting development. The inference might then be drawn that a prayer uttered for someone now dead could have effect. Such a deduction is not likely to be made by many Baptists, and it is wiser to understand the choice of the *Nunc Dimittis* as a result of its having words which seemed generally to fit.

The blessing is the Celtic prayer

> Deep peace of the running wave to you,
> deep peace of the flowing air to you,
> deep peace of the quiet earth to you,
> deep peace of the shining stars to you,
> deep peace of the Son of peace to you.

A Service of Thanksgiving is proposed either for the same day or at a later date. In terms of satisfactory grieving and of proper separation and incorporation, I would suspect that a thanksgiving would be better delayed where possible. The central feature of the service is a sermon to which the following rubric is attached:

> The emphasis will be on thanksgiving for the person's life and on a triumphant proclamation of the resurrection hope.

The prayers that follow express the rubric's agenda in terms that give no hint of the darkness of grief and bereavement. I am strongly in favour of proclaiming the resurrection at the funeral, but only in the context of the death of Christ. For me the transition here is too abrupt.

---

[22] I recognise, of course, that it is the Nicene form of the Creed that is used at the Eucharist; but the placing of the coffin before the communion table evokes the Eucharistic action. I have asked many Baptist ministers what the relevant words of the prayer meant to them. Not one made the connection with the Creed.

[23] *Alternative Service Book*: section 58.

SECOND PATTERN

Here is a more traditional form of service. After the opening sentences – one of which is the powerful Jn 5.25 – a welcome outlines the purpose of the service. The purpose is effectively fourfold: to honour the dead person; to listen to the great words of the Christian faith; to give thanks for the life of the deceased; to renew trust in God.

The assumption of the service is that the person who has died was a Christian. The prayer of remembrance and thanksgiving includes the words "we bless you that his/her sins are forgiven" which Baptists, with their Evangelical stance, will clearly attach to those who have professed faith.

The main interest for the liturgist in this pattern of service lies in two prayers, which form part of the commendation and the committal. First to be offered, as a prayer of commendation, is a form of the *Proficiscere*. For some reason (presumably to avoid what was felt to be an archaism), the traditional 'Go Forth' has been replaced by the word 'Depart'. The effect is not a happy one. 'Depart' in this imperative mood is redolent of the words of Simon Peter: "Depart from me, for I am a sinful man, O Lord"; or, worse, of the words in the parable of the sheep and the goats: "Depart from me, you cursed, into the eternal fire prepared for the devil and his angels."

The old form has much to commend it and 'Go forth' is not so obscure that it requires alteration. What is more interesting is that so Catholic a prayer should have been proposed in a book intended for those of a very different tradition.[24]

The second prayer of note is a selection of words from the *Te Deum*.[25] Once again, it is good to see the use of the ancient texts of the Christian Church in a book meant for those who are often suspicious of church tradition. How many will recognise the source of the words is open to question. The earlier comments about Baptist recognition of the origin of liturgical texts apply here also.

Summary

Beyond these two main patterns of service, other prayers and readings are proposed for special circumstances: a stillborn or newly born child; a child; a sudden or violent death; a victim of violence. The selection is useful and offers perhaps the best contribution to funeral liturgy from the material offered in the book.

One other observation should be noted. A comment is made about memorial services for public tragedies. In the course of what is said, the following appears.

> A memorial service is not a funeral. Funerals are personal and relate more immediately to the release of the body. A memorial service is part of the reflective and healing process. Survivors need time to recover physically, and the service may be three, six, or even twelve months after the event.

---

[24] This form of the prayer was used in the previous Baptist worship book, *Praise God*, (1980: Baptist Union of Great Britain and Ireland, edd., A. Gilmore, E. Smalley, M. Walker).

[25] In the acknowledgements at the end of *Patterns and Prayers* the source of the versions used is given as the United Reformed Church's 1989 *Service Book*. While this form of the *Te Deum* is indeed found in the URC's book, the attribution is incorrect. It is in origin a text of the International Consultation on English Texts (ICET), as the *Alternative Service Book 1980*, in which the full text appears, makes clear.

This is an important recognition that the funeral is primarily an act of separation and that memorial services are much more part of the transitional and incorporative phases of death rites. The patterns of service, like the funeral services in some other traditions at which we are looking, do not keep that distinction sufficiently in view. Funerals still have to bear too much ritual weight. Baptists are no better at avoiding this than others.

At the time of writing, the Baptist Union of Great Britain and Ireland was preparing a revision of *Patterns and Prayers for Christian Worship*. The revision was to be so complete as to constitute a new book of worship resources. Included were to be funerary texts.[26]

---

[26] The present writer was a member of the revision group. It was probable that some of the funeral resources would be based upon his work published in *In Sure and Certain Hope* (Canterbury Press: 2003).

The Methodist Conference[27]

The Methodist Worship Book (1999)

The *Methodist Worship Book* was published in 1999 for use by British Methodists. It succeeded the *Methodist Service Book* of 1975. In common with many of their sister churches, Methodists have significantly increased the range of material for use at or near the time of death. "Prayer with the Dying" is part of a section of the book entitled Healing and Reconciliation. This is followed by a section entitled Funeral and Related Services, which contains the following material:

— Prayers in the Home or Hospital after a Death
— An Office of Commendation
— A Vigil
— A Funeral Service in a Church, a Crematorium, or a Cemetery, leading to Committal
— A Funeral Service at a Crematorium or Cemetery followed by a Service of Thanksgiving in Church
— A Funeral Service for a Child
— A Funeral Service for a Stillborn Child
— A Service for the Burial of Ashes

PRAYER WITH THE DYING
The service begins with a salutation of peace and the words of the Grace. Opening sentences of scripture may be said and followed by a prayer for the dying person, seeking the comfort of the promise of eternal life found in the resurrection of Christ. A psalm precedes the confession,[28] which uses either a responsive form of the *Kyrie* or the General Confession, and absolution. The minister says the *Nunc Dimittis* followed by prayers for those close to death and for those close to bereavement and the Lord's Prayer. A prayer is said,[29] and the service ends with words of peace drawn from Phil 4.7.

This prayer service is direct in its reference to approaching death and the accompanying pastoral note comments:

> The way in which this service is used will depend greatly on the condition of the one who is dying. Even if the dying person cannot register a response, it is still

---

[27] There will be some Methodists who will find the description of them as belonging to a Church of the Reformation somewhat difficult to accept. To them I apologise; I hope that they will find it in their hearts to forgive me.

[28] Ps 23 or Ps 121 or Ps 131.1-2a.

[29] Either a form of the *Proficiscere*, or a formula derived from the *Proficiscere* with the refrain "have mercy on you", or a simple prayer of commendation.

appropriate to pray with her or him. If necessary, the words printed in **bold** type may
be said by the leader alone.

There is no doubt that used with care a service of this kind can be a most helpful
pastoral occasion. With family and friends gathered around the bedside of one who is
dying, a great deal of "unfinished business" may be concluded in this pastoral rite,
making the subsequent funeral much easier to bear.

PRAYERS IN THE HOME OR HOSPITAL AFTER A DEATH

The prayers here proposed mark the first stage of the Church's ministry after death and
are intended for use by the minister or other pastoral visitor on the first visit after the
death.

An opening sentence, using Matt 5.4, invites those present to keep an initial silence.
This is followed by the reading of scripture (Jn 14.1-6, 27 or some other suitable
passage). The Lord's Prayer is said along with other prayers. Among those suggested is
the kontakion "All of us go down to the dust; yet even in the grave we make our song".
The prayers end with the formula from Phil 4.7.

AN OFFICE OF COMMENDATION

This Office provides a form of commendation for use (whether on the day of the funeral
or on hearing of the death) among those who cannot otherwise be at the funeral. The
pastoral note suggests that it is most appropriate when someone has died abroad and the
immediate family cannot be present at the funeral.

Opening sentences are drawn from Mal 4.2 ("your healing shall spring up like the
dawn") and 1 Cor 15.52 ("the trumpet shall sound"). A prayer for comfort may be said,
a hymn sung, and a psalm and other scripture read.[30] These may be followed by the
sharing of memories of the one who has died. Prayers follow, concluding with the
Lord's Prayer. The service ends with a dismissal, using either a form of the *Kaddish* or
the words of Jude 24-25, and the service ends with the formula from Phil 4.7.

In effect, this is a shortened form of funeral rite rather than a form of commendation;
it is a funeral without the body. Such a rite may become increasingly significant as more
and more people undertake travel abroad (whether on business or for pleasure);
inevitably some travellers will die whether from natural causes, from an accident, or
from suicide or homicide. Getting the body home is not always possible. Equally, any
bereaved who are abroad may not be able to return in time for a funeral back home.
Given these considerations, it is an interesting development to provide such a rite.

If it is, as I suggest, a funeral without the body, then it may also have a purpose in
those situations where a body cannot be recovered; air or rail crashes or acts of
terrorism may leave no identifiable remains. Memories of the deceased may not then be
enough; the circumstance may demand "words against death" of a more structured and
formal kind.

---

[30] The following psalms are suggested: Pss 23; 42; 43; 121; 130; 139.
  Scriptures include: Jn 11.21-27; Jn 14.1-3; Rom 6.3-9; Phil 1.20-26.

A VIGIL
The service begins with a greeting and prayer. There follow readings from scripture and further prayers, concluding with a dismissal.

The Ministry of the Word includes three suggested passages of scripture, of which any or all may be read.[31] The prayers that follow use the versicle and response:

Lord, have mercy.
Christ, have mercy.

and, using scriptural images of Christ, make petition for those present:

Crucified Saviour,
save us from the fear of death:
Risen Lord,
raise us to glory:
Gentle Shepherd,
bring rest to our souls:
Lamb of God,
grant us with N your peace for ever:
Son of Mary,
bless those who mourn:

The final prayers may include material from *St.Patrick's Breastplate* ("Christ be with me, Christ within me") and a petition that Christ who gave himself up to death will receive the one who has now died and grant peace to those who grieve.

This Vigil rite may be used in a variety of locations (at home or in church or a chapel of rest) whether the body is present or not. It is designed for evening use and provides a helpful place for quiet and directed prayer for peace.

A FUNERAL SERVICE IN A CHURCH, A CREMATORIUM, OR A CEMETERY, LEADING TO COMMITTAL
This is the conventional form of funeral service. Its structure is akin to those of other traditions and in itself requires little comment.

Gathering
The service begins with Jn 11.25-26 and other optional sentences.[32] A hymn is followed by an opening prayer seeking deliverance from sorrow and grace to receive God's promises.

The Ministry of the Word
Readings from scripture are introduced by a reminder that the assembly gathers to worship God, to give thanks for the life of the one who has died and to commend the deceased to God's care. A choice of psalms is proposed,[33] and a Gospel passage is

---

[31] Ps 27 (selected verses); 2 Cor 5.1, 6-10 (the earthly tent and the house not made with hands); Jn 11.17-26a (I am the resurrection and the life).
[32] Matt 5.4; Jn 3.16; Lam 3.22-23; Jn 16.33b; Ps 46.1.
[33] PSALMS: Pss 130; 23; 103.8-18. This selection is not intended to be exclusive; other psalms may be used.

read.[34] The psalm and gospel may be accompanied by other passages of scripture.[35] Following the reading of scripture, a sermon is preached.

The Response
Prayers are offered in which the death and resurrection give rise to the praise of God; the faithful witness of previous generations is recalled and the one who has now died is commended to God's care with thanks for deliverance from tribulation and death. The final prayer is for those who mourn and is a form of the well known prayer "deal graciously with those who mourn". A hymn may then be sung.

The Commendation
The minister commends the deceased to God and the congregation says the Lord's Prayer. At the place of committal, the minister begins with the words of Phil 4.7 and may continue with other suggested scripture sentences.[36]

The Committal
A version of the traditional formula ("Since the earthly life of *N* has come to an end") may be used, or the following:

> God alone is holy and just and good.
> In this certainty we have commended *N* to God.
> We therefore commit *her/his* body
> *to be cremated/to the elements/to be buried*,
> earth to earth, ashes to ashes, dust to dust;
> trusting in the infinite mercy of God,
> through Jesus Christ our Lord. Amen.
> Blessèd are the dead who die in the Lord;
> for they rest from their labours.

There is a choice of five additional prayers of which one or more may be said.

— We pray for those we love but see no longer – let light perpetual shine upon them.

— You have made nothing vain and love all you have made.

— In our duties your help, in our perplexities your guidance, in our dangers your protection, in our sorrows your peace.

— Support us till the shadows lengthen, the evening comes.

— Bring us into the house and gate of heaven – one equal light, one equal music.

---

[34] GOSPEL: Jn 14.1-6, 27; Jn 6.35-40.

[35] ADDITIONAL SCRIPTURES: 1 Cor 15.3-5; 1 Cor 15.20-24; 1 Pet 1.3-9; Rom 8.28, 31b-35, 38-39.

An appendix of further readings suggests the following: Job 19.1, 21-27a; Pss 8; 16; 27; 30; 42.1-8; 43.3-5; 46; 90; 103; 116; 118.14-21, 28-29; 121; 138; 139.1-14, 17-18, 23; Isa 25.6-9; Isa 40.1-6, 8-11, 28-31; Isa 43.1-3a, 5-7, 13, 15, 18-19, 25; Isa 44.6, 8a; Isa 55.1-3, 6-13; Isa 61.1-3; Lam 3.17-26, 31-33; Eccl 3.1-15; Lk 24.13-35; Jn 5.19-25; Jn 6.35-40; Jn 11.1-6, 17-27, 32-35, 38-44; 2 Cor 4.16-5.10; Eph 1.15-23; Eph 2.1, 4-10; Phil 3.10-21; 1 Thess 4.13-18; 2 Tim 2.8-12a; 1 Jn 3.1-2; 1 Jn 4.7-18a; Rev 7.9-17; Rev 21.1-7; Rev 21.22-27; Rev 22.1-5.

[36] Those suggested are: Ps 103.13; 2 Cor 1.3-4; Rom 14.9.

The service ends with the dismissal. Two forms are suggested:

> Grant to the living, grace;
> to the departed, rest;
> to the world, peace;
> and the blessing of God,
> the Father, the Son and the Holy Spirit,
> be with *you/us* now and for ever. **Amen.**

> May God in his infinite love and mercy
> bring the whole Church,
> living and departed in the Lord Jesus,
> to a joyful resurrection
> and the fulfilment of his eternal kingdom;
> and the blessing of God,
> the Father, the Son and the Holy Spirit,
> remain with *you/us* always. **Amen.**

The formulae and prayers used in this service, while couched in modern language, look back to the continuing tradition of the Church. They mark a Catholic expression of Free Church life that echoes John Wesley's spirituality.

The rite has a strong sense of the passage from earth to heaven from death to life eternal and in this way expresses well a rite of passage for the dead.

A FUNERAL SERVICE AT A CREMATORIUM OR CEMETERY FOLLOWED BY A SERVICE OF THANKSGIVING IN CHURCH

This rite begins at the place of committal and then returns to church for a service of thanksgiving. The committal forms are those commented on above and really demand no further comment.

The service in church visualises the possibility that it occurs either on the day of the committal or at a later date, when ashes may be placed in church. In the latter event, the urn or casket is placed in front of the communion table on another table covered in a white cloth. The service takes the following simple form:

— Gathering
— Ministry of the Word
— Response

The Gathering

An opening scripture introduces a hymn. The minister concludes this section with an acclamation or prayer.

The Ministry of the Word

The minister reminds the congregation of the risen Christ and calls them to give thanks for the one who has died and to support those who mourn. Scripture is then read. The only provision is that where the service occurs on the same day as the committal service, the scriptures should be different from those used at the committal. There follow a sermon and hymn.

The Response

This section begins with an extract from the *Te Deum* ("You, Christ, are the king of glory"). The prayers that follow use the versicle and response:

Lord, in your mercy,
hear our prayer.

Thanks are given for the life and witness of the Church on earth and for support given in times of sorrow. Silent or extempore uttered prayer may be offered by the congregation, and the time of prayer is brought to a close with the following:

Almighty God, we thank you
that you have joined together your faithful people
in one communion and fellowship
in the mystical body of your Son.
Give us grace so to follow your blessèd saints
in all virtuous and godly living,
that we may come to those inexpressible joys
which you have prepared for those who love you;
through Jesus Christ our Lord.
Amen.

The congregation join to say the Lord's Prayer and to sing a hymn. The service ends with the same choice of prayer as given in the funeral service leading to committal.

God grant to the living, grace;
to the departed, rest;
to the world, peace;
and to us and all the faithful, life everlasting;
and the blessing of God,
the Father, the Son and the Holy Spirit,
be with *you/us* now and for ever.
Amen.

The peace of God,
which passes all understanding,
keep *your/our* hearts and minds
in the knowledge and love of God
and of his Son, Jesus Christ our Lord;
and the blessing of God,
the Father, the Son and the Holy Spirit,
be with *you/us* now and for ever.
Amen.

This form of service allows the close family and friends to observe the committal rite on their own and then to invite the wider congregation to give thanks with them at a later stage.

As long as the initial rites do not exclude those who want to say farewell, there is much to commend this practice. There is no long delay between a funeral and reception while the family disappears to a distant place of disposal – a gap when some, who might otherwise stay to console the close mourners, drift away to other things.[37]

A FUNERAL SERVICE FOR A CHILD
The Funeral Service for a Child follows the same structure as the Funeral Service leading to Committal. I shall therefore only consider the particular variations proposed for use in these particular circumstances.

The Gathering
The opening scripture sentences are varied to meet the particular circumstances of a child's death.[38] The gathering sentence names the child and the parents (or parent) and calls the congregation to pray for the support of those who mourn. Silence precedes a further prayer. There are two suggested texts, of which one should be used. The first approaches God "our help in every time of trouble" and asks that those present may be enabled to worship in the presence of death and to trust in God's mercy and goodness. The second prayer starts with God as the father of a son who has suffered and died, but who raised him to glory. Again trust is sought and patience in the time of darkness.

The Ministry of the Word
Among the passages proposed is Mk 10.13-16, with its reference to the children brought to Jesus for blessing and his insistence that the kingdom of God belongs to the childlike.

The Commendation
Echoes of Mk 10.13-16 continue to be found. At the committal, Isa 66.13 is suggested along with Isa 40.11.

The Committal
The intercessory prayers refer to the death of Lazarus, seek release from any burden of guilt and healing for painful memories and ask that sins be forgiven. They call the mourners to newness of life and, referring to Mary at the Cross, call for strength at a time of grief for a child. They conclude with petitions for confident faith, a love which binds the family together and for that time when

---

[37] Where the only concern is not to lose those who might otherwise stay, it may be better to commit the body into the hearse and allow the disposal to proceed unattended. If this course is taken, it may give the impression that the body is unimportant. My own view is that wherever possible at least one person from those who mourn should be present at the graveside or at the crematorium.

   Another possibility is to delay the disposal of the body until after the reception. In this way the family and close friends may greet other mourners after the service.

[38] The opening scripture sentences include several additional texts, while omitting others. Added at this point are: Ps 103.13; Isa 66.13; Mk 10.13; Jn 14.1 and Rom 8.39. Omitted at this point are: Jn 3.16; Lam 3.22-23; Jn 16.33b and Ps 46.1.

we may be united with all your children
in the brightness of your glory.

Concluding prayers for the family are said, followed by the Lord's Prayer and the dismissal, which may include an additional prayer to Christ the Good Shepherd.

Understandably, Mk 10.13-16 is a key verse; after all, the pastoral note that Jesus, who welcomed little children, will welcome this one is natural to make. However, the children brought to Jesus were alive and this child is dead. That is why the other verses and references are needed; death must not be minimised. The Church of Scotland's poignant use of the text "Is all well with the child?" is not found here.

A FUNERAL SERVICE FOR A STILLBORN CHILD
Once again, the structure of the service remains constant, and only the variations call for comment. However, this service attends very closely to the need to recognise the personhood of a stillborn child. It is impossible to quantify grief, but to have carried a child to term and then to be delivered of that infant stillborn must be one of the most traumatic experiences for any woman (and, indeed, for any father). Hope has been invested, a nursery prepared, clothes bought, and all for – well, what? "Nothing" seems far too casual a word; the taste of ashes in the mouth must be very bitter.

The Gathering
The minister greets the congregation, and where a name had been given, it is announced at the very outset (and throughout the service the baby is named). "You have known us from the very beginning," says the opening prayer. The poignancy of the circumstance keeps the words brief.

The Ministry of the Word
Pss 23 and 139.1, 13-18 are proposed for use. Three New Testament texts are also suggested: Matt 18.1-5 (the Matthaean parallel to Mk 10.13-16), Matt 11.27-30 (Come to me, all who carry heavy burdens) and 2 Cor 1.3-7 (the Father of mercies and God of all consolation). A short address or reflection follows.

Although in general I have taken the view that a sermon should be preached at funerals, the circumstances of stillbirth are likely to leave us all bereft of speech. Words here should be kept to a minimum; and they must be words against death. The most important words will be prayer.

The Commendation
There is a time of silence. The first prayer names the child as an heir of God's promises,

sharing in the humanity
that you have redeemed in Christ.

There follows a form of commendation; and at the place of committal, verses used in the funeral of a child are here used.

<u>The Committal</u>
Four optional prayers invoke God as a loving parent, the Father of all, the one whose loving arms enfold us in our grief. The third prayer intercedes specifically for the parents:

> Gracious God,
> may your loving arms enfold us in our grief.
> Support *N*'s mother *B*,
> who with love has carried her/him to birth.
> Uphold *N*'s father *A*,
> who has watched and waited.
> Be with them now
> in their emptiness and pain;
> through him who bears our grief and carries our sorrows,
> Jesus Christ our Lord.
> **Amen.**[39]

The congregation says the Lord's Prayer, and the dismissal follows using either the words of Phil 4.7 or the prayer beginning "Christ the Good Shepherd enfold *you/us* with love".

This service responds to a need that until comparatively recently had been swept under the carpet. A woman whose child had been stillborn was likely to be told to have another, as though grief for the dead child could be assuaged by the arrival of the latter. Many women did just that, but it is becoming increasingly clear that the proposed cure solved little. The Church has taken an important step in acknowledging and marking what has occurred. It raises the parallel question about miscarriages. Where the baby is not carried to term, how are we to mark its death? The issue is not an easy one, but those who draft rites for the stillborn may yet be asked to apply themselves to a similar task for the miscarried.

A SERVICE FOR THE BURIAL OF ASHES
Where a body has been cremated, the mourners may wish to dispose of the ashes other than by leaving them in the crematorium's garden of remembrance.

For some Christian traditions, the scattering of ashes (as distinct from their burial) is not permitted. There is concern that scattering violates the integrity and unity of the body. The rite now under consideration specifically permits scattering of ashes.

The service takes a simple form:

— Gathering
— Ministry of the Word
— Burial (or scattering)
— Dismissal and Blessing

---

[39]   In many ways this is a good prayer; though why the mother (who is named first) should be *B* and the father (who is named second) should be *A*, seems rather strange!

Gathering
The minister greets the people, reminding the congregation that, "although our bodies return to dust, we shall be raised with Christ in glory".

The Ministry of the Word
Scripture sentences are provided of which one or more or some other may be used.[40] These are followed by a prayer that those present might be lifted from the darkness of grief by the light of God's presence.

Burial
The minister says a short prayer as the ashes are returned to the earth. There are three additional prayers for optional use, and the Lord's Prayer follows.

Dismissal and Blessing
Two short prayers are proposed.

Summary

I have reserved until now any comment about the Lord's Prayer, but it ought not to escape our attention that the Methodist Conference authorised for use two versions – the Modified Traditional ("Our Father who art in heaven") and the ELLC text ("Our Father in heaven"). Unlike the Church of England, the Methodists have not altered the ELLC text. The two versions are always printed in parallel, with the ELLC text to the left, as is the case throughout *The Methodist Worship Book*. In a subtle yet clear way, this indicates that in using modern English service texts the ecumenically agreed modern English form of the Lord's Prayer is preferred for use.[41]

The Methodist funerary texts examined in the foregoing section share a vision of death as the gate to glory. The range and diversity of pastoral circumstances for which ministry is offered is impressive. The texts offer a rite of passage for the deceased and the bereaved and articulate a strong Christian belief in the resurrection. They are sensitive to a previous tradition of funerary liturgy, but they do move in a new direction – both in the particularity of the pastoral circumstances they seek to address and in the contemporary freedom among churches to borrow texts from one another without compromising their own integrity.

---

[40] Rom 6.8-9a; 2 Cor 5.1; Rev 7.17.
[41] The United Reformed Church, the Church of Scotland and the Scottish Episcopal Church also use the ELLC text.

The Church of Scotland

Common Order (1994)

On 15 May 1994, the Panel of Worship of the Church of Scotland presented the Moderator with a specially bound edition of *Common Order* at the official launch of the book in John Knox's House, Edinburgh. The Convenor of the Panel remarked that it was 300 years – almost to the month – since the publication in 1694 of John Knox's *Genevan Service Book*. While the new *Common Order* affirms its Genevan past, there was introduced alongside that heritage the tradition of Celtic Christianity, which is an equal part of the Church of Scotland's inheritance. That combination of Celtic and Genevan traditions is to be found in the new funeral rites of the Church of Scotland.

The book offers two main funeral orders, suggestions of material to be used in distressing circumstances, additional prayers for funeral services, an order for a child's funeral, an order for a stillborn child, and an order for the disposal of ashes. There is also an order for the dedication of a churchyard or burial ground.[42] It is not my intention to look at all these in detail, but to draw attention to what is liturgically, ritually, or theologically of particular interest.[43]

FIRST ORDER FOR A FUNERAL SERVICE

The service begins with the grace. A wide selection of texts is then offered for the call to worship. Along with the traditional sentences there are to be found texts promising the continuing and unfailing presence of God (Josh 1.5; Matt 28.20), declaring the beauty and mystery of God (Ps 27.1; 1 Cor 2.9); warning of judgement (Rom 2.2-3); and asserting the safety of the faithful in the hands of God (Wisd 1.1, 3). The range is wider than is commonly found, and is the more helpful for that.

The opening prayers seek comfort for those who mourn and forgiveness for those who

> . . . remember with sorrow
> how we have failed one another
> and grieved your heart.[44]

At the outset this sounds an important confessional note, reminding all present that the living and the departed each rely on the forgiveness we offer one another and receive from God.

There follow the readings from scripture. The order suggests Old Testament, a Psalm (sung or said), and New Testament ending with a Gospel.[45] This is a very full

---

[42] The order for dedication of a Churchyard or Burial Ground is separate from the other funerary rites in *Common Order*, but is intended to form part of the overall provision.

[43] I shall not comment at all on the order for interment or scattering of ashes, which is really simply an extension of the committal and says nothing significantly new.

[44] *Common Order*: 254.

[45] The readings are produced separately from the orders of service at page 269ff.

provision, and whether it is honoured in the breach or the observance, it may be too soon to say. However, as the Moderator of the Church of Scotland remarked, the book is not mandatory, and there will be some who will never open it.[46]

A sermon, called here an Address, is not optional. In the opening rubric to the service there is a clear directive that the address

> which may include reference by way of tribute to the deceased should proclaim the Gospel of the Resurrection.

The rubric adds that any separate tribute should be added after the address and before the prayers.[47]

The prayer which follows begins by thanking God for Jesus who brought "life and immortality to light" (cf. 2 Tim 1.10) and then paraphrases the line from William Bright's hymn "only look on us as found in him",[48] looking for deliverance from judgement to "the joy and peace of your presence". The prayer which follows is "Eternal God, you hold all souls in life", which is to be found in the Church of England's *Alternative Service Book*. Thankful remembrance is then made of the deceased and those who mourn are commended to the consoling love of God.

Two prayers mark the commendation. The *Alternative Service Book*'s "Heavenly Father, by your mighty power" is slightly amended and avoids masculine language for God. It now reads "Gracious God, by your power". The second prayer is the ancient couplet

> Rest eternal grant unto *him*, O Lord.
> And let light perpetual shine upon *him*.

This use of the *Requiem aeternam* is a bold stroke for a church so very much aware of its Genevan tradition. An ascription of glory and a blessing are pronounced before the committal, which presumably follows at another place.

The committal is commendably brief. Opening sentences of scripture and the words of committal themselves are followed by the *Nunc Dimittis* and a modern-language

---

OT: Job 14.1-2, 5; Eccl 3.1-8, 11, 14; Isa 25.8-9; Isa 26.3-4; Isa 40.28-31; Lam 3.17-18, 21-26; Wisd 3.1-5; Wisd 4.7-11, 13-15.

PSALMS: Pss 23; 103.8-18; 121; 130. Also: 8; 16.8-11; 39.4-7, 12; 42.1-8; 43.3-5; 46; 62.5-8; 90.1-6, 10, 12; 116; 118.14-21, 28-29; 138; 139.1-14, 17-18, 23.

EPISTLE: Rom 8.18, 28, 31-36a, 37-39; Rom 14.7-12; 1 Cor 15.19-23, 35-38, 42-44, 50, 53-55, 57-58; 2 Cor 1.3-4; 1 Thess 4.13-14, 18; Rev 21.1-4; 22.3b-5. (Also: Acts 10.34-43; Rom 5.5-11; Rom 6.3-9; Rom 8.14-24a; 2 Cor 4.7-18; 2 Cor 4.15-5.1; 2 Cor 5.1, 6-10; Eph 2.4-9a; 1 Thess 4.13-18; 1 Thess 5.9-11, 23-24; 2 Tim 2.8-13; 1 Pet 1.3-9; Rev 7.9-17.)

GOSPEL: Jn 6.37-40; Jn 14.1-4, 6-7, 27. Also: Mk 16.1-8a; Lk 7.11-16; Jn 11.17-27; Jn 20.24-29.

[46] This observation was made in the Moderator's short speech of welcome to the book at the launch in John Knox's House. He himself looked forward to using the new *Common Order*, but his comment about those ministers of the Kirk whose allegiance to previous service books had been at best occasional drew wry laughter from those present.

[47] *Common Order*: 251.

[48] "And now, O Father, mindful of the love".

form of the prayer from the 1928 *Book of Common Prayer* ". . . you have given us new birth into a living hope. . ." The service ends with the blessing.

SECOND ORDER FOR A FUNERAL SERVICE

In place of the usual sentences of scripture the introduction to this order of service offers a reflection of the nature of death, which it describes as "always a mystery". It continues

> Whenever it comes, it is never an end,
> but is always a beginning

and links the present death with the death and resurrection of Jesus. This represents something of what I have argued throughout this book – although I would rather say that death is both an end and a beginning. It may therefore seem a little churlish if I suggest that, while there is a genuine attempt to use poetic language, the overall effect is rather didactic. The information needs to be the poetry, rather than being carried by it. The idea is excellent, and it only fails in execution by the slightest touch; but in poetry execution is everything. The language itself must be the meaning.

The theme of the service is light and darkness, and the references to the sun as symbolic of the light of Christ are many. In the prayer that follows the first hymn this theme is very clearly expressed:

> Living God,
> you have lit the day with the sun's light
> and the midnight with shining stars.
> Lighten our saddened hearts with the bright beams
> of the Sun of Righteousness
> risen with healing in his wings,
> even Jesus Christ our Lord.
> And so preserve us in the doing of your will,
> that at the last we may shine
> as the stars for ever;
> through Jesus Christ our Lord. **Amen.**

This is far more successful as a piece of liturgy than the introductory material, since it is not at all didactic. The petition arises simply from adoration. The words are the message.

After the reading from scripture and the address, there follow prayers of petition and intercession. Here again the poetry of the prayers is resonant, although at times lacking complete assurance of rhythm and metre.

> You deliver our eyes from tears,
> our feet from falling
> and our souls from death . . .
> Help us to walk amid the things of this world
> with our eyes wide open to your glory . . .

The second excerpt is a little ungainly and would have gained from two slight emendations to retain the metrical pulse:

> Help us to walk amid this world
> with eyes wide open to your glory . . .

However, the prayers are illuminated with metaphor, and show a real determination to avoid the impersonal prose that makes for unsatisfactory liturgical language. These prayers are alive with direct address and concrete allusion.[49]

FOR USE IN DISTRESSING CIRCUMSTANCES
The Church of Scotland offers a collection of supplementary material for use in addition to or substitution for that provided in the first or second orders. Extra opening sentences are suggested, an additional opening prayer, and two further passages of scripture.[50] There follow prayers for various circum-stances. The list is headed by a prayer that begins with the opening two paragraphs of the *Te Deum* before concluding:

> Chase away the darkness of our night
> and restore morning to the world.
> Enlighten us with the healing beams of your love
> and guide our feet into the way of peace.

The switch is quite abrupt and while the favoured theme of darkness and light is continued, there is a slight problem for the ear, which does not appear on the page. The visual contrast between night and morning is clear, but the aural impression may be confusing. I wonder how many congregations will hear "restore *mourning* to the world"? My own impression is that here the liturgists have pushed their imagery too far. Other prayers are grouped under themes: after a wasting illness; after a suicide; after violence.

ADDITIONAL PRAYERS FOR FUNERAL SERVICES
Additional prayers are offered for various sections of the two orders. There is a rich and wide provision dealing with the approach, the reading of scripture (before and after), thanksgiving, those who mourn, the offering of life, petition, the communion of saints, facing death, commendation, and committal. Some suggestions are given for those situations when no body has been recovered. This additional material forms twenty seven different prayers and suggestions. I do not intend here to offer any detailed commentary.

---

[49]   They are also remarkable for the use of the third person singular pronoun. Where often *he/him* is made to do common duty, here the Panel of Worship has given the same role to *she/her*. However, the texts are not consistent in this matter; elsewhere *he/him* re-surfaces.

[50]   OPENING SENTENCES: Ps 46.1-2; Lam 3:22; 1 Pet 5.7; Isa 35.10b; Heb 13.5b; Matt 11.28
     SCRIPTURE READINGS: Ps 22.1-2, 4-5, 19; Jn 5.24-25.

ORDER FOR THE FUNERAL OF A CHILD

This order represents a clear decision to create a distinct rite rather than adapting existing liturgy by patching on a few new texts and prayers. The opening sentences of scripture demonstrate this from the outset. Three verses in particular stand out:[51]

> As a mother comforts her child,
> so shall I myself comfort you.

> Is all well with the child?
> All is well.

> Jerusalem will be called the City of Faithfulness:
> and the city will be full of boys and girls
> playing in the streets.

The prayers that precede the reading of scripture include a litany linking the life, death and resurrection of Jesus with children and parents.

> Lord Jesus Christ,
> you became a little child for our sake,
> sharing our human life:
> **bless us and keep us.**

> You grew in wisdom and grace,
> learning obedience:
> **bless us and keep us.**

> You welcomed little children,
> promising them the kingdom of heaven:
> **bless us and keep us.**

> You comforted those who mourned,
> grieving for their children:
> **bless us and keep us.**

> You took upon yourself
> the suffering of us all:
> **bless us and keep us.**

> Lord Jesus Christ,
> you rose from the dead
> bringing life eternal:
> **bless us and keep us.**
> **Amen.**

Among the scriptures proposed, there stands out as an interesting and creative choice the passage Matt 18.1-5, 10-14 in which two distinct pericopes are made to stand in juxtaposition. New Testament scholars may well have qualms about such a use of the text, but the effect is remarkable. Words of Jesus about who is greatest in the kingdom

---

[51]   Isa 66.13; 2 Kgs 4.26; Zech 8.3, 5

of heaven in which he points to the child whom he has called to stand in front of his disciples conclude with the phrase:

> they have their angels in heaven,
> who look continually
> on the face of my heavenly Father.

There follows, without ado, the parable of the straying sheep. The shepherd leaves the ninety-nine on the hills to look for the stray. The conclusion refers to the delight of the shepherd in his finding and adds:

> In the same way,
> it is not your heavenly Father's will
> that one of these little ones should be lost.[52]

Prayers of petition and intercession follow an address.

At the committal prayers are used which unambiguously declare that the deceased child has been welcomed into the loving presence of God. This is a bold affirmation other traditions have not always felt able to make.[53] Presumably, pastoral considerations have been uppermost here. But many traditions, who are glad to make a special commendation of children to God's parental loving care, are diffident about declaring that the child has been welcomed "into the light and love of your presence". One admires and approves Scots courage.

ORDER FOR THE FUNERAL OF A STILLBORN CHILD

Introductory words to this rite declare that "All that has happened seems futile and pointless", but add that God's love is constant and

> that his strength is available for us,
> especially at those times when we feel
> that we have no strength of our own.

Among the scriptures chosen for reading is a selection from 1 Cor 13, with its reference both to "puzzling reflections" in a mirror and to the eternal nature of faith, hope and love. This is a scripture that can usefully become the text for an address, for it confronts the desolate emptiness of stillbirth with the gentleness of God's love. In the middle of the passage, these words shine out:

> There is nothing love cannot face;
> there is no limit to its faith,
> its hope, its endurance.

---

[52] The intervening material is understandably omitted. It contains two warnings. The first is about millstones and the sea being a better fate than what awaits those who mislead children. The second is about mutilation being preferable to damnation. However keen one is about not using scissors and paste with the scriptures, I think that this is one exception to which all would agree! Of course, it does raise a ticklish question about what texts might be suitable at the funeral of a convicted paedophile.

[53] Cf. the Church of England's form of committal in the *Alternative Service Book* (page 321), which provides no extra prayer beyond what is normally said at the committal of an adult.

A preacher who can link this love of God with the hurt and anger of parents denied the expected opportunities to love the child they have lost will have spoken a powerful word of God.[54]

In this order there is no mention of an address. Silence may be all that can be offered, and the prayers that follow may have to do the duty of speaking not only to God but also to those who mourn. These prayers, like those in the previous order, unambiguously place the child in the fullness of God's presence:

> Grant us such trust
> in the finished work of your Son our Saviour,
> that we shall look with hope
> towards a full knowledge of *N.* . . . ,
> whose earthly life we have so little shared
> but who is now complete with Christ in you.[55]

They seek that the family may be assured that "with you nothing is wasted or incomplete".

Increasingly orders of service are being prepared for the funerals for stillbirths and neo-natal deaths. In large measure, this is a result of greater awareness of the particular grief of those in such circumstances. Although I have argued strongly elsewhere for there to be a sermon, I accept fully – particularly in these cases – that words may do more damage than good. It will demand high pastoral sensitivity to speak for the resurrection in this awful sadness.

ORDER FOR THE DEDICATION OF A CHURCHYARD OR BURIAL GROUND
The interest in this order lies in two considerations; the setting aside of places of burial, and the anthropological assumptions made about human remains.

The order provides for a statement of the purpose of having a burial place.[56] It observes the ancient tradition of linking the burial of Jesus with the graves of the faithful. The well-established connection made with Abraham's story is also made.[57]

The anthropology of human remains is covered in the prayers:

> Holy Spirit of God,
> you strengthen us in weakness,
> and wipe away all tears from our eyes.
> Comfort those who sorrow here,
> that by your power

---

[54]   Of course, those who have suffered this trauma or that of neo-natal death may never lose the memory of that short opportunity to love and cradle the child. But to love that child through each stage of normal human development is lost, and that loss is a gaping void which can never be made good.

[55]   *Common Order*: 323. Prayer (c).

[56]   *Common Order*: 394.

[57]   Gen 23 forms the source text of the link with Abraham. The courtly dealings between Abraham and the Hittites as each offers the other a better deal conceal issues relating to property rights and their accompanying financial responsibilities. Abraham only wants a burial site, not the whole tract of land. The Hittites do not want to keep the field with Abraham and his family traipsing across on occasional visits to Sarah's grave. The to-ing and fro-ing signify not so much generosity as haggling.

they may find light in darkness,
hope in distress,
and faith in the midst of doubt.
Assure them that the souls of our loved ones
who lie buried in peace,
are safe in your everlasting arms;
through Jesus Christ our Lord. *Amen.*

The body-soul model abides.

Summary

The Church of Scotland provides in *Common Order* funeral rites offering new and imaginative liturgical forms and vivid language. However, in its anthropological stance there is no change. Death is the separation of the soul from the body. Is this old wine in new skins?

There is, however, a strong sense of the life to come, and in this way the journey nature of death and the funeral is displayed.

Presbyterian Church in the United States of America

Book of Common Worship (1993)

The 1993 *Book of Common Worship* (*BCW*) of the Presbyterian Church in the United States of America (PCUSA) gives its funeral service a subtitle: "A Service of Witness to the Resurrection". Four main sections are provided:

— Comforting the Bereaved

— The Funeral

— The Committal

— Scripture Readings for Services on Occasions of Death

COMFORTING THE BEREAVED
An opening pastoral note suggests that it is appropriate for family and friends to gather for prayer (either at home or at the funeral establishment) on the day or night before the funeral. The proposed resources may be adapted as necessary and the service may be led by the minister or another representative of the church.

The service takes the following shape:

— Scripture Sentences[58]

— Prayer

— Hymn

— Psalm[59]

— Reading(s) from Scripture[60]

— Prayer

---

[58]   The following scripture sentences are suggested, though others may be used: Rom 15.13; Ps 46.1; Deut 33.27; Matt 5.4; 2 Cor 1.3-4.

[59]   The following are suggested for use: Pss 16.5-11; 23; 27.1, 4-9a, 13-14; 39.4-5, 12; 42.1-6a; 43; 46.1-5, 10-11; 90.1-10, 12; 91; 103; 106.1-5; 116.1-9, 15; 118; 121; 130; 139.1-12; 145; 146.

[60]   OLD TESTAMENT: Job 19.23-27; Isa 25.6-9; Isa 40.1-11, 28-31; Isa 40.28-31; Isa 43.1-3a, 18-19, 25; Isa 44.6-8; Isa 55.1-3, 6-13; Isa 61.1-4, 10-11; Isa 65.17-25; Lam 3.19-26, 31b-32; Dan 12.1-3; Joel 2.12-13, 23-24, 26-29; Wisd 3.1-7, 9; 5.15-16. At the loss of a child: Zech 8.1-8; Isa 65.17-25. For those whose faith is unknown: Eccl 3.1-15; Lam 3.1-9, 19-23.

EPISTLE: Rom 5.1-11; Rom 6.3-9; Rom 8.14-23, 31-39; Rom 14.7-9, 10b-12; 1 Cor 15.3-8, 12-20a; 1 Cor 15.20-24a; 1 Cor 15.20-26, 35-38, 42-44, 50, 53-58; 1 Cor 15.35-44; 1 Cor 15.50-57; 2 Cor 4.16-5.1; 2 Cor 5.1-10; Eph 1.11-2.1, 4-10; Phil 3.7-11; Phil 3.20-21; Col 3.1-17; 1 Thess 4.13-18; 2 Tim 2.8-13; Heb 2.14-18; Heb 11.1-3, 13-16; 12.1-2; 1 Pet 1.3-9; 1 Pet 3.18-22; 4.6; 1 Jn 3.1-3; Rev 7.2-3, 9-17; Rev 14.1-3, 6-7, 12-13; Rev 21.1-4, 22-25; 22.3-5; Rev 22.1-5. For those whose faith is unknown: Rom 2.12-16; Rom 14.7-9, 10c-12.

GOSPELS: Matt 5.1-12; Matt 11.25-30; Matt 25.1-13; Matt 25.31-46; Lk 7.11-17; Lk 18.15-17; Lk 23.33, 39-43; Jn 3.16-21; Jn 5.24-29; Jn 6.37-40; Jn 6.47-58; Jn 11.38-44; Jn 14.1-6, 25-27. At the loss of a child: Matt 18.1-5, 10; Mk 10.13-16. For those whose faith is unknown: Matt 25.31-46.

—   Lord's Prayer

—   Blessing

Prayer

Two prayer texts are proposed. The first originally appeared in PCUSA's 1986 book of funeral rites, now incorporated in *BCW*; the second is drawn from ECUSA's 1977 *Book of Common Prayer*.

Psalm and Reading(s) from Scripture

An extraordinarily wide range of texts is included, with separate provisions for the loss of a child and for those whose faith is unknown. The latter provision will help many ministers and officiants who frequently find themselves taking Christian funeral rites for those about whose faith they are uncertain.

It is also worth noting that *BCW* does not flinch from readings of scripture that speak clearly of a final judgement. Given our contemporary preoccupation with avoiding saying nasty things about those who have died – *nil nisi bonum de mortuis* is not a Christian tag – such a clear reminder that death and judgement are intimately related is, in my view, a welcome corrective.

Prayer

Five prayer texts are offered in the main body of the text. Where not otherwise indicated, they are original to the 1986 edition of the rite.

The first gives thanks for the one who has died and for the hope of eternal life made possible by the death and resurrection of Jesus Christ.

The next two are for those who mourn; of these the first is attributed to ECUSA's 1977 *Book of Common Prayer*, though it is not in itself original to ECUSA:

> Almighty God, source of all mercy and giver of comfort:
> Deal graciously with those who mourn,
> that, casting all their sorrow on you,
> they may know the consolation of your love;
> through your Son, Jesus Christ our Lord.
> **Amen.**

The final two texts are for use at the death of a child. The first of these draws on the passage in Mk 10.13-16 (and parallels) and is once again drawn from ECUSA's 1977 *Book of Common Prayer*. The second is an original PCUSA text:

> Holy God,
> yours is the beauty of childhood
> and yours is the fullness of years.
> Comfort us in our sorrow,
> strengthen us with hope,
> and breathe peace into our troubled hearts.
> Assure us that the life in which we rejoiced for a time is not lost,
> and that *N.* is with you,
> safe in your eternal love and care.

We ask this in the name of Jesus Christ,
who took little children into his arms and blessed them.
Amen.

One wonders what kind of prayer might be fashioned for a less angelic child – one perhaps who had reached "the terrible twos" or "frantic fours" and who was not forever sweetness and light! This prayer is not in itself a bad prayer; however, it offers a view of children like the little Lord Jesus asleep on the hay. "No crying he makes" is not the experience most parents have of children. Of course, at the funeral of a child, grief may be particularly bittersweet, and one does not want a prayer too robust. However, PCUSA's text raises the issue simply because it has such an interesting opening.

Lord's Prayer
The Lord's Prayer is printed in parallel columns. The unamended ELLC text appears to the left and the Modified Traditional form takes its place on the right.

Blessing
The service ends with a blessing:

The Lord bless us,
defend us from all evil,
and bring us to everlasting life.
Amen.

There is a wealth of material here for use in what is a preparatory rite. The strong emphasis on pastoral care springs from the deliberate decision that this is the purpose of such a gathering. There is good attention to the feelings of bewilderment and apprehension so often attendant on such occasions. Equally, there is a clear expression of the reality of death and judgement and of the resurrection hope. The strong notes of the Reformation still resound.

THE FUNERAL
The funeral service itself uses the following outline:
—   [Placing of the Pall]
—   Sentences of Scripture
—   Psalm, Hymn, or Spiritual
—   Prayer
—   [Confession and Pardon]
—   Readings from Scripture
—   Sermon
—   Affirmation of Faith
—   [Hymn]

— Prayers of Thanksgiving, Supplication, and Intercession

> Lord's Prayer   *Or*   •   Psalm, Hymn, or Spiritual
>
>   •   Invitation to the Table
>
>   •   Great Thanksgiving
>
>   •   Lord's Prayer
>
>   •   Breaking of the Bread
>
>   •   Communion of the People

— Commendation
— Blessing
— Procession (Psalm, Hymn, or Biblical Song)

The pastoral notes preceding the service suggest that:

> Except for compelling reasons, the service for a believing Christian is normally held in church, at a time when the congregation can be present. When the deceased was not known to be a believer or had no connection with a church, then it is appropriate to hold the service elsewhere and to omit or adapt portions of it as seems fitting. The ceremonies and rites of fraternal, civic, or military organizations, if any, should occur at some other time and place.

Placing of the Pall
This is an optional action of the rite, appropriate to one who has been baptised. The pall should be white; and as it is placed over the coffin, the minister pronounces a baptismal text – either Gal 3.27 or Rom 6.3-5.

Sentences of Scripture
Opening sentences of scripture are provided for use.[61] Once again, what is impressive is the range of scripture proposed. Here is a resource of exemplary depth and breadth.

Prayer
Four prayer texts are offered. The first is divided into three paragraphs, addressed successively to the Father (giver of the breath of life), the Son (who has tasted death and risen to eternal life) and the Holy Spirit (the comforter).

The prayers beginning, "O God who gave us birth, you are ever more ready to hear than we are to pray" and "Eternal God, we bless you for the great company of those who have kept the faith", have been amended from the 1992 *United Methodist Book of Worship.*

The final text, "Eternal God, we acknowledge the uncertainty of our life on earth", is a PCUSA text amended from the 1946 *Book of Common Worship* (renewed 1974).

Each prayer names death and moves to the hope of glory. In this way the processional note of the rite is struck. Although its second line is somewhat

---

[61] Ps 124.8; Rom 6.3-5; Jn 11.25-26; Rev 21.6; 22.13; 1.17-18 and Jn 14.19; Matt 11.28; 1 Pet 1.3-4; Ps 46.1; Jn 14.27; Ps 103.13 and Isa 66.13; Deut 33.27; Rom 8.38-39; Rev 1.17-18; Isa 41.10; Matt 5.4; 2 Cor 1.3-4; 1 Thess 4.14, 17-18; Rom 14.8; Rev 14.13; Jn 10.14 and Isa 40.11.

cumbersome (why not "our life on earth is uncertain"?), the fourth prayer is noteworthy for its cumulative use of scriptural imagery:

> Eternal God,
> we acknowledge the uncertainty of our life on earth.
> We are given a mere handful of days,
> and our span of life seems nothing in your sight.
> All flesh is as grass;
> and all its beauty is like the flowers of the field.
> The grass withers, the flower fades;
> but your word will stand forever.
> In this is our hope, for you are our God.
> Even in the valley of the shadow of death,
> you are with us.
> O Lord, let us know our end
> and the number of our days,
> that we may learn how fleeting life is.
> Turn your ear to our cry, and hear our prayer.
> Do not be silent at our tears,
> for we live as strangers before you,
> wandering pilgrims as all our ancestors were.
> But you are the same
> and your years shall have no end.
> **Amen.**

Confession and Pardon

This section is optional. The proposed prayer text is for use by the whole congregation. It was originally drafted for the 1986 edition of the Funeral Service and was subsequently included in *BCW*. The minister pronounces a declaration of forgiveness. Two forms are proposed; the first uses Rom 8.34 and 2 Cor 5.17, the second draws on Ps 103.17.

Readings from Scripture

A prayer for illumination precedes the reading of scripture. Two texts are suggested. The first was originally drafted for the 1986 edition of the Funeral Service:

> Source of all true wisdom,
> calm the troubled waters of our hearts,
> and still all other voices but your own,
> that we may hear and obey
> what you tell us in your Word,
> through the power of your Spirit.

The second is an amended version of a prayer originally found in the 1946 *Book of Common Worship*: "Eternal God, your love for us is everlasting . . . speak to us of eternal things . . ."

The list of scripture readings is that commonly proposed for all PCUSA's funeral rites and alluded to in this commentary under the provisions for "Comforting the Bereaved".

Sermon
The accompanying rubric advocates a brief exposition of the scriptures that have been read. This may be followed by "expressions of gratitude to God for the life of the deceased".

Affirmation of Faith
The ELLC text of the Apostles' Creed is printed for use. It may be replaced or followed by the *Te Deum* (also ELLC text). Alternatively, two other credal texts are proposed. Each is of PCUSA origin; the first is based on 1 Cor 15.1-6, Mk 16.9, Matt 16.16, Rev 22.13 and Jn 20.28.

> **This is the good news which we have received,**
> **in which we stand,**
> **and by which we are saved,**
> **if we hold it fast:**
> **that Christ died for our sins**
> **according to the scriptures,**
> **that he was buried,**
> **that he was raised on the third day,**
> **and that he appeared**
> **first to the women,**
> **then to Peter, and to the Twelve,**
> **and then to many faithful witnesses.**
> **We believe that Jesus is the Christ,**
> **the Son of the living God.**
> **Jesus Christ is the first and the last,**
> **the beginning and the end;**
> **he is our Lord and our God. Amen.**

The second begins "We believe" and is followed by Rom 8.1, 28, 38-39.

Whether one could use either of these texts as a regular credal formula is debatable, since they relate exclusively to Jesus and to this extent fail to express the Trinitarian nature of Christian belief. However, in this context (the occasional, and specific) they offer a helpful focus on the redemptive nature of Christ's death.[62]

Prayers of Thanksgiving, Supplication, and Intercession
Seven prayer texts are offered for use; four for general use and three for the funeral of a child.

---

[62] These texts appear with three others as alternative credal statements for use on the Lord's Day. The first of the five is a full-blown Trinitarian confession: the remaining four are scriptural formulae about Jesus; the two described in the commentary above, and the others based on Col 1.15-20 and Phil 2.5-11 – two early Christian hymns.

The prayers beginning "O God of grace, you have given us a new and living hope in Jesus Christ", "O God, before whom generations rise and pass away" and "Almighty God, in Jesus Christ you promised many rooms within your house" are drawn from PCUSA's 1970 *The Worshipbook: Services*. The first of these continues by reference to the resurrection of Christ and concludes citing Rom 8.38-39. The second describes the baptism of the one who has died as being completed by death and gives thanks that death is past and pain is ended. The third prayer, having begun with the reference to Jn 14, concludes:

> Lift heavy sorrow
> and give us good hope in Jesus,
> so that we may bravely walk our earthly way,
> and look forward to glad reunion in the life to come,
> through Jesus Christ our Lord.
> **Amen.**

The final prayer of this quartet is the litany from the Roman Catholic *Order of Christian Funerals* that alludes to Martha and Mary and the grave of Lazarus, and to the repentant thief. It refers to the deceased's baptism, anointing in the Holy Spirit and participation in the eucharist during his/her earthly life, and seeks his/her participation in the heavenly banquet.

The three texts for use at a child's funeral are all PCUSA texts. The first ("Loving God, you are nearest to us when we need you most") comes with some amendment from the 1986 Funeral Service text. The second ("O God, your love cares for us in life and watches over us in death") was originally found in the 1946 *Book of Common Worship*. The third prayer is for use after a sudden death:

> O God of compassion,
> comfort us with the great power of your love
> as we mourn the first sudden death of N.
> In our grief and confusion,
> help us find peace
> in the knowledge of your loving mercy to all your children,
> and give us light to guide us
> into the assurance of your love;
> through Jesus Christ our Lord.
> **Amen.**

The service may now take a eucharistic or non-eucharistic form.

NON-EUCHARISTIC SERVICE
Lord's Prayer
ELLC text and Modified Traditional forms are printed in parallel (with ELLC to the left). The remainder of the service continues with the commendation and procession. The commentary will deal with these at the appropriate point in the Eucharistic form of the funeral service.

EUCHARISTIC SERVICE
Two forms of invitation are provided: the first draws on Matt 11.28, Jn 6.35 and Matt 5.6 (*sic*, not 5.4); the second supplements 1 Cor 11.32-36 with Lk 22.19-20. Where the second form is used, the words of institution are omitted from any later stage (either the great thanksgiving, or the breaking of the bread).

The eucharistic prayer follows the customary PCUSA forms with proper texts for the dead. Two forms of the Lord's Prayer are reproduced: ELLC and Modified Traditional. Bread is broken and the people are communicated. The funeral service resumes with the Commendation.

Commendation
The Commendation begins with the kontakion commented upon throughout this commentary. Two prayers follow drawn from ECUSA's 1977 *Book of Common Prayer* and United Church of Christ's 1986 *Book of Worship*.

Blessing
Three forms of blessing are given. The first two are the formulae derived respectively from Heb 13.20-21 and Phil 4.7. The third is a form of the classic funerary blessing:

> May God in endless mercy
> bring the whole Church,
> the living and departed,
> to a joyful resurrection
> in the fulfillment of the eternal kingdom.
> **Amen.**

Procession (Psalm, Hymn, or Biblical Song)
The pall is removed from the coffin and the procession from Church may be accompanied by a hymn or psalm. Alternatively, the *Nunc Dimittis* may be sung or said together with the *Gloria Patri*.

THE COMMITTAL
The rite of Committal takes the following shape:
— Scripture Sentences[63]
— Committal
— Lord's Prayer
— Prayers
— Blessing[64]

The opening pastoral note suggests that the Committal may take place before the funeral service itself.

---

[63] Job 19.25; Jn 11.25-26; 2 Cor 5.1; Rev 1.17-18 and Jn 14.19; Rom 14.8; Ps 16.11; Jn 6.68.

[64] SOURCE TEXTS: 2 Cor 13.14; Num 6.24-26; Phil 4.7; Heb 13.20-21.

Scripture Sentences

In addition to the proposed scripture sentences there is to be found the text from the kontakion:

> Christ is risen from the dead,
> trampling down death by death,
> and giving life to those in the tomb.

Committal

Whether disposal of the body is by burial in the earth or at sea or by cremation, the common scripture text used is Rev 14.13. In turn, this is preceded by the formula

> In sure and certain hope of the resurrection to eternal life,
> through our Lord Jesus Christ,
> we commend to Almighty God our *brother/sister N.*,

Varying forms of committal are provided for use at burial, burial at sea, or cremation.

Lord's Prayer

As elsewhere in *BCW*, the ELLC text and Modified Traditional form of the Lord's Prayer are set in parallel, with the ELLC text to the left.

Prayers

Twelve prayer texts are printed; the first ten for use at the funeral of adults.

1. "O Lord, support us all the day long until the shadows lengthen" is attributed to ECUSA's 1977 Book of Common Prayer.
2. "O God, you have designed this world, and know all things good for us" is a PCUSA text.
3. "God of all mercies and giver of all comfort" is attributed to the Uniting Church in Australia's 1988 Uniting in Worship.
4. "Almighty God,
    Father of the whole family in heaven and on earth;
    Stand by those who sorrow,
    that, as they lean on your strength,
    they may be upheld,
    and believe the good news of life beyond life;
    through Jesus Christ our Lord. **Amen.**" is unattributed.
5. "God of boundless compassion, our only sure comfort in distress" and
6. "Merciful God, you heal the broken in heart" are PCUSA texts.
7. "God of all consolation, our refuge and strength in sorrow" and
8. "Gracious God, your mercies are beyond number" come from the Uniting Church in Australia's *Uniting in Worship*.
9. "God, whose days are without end: Help us always to remember how brief life is" is a PCUSA text.

10.   "Rest eternal grant *him/her*, O Lord; and let light perpetual shine upon
       him/her" is acknowledged as amended from the 1990 Roman Catholic
       Order of Christian Funerals.

The remaining two prayers are for use at the funeral of a child.

What this range of sources shows is the increasingly ecumenical nature of liturgical
text-drafting. While some material is inevitably peculiar to a tradition, increasingly we
encounter borrowing and lending across the old doctrinal and ecclesial boundaries.

SCRIPTURE READINGS FOR SERVICES ON OCCASIONS OF DEATH
These have been listed earlier in the footnotes of the commentary relating to those
points where scripture is read. No further comment need be made here.

Summary

Throughout PCUSA's funeral resources, certain characteristics appear. There is a
willingness to borrow from other traditions, particularly from PCUSA's sister church in
the United States of America, ECUSA. At the same time, there is a breadth in the range
of scriptures provided for use and a willingness not to avoid the difficult issue of
judgement. These Reformation notes are evidence of PCUSA's strong attachment to its
roots.

The United Reformed Church

Service Book (1989)

Of the mainline English Free Churches, the United Reformed Church (URC) is most keenly aware of the Calvinist Reformed tradition. Yet it is a church avowedly ecumenical in its beginnings and in its continuing life, and is committed more clearly than any other to continuous revision. Such change is seen both in its commitment to widen its denominational membership and its commitment to gender issues. Although it had produced a service book only a few years previously, an Assembly decision to use only gender inclusive language led to an immediate revision of liturgy and to the production of a new hymn book.

The funeral liturgy is subtitled "A Service of Witness to the Resurrection", and after the opening sentences offers a preface which comes in two alternative forms. The first version expresses the purpose of gathering to be fourfold: the worship of God, the thankful remembrance of the deceased, the prayer for comfort and strength for the bereaved, and the affirmation that "death is not the end - but a new beginning". The second delineates the purpose in the following terms: the worship of God, the thankful remembrance of the deceased, the sharing of grief, and the expression of the faith that "death is not the ultimate calamity that it seems". The prayers that follow (from which one should be selected) speak of light in darkness and comfort in the word of God, and form an introduction to the Liturgy of the Word.

The principal readings of scripture are printed in full with further readings suggested.[65] There is plenty of material here from the Old Testament. However, the problem referred to earlier also applies here, since the provision of lists of readings does not ensure their use. A rubric indicating that one Old Testament text should be read in addition to any other(s) would remove the difficulty. The usual objection given to the use of two readings is that at the service in a crematorium chapel there is not adequate time. From my own experience, I do not believe this to be true. It is possible to use a selection from the Psalter as well as readings from both Old and New Testaments, and to preach a homily. If the entire service has to be in the crematorium, then brevity and conciseness are necessary and possible.

The URC is true to its Reformed inheritance in its clear provision of a sermon. The sermon is to be on the Christian Hope. Knox and Calvin would have wanted this to

---

[65]   Printed in full are: Rom 8.16-18, 28, 31-35, 37-39; 1 Cor 13.1-13; 1 Cor 15.19-26, 35-38, 42-44, 50-58; Rev 21.1-7; Rev 22.1-5; Jn 14.1-6, 18-19, 27.
Additional readings are listed:

PSALMS: Pss 23; 103.8-18; 123; 121; 90:1-6, 10, 12; 139:13-18.

OT: Isa 25.6-9; Isa 26.3-4; Isa 61.1-3; Isa 40.6-10, 28-31; Isa 11.6-9; Lam 3.17-26, 31, 33; Job 19.1, 23-27b.

NT: 1 Jn 3.1-2; Jn 6.37-40; Jn 11.17-27.

include the theme of Judgement; but the sermon is here described as a *sermon* and not an address, and it is not optional.

Prayers of thanksgiving for the victory of Christ and of commendation of the departed follow. Two alternative prayers of thanksgiving are provided. The first contains a central clause that speaks of the life and death of Jesus as showing the ways of God in human life and demonstrating the limitless power of divine life. The second draws on the divine promise to Joshua ("I will not leave you or forsake you"), the theme of *Christus Victor*, and the final verse of Rom 8.

The commendation, which includes the usual opportunity for silent remembrance, is followed by petitions for the bereaved. Commendation, petition and intercession are offered in a variety of forms. Of these, the most original begins with a prayer that seeks to lay the past to rest. Part of this (the last) form is reproduced below:

Intimate God,
you are able to accept in us
what we cannot even acknowledge;
you have named in us
what we cannot bear to speak of;
you hold in your memory
what we have tried to forget;
you will hold out to us
a glory we cannot imagine.
Reconcile us through your cross
to all that we have rejected in ourselves,
that we may find no part of your creation
to be alien or strange to us,
and that we ourselves may be made whole,
through Jesus Christ, our lover and our friend,
Amen.

It concludes with petitions and intercessions that declare:

. . . since we have all been but a hair's breadth from death since birth, teach us, O God, how close we are to that life in all its fullness which Christ alone can give . . .

Silence

Let us pray for... *(members of the bereaved family are named)* and all whom they love. For them we ask for resources stronger that anything we can offer: peace, joy, and hope; gifts that no one, no grief, can take away. May they grieve, but not as those without hope.

Silence

Sustaining and all-loving God, we pray also for others around the world who bear pain and grief, guilt and fear. May they find the peace and the wholeness, the healing and the joy we seek.

The Lord's Prayer is said before the service moves to the committal. The committal includes the same section of the *Te Deum* that is chosen in Baptist Pattern Two. Two concluding prayers are offered. The first refers to the Church militant and triumphant (though not expectant!) and asks for the strength to move from the sadness of grief to "return to the duties which await us in the world" and to greater faithfulness to God in the service of one another. This should probably be seen as a move from separation into transition and incorporation, which is presumably its intention. The second prayer is a slight rewording of the well-known prayer "O Lord, support us all the day long of this troublous life". The blessing is then pronounced.

A short appendix offers prayers for special circumstances: the death of a child; the funeral of a stillborn child; particularly distressing circumstances; and the burial or scattering of ashes.

Summary

The texts reviewed here are described as a "Witness to the Resurrection"; the difficulty with such a title is that the move from death may be too quick. We are almost in the land of "death is nothing at all". The texts themselves do not, in my judgement, give officiants the pretext to take such a view, but in practice we are close to the celebratory understanding of death. What has to be borne in mind is that any Christian celebration of death is prospective rather than retrospective; where it is retrospective, the backward look is to the death of Christ.

In 2000 the United Reformed Church began the process of revising its funerary texts. Whether this will mean the usual proliferation of services, or options within a common core remained uncertain at the time of writing this. To watchers of current trends, the latter course seemed unlikely.

CHAPTER 6

Ecumenical Churches

Introduction

The churches whose liturgies appear in this chapter mark the twentieth-century ecumenical reformation. Born from concerns of mission, the ecumenical movement represents a considerable challenge to inherited ways of "being church". The healing of old wounds and the mending of fences is a slow and laborious business, and ecumenical enthusiasts (some of whom do not seem to understand the size of the project) can become impatient and even despairing at the pace of change.

Liturgists are confronted with the task of drafting texts which can command assent and joyful acceptance across the traditions. The perils of a "lowest common denominator" approach or of too great an eclecticism are well established. *Creatio ex nihilo* is not a possibility for those working in this field; the several histories have to be honoured, but without their becoming a leash that inhibits the future.

Australian Uniting Church

The Australian Uniting Church is not itself one of the ancient Reformation churches. Like the United Reformed Church in Great Britain, it is (as its name implies) an ecumenical marriage. Not the least of the interests of the Australian Uniting Church from a liturgical point of view arises from this ecumenicity. Its 1988 book *Uniting in Worship* (*UW*) manifests a clear commitment to the use of ecumenical texts wherever possible. In practice, this means that it has adopted the ELLC texts published in *Praying Together*[1] as well as working cross-denominationally on its own texts. At the time of writing, the funeral texts published in *UW* and the service in the 1994 texts for use in circumstances of a stillbirth or perinatal death were subject to the work of a revision committee. Revised texts were to be prepared for publication in 2003.

This commentary will examine the 1988 and 1994 texts and suggest some of the areas to which the revisers may be paying attention.

Uniting in Worship (1988)

UW provides resources for ministry at the time of death, a funeral service in church, and a service at the cemetery or in the crematorium chapel.

MINISTRY AT THE TIME OF DEATH
Here are provided:

— Prayers with the dying
— Prayers with the family after a death

In neither case is a full-blown order of service suggested; what are offered are scripture sentences and prayers, no more.

Prayers with the dying
Scripture sentences are suggested[2] and six short prayer texts are offered for use. The first prayer text draws on Lk 23.46, the second and sixth are forms of the *Proficiscere*; the remaining three commend the dying person to the mercy of God and refer in turn to the resurrection of Christ, the everlasting arms, and the assurance of forgiveness.

Prayers with the family after a death
The opening scripture sentences[3] are followed by three prayer texts. All three draw on scriptural images; the second on Jesus' tears at the grave of Lazarus, the third on the suffering of Christ before his death and entry into glory. The first prayer uses a range of images shifting quickly from one to the next, and is reproduced here:

---

[1] *Praying Together* (The Canterbury Press: 1988).
[2] Lam 3.22-23; 1 Cor 2.9; 2 Cor 5.17-18; Matt 28.20b; Lk 23.46.
[3] Isa 30.15; Rom 8.38-39; 2 Cor 1.3; Matt 5.4; Matt 11.28-29.

O God our Father,
we know that you are afflicted with our afflictions.
We come to you today in sorrow,
that we may receive from you
the comfort you alone can give.
Enable us to see that in perfect wisdom,
perfect love and perfect power
you are always working for our good.
You are our dwelling-place, O God,
and underneath us are your everlasting arms.
Make us so sure of your love
that we will be able to accept
what we cannot understand.
Help us today to be thinking
not only of the darkness of death,
but of the splendour of eternal life.

Enable us even now to face life with courage and hope;
give us the grace and the strength to go on,
knowing that the best tribute we can pay our loved one
is to let his/her life be a continuing inspiration to us,
and knowing that we are constantly surrounded
by the unseen cloud of witnesses.

Comfort and uphold us,
until we share with them the light of your glory
and the peace of your eternal presence;
through Jesus Christ our Lord.
Amen.

Of the three prayers proposed, this is perhaps the least focussed. Its use of diverse scriptural allusions and its plea that the life of the departed (rather than the life of Christ) should be our continuing inspiration contribute to the slight confusion and lack of clarity. The other prayer texts use one scriptural allusion and relate the petition directly to the scripture, producing a more direct and assimilable effect.

THE FUNERAL SERVICE IN CHURCH
The service adopts the following structure:

— Introduction
— Prayers
— Hymn
— The Promises of God
— Preaching of the Word
— Prayers of the People
— Commendation

- The Lord's Prayer
- Hymn
- Prayer

Introductory pastoral notes offer a threefold agenda for the funeral service:

(a)   to worship God, celebrating the death and resurrection of Jesus Christ which witness to the faithfulness of God in life and death;

(b)   to give thanks for a specific person's life and mourn that person's death;

(c)   to dispose reverently of the body

The notes continue:

> The Funeral Service witnesses to the fact that death is a reality and a basic part of our common humanity that all people must face. However, as each human life is of individual worth to God, the minister should make each funeral a unique occasion.

Both emphases are important: our common mortality and our individual worth. The Uniting Church of Australia does well to call our attention to this bi-polarity of the rite in addition to its reminder that the first task of the Funeral Service is the worship of God revealed in the death and resurrection of Jesus.

The opening notes also propose a wide range of scriptural passages suitable for use. These will be noted under the section "The Promises of God".

Introduction
The minister greets the congregation and reminds those present

> that while death is the end of human life,
> it marks a new beginning in our relationship with God.

Death is both end and beginning. A more explicit declaration of the nature of the rite as a rite of passage could scarcely be given. The minister continues with scriptural sentences,[4] followed by opening prayers.

Prayers
The first prayer addresses God who "alone can turn the shadow of death into the brightness of the morning light", while the second prayer is a clear prayer of confession which confronts the reality of sin's power to distort and break relationships:

> Merciful Father, our Maker and Redeemer,
> we confess that we have not always lived
> as your grateful children;
> we have not loved as Christ loved us.
> Father, forgive us
> if there have been times when we failed N.
>
> Enable us by your grace
> to forgive anything that was hurtful to us.

---

[4]   Jn 11.25-26 and/or 1 Pet 1.3.

Lord, have mercy on us;
set us free from our sins,
and grant us healing and wholeness;
through Jesus Christ our Lord.
Amen.

Two other prayer texts are offered for optional use. The first asks for "those things for which we are unworthy to ask and those things we are too blind to know we need". The second asks for faith to trust in "the communion of saints, the forgiveness of sins, and the resurrection to life everlasting". This is a clear reference to (if a slight adjustment of) the Apostles' Creed, which in the ELLC text reads:

the communion of saints,
the forgiveness of sins,
the resurrection *of the body*
and the life everlasting.

What significance there is (if any)[5] in the omission of the italicised phrase in the prayers of the Uniting Church it is difficult to say, but the omission is noticeable precisely because of the adherence in the remainder of the prayer to the ELLC text.

Where the above optional texts are not used, free prayer may be made. A hymn of praise or faith may follow.

The Promises of God
Whatever other passages of scripture may be read, an opening rubric declares that "a gospel reading shall be included." Several texts are printed in full;[6] additional passages (as noted earlier) are suggested in the opening pastoral notes.[7]

Preaching of the Word
Pastoral note vii is clear that the faith of the church is to be proclaimed at this point in the service:

Provision is made in this order for the Preaching of the Word, following the reading
of Bible passages. The purpose of the Funeral Service is not only to assist people to
honour the life and death of a specific person but also to acknowledge God's gift of
life and to witness to the faithfulness of God in both life and death. The preference,
therefore, is for a brief sermon. Alternatively, the minister or a family member or

---

[5]   It is dangerous to argue from silence, but the omission is surely not accidental! The italics in the ELLC
text are mine.

[6]   Lam 3.17-26, 31-33; Ps 23; Ps 90.1-2, 4-6, 10, 12, 14-17; Ps 121; Ps 139.1-12, 17-18; Rom 8.18, 28, 31b-
35, 37-39; 1 Cor 15.19-26, 35-38, 42-44, 50, 53-58; Eph 3.14-19; 1 Pet 1.3-9; Jn 6.35-40; Jn 10.14-15,
27-30 (suitable for a child's funeral); Jn 14.1-6, 18-19, 27.

[7]   OT: Job 19.1, 23-27b; Eccl 3.1-11; Isa 25.6-9; Wisd 3.1-5; Ecclus 44.1-5.

PSALMS: Pss 27; 42; 118.14-21, 28-29; 130.

NT: Acts 10.34-43; Rom 5.5-11; Rom 6.3-11; Rom 14.7-9; 2 Cor 1.3-7; 2 Cor 4.7-15; 2 Cor 4.16-5 10;
Phil 3.8-11, 20-21; 1 Thess 4.13-18; Rev 7.9-17; Rev 21.1-7; Rev 22.1-7.

GOSPEL: Matt 5.1-12; Matt 11.25-30; Lk 23.33, 39-43; Lk 24.1-9; Jn 5.19-24; Jn 11.17-27.

FOR THE FUNERAL OF A CHILD: Isa 11.6-9; Ps 103.8-19; 1 Jn 3.1-2.

friend may give a brief tribute, which may be placed prior to the Bible readings; a brief witness to the resurrection of Christ and the Christian hope of all who believe in him shall then follow after the readings. Where there is inadequate time to give a brief sermon or a tribute/sermon, or where it seems inappropriate to do so, the minister shall, at the very least, give a brief personal witness to the faith of the church in the risen Lord and his promises.

Given the clarity of the note about the need to proclaim the Christian hope, one wonders what circumstances render a brief sermon "inappropriate". If what is meant is a lack of faith among those present and the one whose funeral it is, perhaps this should have been made clear. What is clear is that a funeral service in church is an act of Christian worship and part of Christian worship is the proclamation of the word. For this unambiguous note, the Uniting Church is to be congratulated.

<u>Prayers of the People</u>
The prayers that follow are arranged in seven sub-sections:
—   Praise for the work of Christ
—   Thanksgiving for life in the Church
—   General prayers of thanksgiving and intercession
—   Prayers of thanksgiving and intercession for use in circumstances of tragic death
—   Prayers of thanksgiving and intercession for use at the funeral of a child
—   General intercessions
—   Alternative prayers.
The first prayer (for the work of Christ) is always to be used.

All glory and honour, thanks and praise,
be to you, eternal God, our Father.
In your great love for the world
you gave your Son to be our Saviour;
to live our life, to know our joy and pain,
and to die our death.

We praise you for raising him from the dead,
and for receiving him at your right hand in glory.
With your Church in every generation
we rejoice that he has conquered sin and death for us,
and opened the kingdom of heaven to all believers.
For this assurance of a new life in Christ,
and for the great company of the faithful
whom you have received into your eternal joy,
all praise and thanks be given to you,
our God, for ever and ever.
Amen.

Other prayers are to be used as appropriate. The prayer texts provided cover the normal range of options and require no particular comment. As with much of the Uniting Church's work in these rites, the strong use of scriptural imagery and the centrality of (and continual reference to) the work of Christ are particularly impressive. We are never in doubt as to the credal and confessional nature of the texts.

The Lord's Prayer should be said here if it is not to be used during the Commendation.

Commendation

Three prayer texts are proposed; two for general use, the third for use at the funeral of a child. The general prayers rejoice in the gift of eternal life and seek that without fear those who mourn may entrust those who have died to God's never-failing love. The third makes allusion to Mk 10.13-16 and the need for childlike trust.

The Lord's Prayer

The Lord's Prayer is set in two forms: the ELLC text first, and then the Modified Traditional version. It may be followed by a hymn celebrating God's love for us, our love for God, the victory of Christ, or the presence of the Spirit.

Prayer

This phase of the rite concludes with a prayer which may be omitted if the whole service is at the cemetery or crematorium chapel. Two prayer texts are proposed; either may be used. The first is the well-known:

> May God in his infinite mercy bring the whole church,
> living and departed in Christ,
> to a joyful resurrection
> in the fulfilment of his eternal kingdom.

The alternative text is simply the words of Heb 13.20-21. In either case, an appropriate blessing may be added.

SERVICE AT THE CEMETERY OR IN THE CREMATORIUM CHAPEL
This section of the rite includes:

— Scripture Sentences
— Committal
— Affirmation of Faith
— Prayers
— Blessing

Where the previous part of the service has been in another place, those present should be welcomed and (to ensure no accidents) the deceased should be named. This is a useful reminder that in many modern crematoria, several funeral groups may be gathering at the same time for services in different chapels.

As the coffin is brought to the place of disposal, scripture sentences may be read.[8] A psalm or other reading may follow these sentences. A choice of three committal sentences is offered.

Affirmation of Faith
It is then suggested that an affirmation of faith be said. Four texts are offered; the first two are scripture sentences,[9] the third and fourth are drawn from the *Te Deum*.

The third text simply reproduces the ELLC text of the *Te Deum* from "You, O Christ, are the king of glory" to "and bring us with your saints to glory everlasting". The fourth text consists of the ELLC text of the Versicles and Responses after the *Te Deum*:

> Save your people, Lord, and bless your inheritance.
> Govern and uphold them now and always.
>
> Day by day we bless you.
> We praise your name for ever.
>
> Keep us today, Lord, from all sin.
> Have mercy on us, Lord, have mercy
>
> Lord, show us your love and mercy,
> for we have put our trust in you.
>
> In you, Lord, is our hope:
> let us never be put to shame.

Such an affirmation of faith serves once again to underline the central note of Christian conviction in these rites.

Prayers and Blessing
Concluding prayers seek faith, comfort and consolation, and hope. The final prayer is a modern language text of the prayer that includes the well known words:

> until the shadows lengthen,
> and the busy world is hushed,
> the fever of life is over, and the evening comes.

The rite concludes with the dismissal. If not previously used, one of the prayers from the final section of the service in church may be said. There follows either the grace (2 Cor 13.14) or a blessing based on Phil 4.7.

1994 SERVICE TO FOLLOW THE BIRTH OF A STILLBORN CHILD, OR THE DEATH OF A NEWLY BORN CHILD
In 1994, a separate text was prepared for use in circumstances of perinatal death and, according to the accompanying pastoral notes, is intended for use "as soon as possible

---

[8] Lam 3.22-23; Isa 30.15; Ps 46.1; Rom 8.38-39; 1 Cor 2.9; 2 Cor 1.3; 2 Cor 5.17-18; Matt 5.4; Matt 11.28-29; Jn 3.16; Jn 11.25-26.

[9] FOR THE FUNERAL OF A CHILD: Isa 40.11; Ps 103.13-14; Matt 5.4.
Rev 14.13 or Rev 7.16-17.

after the death has occurred, though in special circumstances some delay may be necessary". The service, which is *not* a funeral service, adopts the following structure:

— Introduction
— Scripture Verses
— Prayer
— The Sign of the Cross
— The Lord's Prayer
— Blessing

What is intended by this service is the pastoral care due to those whose child is lost to them in the moment of birth. A separate funeral service will normally be held at a later stage. The pastoral notes suggest the need for privacy and quiet – usually at the place where the birth has just occurred. As well as the parents, other family members, hospital staff and "an elder of the local congregation" may be present. Normally, a hospital chaplain will take the service – although, if the parents are churchgoers, it may be more appropriate for their minister to take responsibility for the service. Other helpful suggestions are made for preparing the room and the parents for the service. Those taking such services are referred to a number of resource books on perinatal death.

Where the child has been given a name, that name should be used throughout the service, and the parents should be encouraged to hold the child.

The minister begins by expressing the overwhelming anguish and emptiness that such a loss occasions, and continues:

Yet we remember, in our confusion and distress,
that the eternal God is here,
the One whose love is seen in Christ Jesus.

On the cross, Jesus bears our pain.
Through the cross, God shares our pain.
In the Spirit, God is with us
offering comfort, peace and love.

The minister then turns to the words of scripture. Two texts are introduced by the bidding, "We cry out to God".[10] Some or all of a series of additional texts may also be used.[11] The proposed passages express the pain of loss and the hope of comfort to be found in Christ and the love of God.

Prayer

Prayer is made, thanking God for "the assurance of your presence" and seeking faith to trust the promises of God. It is then suggested that ex tempore prayers be offered, and the time of intercession concludes with a short prayer.

---

[10] Ps 13.1-2; Ps 22.1-2.
[11] Lam 3.22-23; Ps 46.1; Matt 11.28-29; Rom 8.35, 37-39.

Surround *N* and *N*, their family and friends,
with your love and grace.

Comfort them in their sorrow and fill them with your peace.
Strengthen their faith in you
and bless them with confidence and courage
to face the future,
through Jesus Christ our Lord. Amen.

There then follows an act potentially open to misunderstanding – despite the clarity of direction in the pastoral notes.

The Sign of the Cross
The pastoral notes accompanying this rite make the following observation.

> Uniting Church practice, along with the practice of the church catholic, clearly indicates that it is inappropriate to do anything in this service which may suggest that it is a baptism. Therefore, water should not be used at any point. It may be necessary to speak in something like the following terms with parents who are requesting a baptismal service.

> It is not the practice of the Uniting Church to baptise in situations such as this. God's love for, and acceptance of, your child does not depend on whether he/she is baptised. However, we do have a service which we believe you may find meaningful and helpful.

The notes then suggest that the service may also be used in the event of miscarriage, simply omitting "The Sign of the Cross".

One quite understands the reservation about post-mortem baptism.[12] However, it is quite appropriate for those who practise infant baptism to baptise a child during a birth where the likelihood of infant mortality is very high. The pastoral notes attached to this service make no reference to this practice. The reason for such an omission is not clear.

When the body is to be signed with the cross, the minister (who may be joined by the parents in so doing) makes the sign of the cross on the child. The minister utters these words from the call of Jeremiah, "Before I formed you in the womb, I knew you" (Jer 1.18) and refers to Jesus' action of taking children in his arms and blessing them (Lk 18.15-17). Then using either the child's given name or the word "all", the minister says:

For *N*/all, he lived.
For *N*/all, he died.
For *N*/all, he rose again.
He has welcomed *N*/this child
into his eternal kingdom.

---

[12]   However, there is the famous *crux interpretum* in 1 Cor 15.29 with its reference to baptism *for* the dead. Perhaps the difficulty of understanding what Paul meant led to the early Church swiftly abandoning the practice!

Therefore, as a mark of that love and grace,
we place on him/her the sign of the cross.

Let us pray:

God of compassion,
help us to believe that N/this child,
a lamb of your flock, is in your gentle care
through the grace of our Lord Jesus Christ. Amen.

The aptness of this prayer is immediately clear, both in its theological rootedness and in its pastoral sensitivity. One is grateful for such a resource. Even those who do not practise infant baptism must feel the value of such a prayer and action.

The Lord's Prayer
The ELLC text of the Lord's Prayer is printed without alternative.

Blessing
The short service concludes with a blessing based either on Phil 4.7 or on the Aaronic blessing of Num 6.24-26.

Summary

The Uniting Church was (at the time of writing) engaged in a complete revision of its funeral texts. The texts reviewed here indicate a strong preference for rites that articulate the finality of death and the hope of resurrection to be found in Christ. There is a clear sense of separation and incorporation and it is unlikely that such emphases will be missing from the forthcoming texts.

Whether the Uniting Church will be able to draw on indigenous traditions, as the Anglicans in New Zealand have, remains to be seen. There is a determination within the reviewing group to strengthen the Christological focus and to express the pastoral concerns of the rites by way of some reference to the threefold structure noted by van Gennep.

Revision groups no longer act in isolation. The rites of different sociological and ecclesiological traditions are studied and used. Undoubtedly, the next round of Australian rites will reflect this collaborative style. It is to be hoped that they will also retain a distinct voice.

The Church of North India

Before turning immediately to the texts of the Church of North India (CNI), it is worth reminding ourselves that hot climates require the prompt management of dead bodies. For this reason, burial or cremation will normally occur within twenty-four hours of death and may, therefore, be undertaken in a home rather than a church setting.

The Book of Worship (1995)

The Book of Worship was published in 1995 to celebrate the Silver Jubilee of the foundation of CNI. The book is descriptive rather than prescriptive; the ecumenical nature of CNI means that in its service books it must offer options which suggest possibilities, while at the same time trying to foster a sense of commonality in a church which practises diversity in unity. Two forms of funeral service are provided: the Burial of an Adult and the Burial of a Child.

BURIAL OF AN ADULT
The service takes the following form:

— Ministry of the Word
— Affirmation of Faith
— The Prayers
— The Committal

The first three sections of the service may be held at home, in church or at a cemetery according to circumstance.

Ministry of the Word
The service begins with opening sentences; Jn 11.25-26 is always said.[13] The minister then says the opening prayer, "O God, our help in every time of trouble . . .".[14] Psalms are said antiphonally and a NT scripture is read.[15] A rubric directs that:

> An address or sermon may be given now or at any other convenient point in the service.

---

[13]   Also proposed for use are: Deut 33.27; Josh 1.5; Ps 55.22; Ps 25.7; Ps 46.1; Matt 5.4; Jn 3.16; Rom 8.38-39; 1 Pet 1.3-4.

[14]   Alternative prayers, psalmody, scripture passages, thanksgivings and prayers of intercession may be found in the earlier order for the burial of the dead.

[15]   Proposed here for use are Pss 23; 90.1-6, 10, 12, 14, 16; 130.

NT: Jn 14.1-6, 27; 1 Cor 15. 20-23, 35-38, 42-44, 53-55, 57-58; Roman 8.18, 28, 35, 37-39.

While the latter two provisions seem to make excessive use of "scissors and paste", the selection from 1 Cor 15 is particularly successful in laying out clearly the core of St. Paul's argument, which can be both lengthy to hear and troublesome to read in full. Many other churches have used this abridgement (or similar).

Structurally, it makes best sense to have the sermon here, emphasising the close link with psalmody and the reading of scripture. It may be that in certain circumstances, it will be convenient to move an address to the graveside, for example.

Affirmation of Faith

The congregation (or the minister alone) may then confess their faith in the words taken from the *Te Deum*.

> O Christ, you are the King of glory,
> the eternal Son of the Father.
> You overcame the sting of death,
> and opened the kingdom of heaven to all believers.
> You are seated at God's right hand in glory;
> we believe that you will come and be our judge.
> Come, then, Lord and help your people,
> bought with the price of your own blood,
> and bring us with your saints
> to everlasting glory.

The Prayers

The minister invites the congregation to pray and the intercessions are prefaced by a threefold Kyrie and the Lord's Prayer.[16] Four prayer texts are offered here: the first entrusts the one who has died to God's mercy; the second prayer is for those who mourn, "Almighty God, Father of all mercies and giver of all comfort . . ." The third and fourth prayers are for all present: "Grant us, Lord, the wisdom and grace to use aright the time that is left to us here on earth . . ." and, finally:

> May God in his infinite love and mercy bring the whole Church, in earth and heaven, to a joyful resurrection and the fulfilment of his eternal kingdom. **Amen.**

This section of the rite concludes with the Grace.

The Committal

The order recognises that disposal may occur by burial on land or at sea or by cremation. The minister may use some of the opening sentence proposed earlier. Jn 6.37, 39-40 may then be read. As the body is committed for disposal, a hymn may be sung or the minister may repeat the words of Ps 103.8, 13-17, continuing with the traditional committal formula, "We have entrusted our brother/sister *N* to God's merciful keeping and we now commit . . ."

The minister then reads the words of Jn 5.24 and says the concluding prayers. The first seeks that those present may in due time be united in the "unclouded vision of your glory." The second is the prayer, "Heavenly Father, in your Son Jesus Christ you have given us a true faith and a sure hope . . ." The third takes the words of Jude 24-25.

---

[16] The Lord's Prayer follows the ELLC text.

The congregation is dismissed with the Blessing.[17]

Where ashes are to be buried, a short order is proposed using elements of the committal order.

BURIAL OF A CHILD

The service is essentially identical to that of the Burial of an Adult. There are variants in the scriptures proposed in the Ministry of the Word;[18] there are similar amendments suggested for the committal stage.[19] At the committal, 'this child' has been substituted for 'our *brother*'.

This form differs from the Western rites for use at the funerals of children, where the sense of tragedy and loss is articulated far more strongly. It does not, therefore, provide a different service from the adult rite; it simply makes minor adjustments.

Summary

The CNI service texts are quite sombre in tone. There is a sense of the prospect of heaven; death is the gateway to life eternal. Compared, however, with rites of the Marthoma Syrians, the CNI rites are modest – almost flat. There is none of the creativity that is found in the rites of Kenya, South Africa or New Zealand.

However, we must never cease to remind ourselves that what is on the page is not the rite. It is only the text. And the texts of CNI – while not exotic – are (like those of CSI) designed to be acceptable to a diversity in unity. In such circumstances, it may well be that some creativity is lost in the political discussion.[20]

---

[17] The suggested text is Heb 13.20-21.

[18] OPENING SENTENCES: Isa 40.11; Rev 7.17; Matt 5.4.

Ps 23 may be used.

NT: Mk 10.13-16.

[19] OPENING SENTENCES: Mk 10.14; Matt 18.14.

AT THE COMMITTAL: Matt 18.10.

[20] The late Michael Vasey once described drafting liturgy which would meet the approval of the General Synod of the Church of England as "like doing embroidery with a bunch of football hooligans"! Committees are rarely creative in the detail.

The Church of South India

The Book of Common Worship (1962)

The 1962 *Book of Common Worship* of the Church of South India (CSI) contains one service for use at funerals. The service may take place at the home or in church. It is important once again to remember that in hot climates disposal of dead bodies is a matter of urgency. The service book speaks of "burial", but cremation is equally possible, and ashes may be buried thereafter.

The service takes the following shape:

— Opening Sentences and Psalmody
— Reading of Scripture and Short Address
— Prayers and Apostles' Creed
— Burial
— Committal
— Lord's Prayer
— Dismissal and Blessing

Opening Sentences and Psalmody
A hymn or other lyric may be sung at the start of the service. Where the service takes place at the house, the sentences are said there. For a service in church, they are spoken as the body is taken into church.[21]

One or more psalms are said or sung; a selection is printed in full. The Gloria follows each.[22]

Reading of Scripture and Short Address
One or more passages of scripture are read, focussing on the hope of the resurrection,[23] and "a short address" may be given. No direction is given to the preacher as to the theme or content of the address; the rubric is bare. After the address, there is a brief greeting

> The Lord be with you:
> **And with thy spirit.**

and this is followed by a threefold Kyrie said antiphonally by minister and congregation.

---

[21] The following texts of scripture are proposed: 2 Cor 1.3-4; Ps 16.11; Ps 30.5; Jn 11.25-26; Jn 14.19; Jn 5.25. At the burial of a child: Isa 40.11; Matt 18.14, 10b.

[22] Pss 90; 130; 23

[23] The selection is quite thin: 1 Cor 15.20-28; 1 Cor 15.35-38; Rev 7.9-17; 21.1-7.

Prayers and Apostles' Creed

The prayers of intercession begin with the Lord's Prayer (printed in the Modified Traditional form), and are introduced as the minister says, "Let us commend our *brother* departed to God".

There follow three prayers.[24] The first is a form of *Deus, apud quem omnia morientia vivunt*, preceded by a versicle and response using Wisd 3.1:

> The souls of the righteous are in the hand of God:
> **And no torment will ever touch them.**

The second is based on Ps 46.1 and Phil 4.7, preceded by a versicle and response using Matt 5.4:

> Blessed are those who mourn:
> **For they shall be comforted.**

The third is the well-known "Heavenly Father, who in thy Son Jesus Christ hast given us a true faith, and a sure hope . . ." It is preceded by a versicle and response using Ps 27.13:

> I believe that I shall see the goodness of the Lord:
> **In the land of the living.**

The prayers are followed by the congregation reciting the Apostles' Creed. By this means, the faith of the Church becomes the way in which the congregation's prayers are gathered up. Whether the theological significance of this is recognised by the congregations who attend funeral services is unclear. However, the Creed is a reminder that what is said by any particular congregation at any particular time is linked to the community of the faithful through time and space, and this is in itself an important pointer to that communion of saints of which the Creed speaks.

A hymn or other lyric is sung and the Grace spoke by minister and people together. As the body is taken from the church or house, there is further singing.

Burial

At the cemetery gate, the minister greets the people in the words of 1 Pet 1.3. The procession makes its way with the body to the grave to the accompaniment of words of scripture.[25] At the graveside the minister uses the prayer "O Lord Jesus Christ, who didst rest in a sepulchre . . ." and these words are followed by the couplet of *Requiem aeternam*, said by minister and people antiphonally.

Committal

The body is lowered into the grave as a lyric or hymn is sung. A traditional committal formula commends the soul and commits the body, concluding with the hope expressed in Phil 3.21 of a resurrection transforming our low estate into the likeness of Christ's glorious body.

---

[24]   In the text as printed there is no appendix of additional prayers for use in various circumstances.

[25]   Where there is a cremation, a parallel course may be taken. The processional scriptures proposed are: 1 Cor 15.20-22; Rev 1.17-18; Ps 23.4.

Lord's Prayer

The service concludes with the Lord's Prayer and a brief antiphonal exchange:

Thou art the King of glory, O Christ:
Thou art the everlasting Son of the Father.

We therefore pray thee, help thy servants, whom thou hast redeemed with thy precious blood:
Make them to be numbered with thy saints, in glory everlasting.

Lord, now lettest thou thy servant depart in peace, according to thy word:
For mine eyes have seen thy salvation.

Dismissal and Blessing

The congregation departs after the minister has read the words of Rev 14.13 and pronounced the blessing, using the formula of Heb 13.20-21.

Summary

The shape and theology of the CSI is traditionally Evangelical. There is a strong processional feel to the rite and a strong proclamation of the resurrection of the dead. The anthropological stance is body-soul.

The text (to a Western commentator) seems dated. In part, this is to do with the language – the text was written in 1962 when SCI was in its infancy and needed a common worship book. In part, it arises from a rather sparse provision, devoid (at least in the text) of much elaboration. This befits a church holding together a variety of ecclesial traditions within its ecumenical structures. The text reflects the common core. However, one cannot imagine a Southern Indian funeral without some liturgical embellishment.

The Book of Common Worship Supplement (1986)

Nearly a quarter of a century after the *Book of Common Worshi*, a supplement was produced (in 1986). An alternative form of burial service was included, offering an alternative to the procession and committal stages of the service found in the 1962 book. Ps 130 may be used as a processional psalm and additional verses may be spoken.[26] A local translation of the Lord's Prayer is offered:

Our Father in heaven, holy be your name, your kingdom come, your will be done, on earth as in heaven. Give us today our daily bread. Forgive us our sins as we forgive those who sin against us. Do not bring us to the test, but deliver us from evil. For the kingdom, the power and the glory are yours, now and for ever. Amen.

---

[26] Jn 5.25-26; 1 Jn 2.1-2 and 3.20; Jn 1.29; 2 Esdr 8.47 and Ecclus 2.18.

There may follow additional prayers, most notable of which is the *Salvator Mundi*. The last prayer text is based on 1 Jn 3.2, making an excellent final reminder of what cannot be seen, heard or imagined yet what is prepared by God for the faithful.

The language of the supplement is less archaic than that of the earlier book, but the provision is scant and cannot be said to represent a revision.

CHAPTER 7

Some Conclusions

General conclusions

Pastoral concern

What this commentary has revealed is overwhelming evidence of pastoral concern in all rites. The focus of attention in the pastoral rites has not always been the same. Rites from more Catholic traditions have paid careful attention to the deceased and to prayers for the dead. The more Protestant churches have generally avoided this emphasis and looked more to the solace of those who mourn. This is fairly predictable and arises from theological convictions.

Phased rites

What has proved more challenging for the liturgist has been to express van Gennep's theory of rites of passage with its phases of separation, transition and incorporation. In particular, there has not been a very clear sense of incorporation into new life for either the dead or the living. The Anglican Church in New Zealand's *Prayers in a House after Death* and the Roman Catholic *Office of the Dead* have been fine (though not sole) exceptions. It is significant that in the case of each of these rites such a move has to come from beyond the main funeral liturgies. Just as there has been over the last few years a special attention given to the funerals of children stillborn and of neonates, perhaps the next work to be attempted is the drafting of post-funeral rites.

Past and present

The work of scholars in uncovering Christian funerary traditions has informed the work of liturgists. This manifests itself in a number of ways, of which the processional nature of funerals is most widespread. We might also note the increasingly widespread use of the psalter to articulate the cry of the dead.

However, the proposed use of white as the liturgical colour for funerals has been less popular; where black has been abandoned, violet has usually been the preferred option.

Personal diversity

One of the clearest things to have emerged is the contemporary desire to provide services to meet as wide a range of pastoral circumstances as possible. The old approach that death abolishes the distinction that life creates – saint and sinner, famous and unknown, rich and poor, young and old – is no longer clear. Our common mortality is obscured by the urgent call to celebrate the individual's life. Any attempt to insist that what is celebrated at a funeral is the mighty act of God in raising Jesus from the dead, rather than the life of the present deceased, is becoming increasingly difficult to make. I have argued that we should, nonetheless, declare that Christological agenda. Failure to do so compromises the foundation of the Church's ministry.

Eschatology

Bryan Spinks, writing a comparative commentary on the funeral rites to be found in *Common Worship* and *Common Order*, concludes with this reflection on the link between personal and cosmic eschatology:

> Can a church which is hesitant about the afterlife give any confident hope about the renewal of the whole cosmos? Can it, logically, express nothing more than a vague pious hope? On the other hand, a church which is confident about its departed has more right to be listened to in terms of its other eschatological hopes.[1]

He then cites the Gelasian prayer "O God of unchangeable power and eternal light", approving its linking of "the eschatological concerns of the funeral, and its witness to the greater eschatological hope of the future of God".

This duality of focus expresses what I have urged in my contention that the Christian funeral is more than a dignified farewell. In linking individual human death with the Paschal Mystery, we declare that those who are created in the image of God are, at the end of their earthly life, brought to that same God in whose image they are made. Death is not simply a private matter; the death of Christ changes the nature of human death. Eschatology is not a matter of survival but of salvation; and salvation is not simply about "my soul", but is the work of God who:

> has made known to us the mystery of his will, according to his good pleasure that he set forth in Christ, as a plan for the fullness of time, to gather up all things in him, things in heaven and things on earth (Eph. 1.9-10).

Personal reflections

Core texts and additional resources

Whether we have been entirely wise in trying to set out in our books what should be done in every conceivable circumstance, I doubt. However clever or prescient we may be, later events will find out the limits of what we know now. It may be better to provide a single core text for each stage of our rituals which officiants may then develop and adapt (by reference to additional resources) to meet the particular circumstances of any given death.

A recent rash of discoveries in Britain that some hospitals have retained organs and other body parts without the knowledge of bereaved families is leading some to ask for second rites of burial or cremation. Whatever the theologian may argue, some bereaved

---

[1]   Spinks and Torrance (1999: 198-199).

people feel that the funeral was invalidated by the fact that some tissue was withheld without consent.[2]

A personal approach

In the original theological preface to the funeral resources I published with the Canterbury Press,[3] I included the following comment:

> Death is, in Christian understanding, both friend and foe. It is the doorway to life eternal and it is the wage paid by sin. Even when death comes as a friend to one who has suffered prolonged illness or catastrophic, irreversible injury, those who are left have no release from the pain of grief.
>
> Death is consuming in its urgency; its advent leaves none unchanged. Other priorities are set aside, and attention is forced, like it or not, upon the immediacy of what has occurred.
>
> The angry, the dazed, the relieved, the numb – all look for help; and when they seek that help from the Christian people of God, they expect to receive all the compassion that our humanity commands. God in Christ calls us to offer more. The Church's funeral rites provide more than a dignified farewell to the deceased and quiet sympathy to the bereaved.
>
> The Christian understanding of our creaturehood leads us to believe that life and death and resurrection are all in the hands of God. Life and death and resurrection are therefore theological concerns, and in Christian understanding must be linked with the life and death and resurrection of Jesus the Christ.
>
> The funeral rites offered here take their stance from these primary beliefs. They relate each instance of human death to the death of Jesus. There is an evangelical dimension to the Christian funeral which is the proclamation of Christ's victory over death in which he binds the strength of death before plundering death of its spoils (cf. Mk 3.27). Christ's death is an offering for all, making all death an offering to God. His death transforms what we naturally fear and resent. The pain of death and bereavement is not diminished by this, but it is transformed.
>
> Nor is the call to the risen life issued to the dead alone. The bereaved, too, are called to newness of life. "Returning to normal" is not a Christian option. The old normality can never be recovered, for God is making all things new.
>
> The ministry of the Church at the funeral is therefore to proclaim the story of Christ, setting the deceased's story within it, to speak of Christ's death and this death, to speak of the resurrection, the light in the darkness. We minister best to the bereaved not by vague generalities, but by careful attention to the details that made up the life of the deceased. We must not ignore the ways in which grief comes, nor must we forget the word of forgiveness which the deceased and bereaved alike need to speak and to hear. "Forgive us our sins, as we forgive those who sin against us," With the death of another we are reminded of that judgement to which we are summoned. We all stand in need of the mercy and forgiveness of God. The measure by which we forgive is the measure by which we are forgiven.

---

[2]   The disposal of such remains needs to be undertaken with pastoral sensitivity – even when what is available may be slice of tissue microns thick on a lab slide. Whether this requires a rite equal to the original funeral is a matter of considerable debate. The matter is extremely delicate.

[3]   *In Sure and Certain Hope*, SCM-Canterbury, Norwich, 2003. My thanks to SCM-Canterbury Press for permission to use this extended extract.

In part, it is the responsibility of the liturgist to devise rites which will enable these considerations to be properly addressed. Whoever leads the service needs to take the structure of the rite and apply it to the particular circumstances of death.

For all these reasons a short homily or sermon is to be provided. For many this is problematic. There is a temptation to offer something along the lines of a sanctified obituary notice. The old tag "nothing but good of the dead" becomes the prevailing imperative, and the need for forgiveness is obscured – one might almost say eradicated – as "beatification precedes interment".

The task of the preacher is to tell the story of the dead person honestly, and to frame that narrative in the story of Jesus, whose death and resurrection assure us that our death is not God's last word.

What we say here addresses the central questions of the funeral and offers a Christian answer. "Where is daddy now?" and "What will God do to our friend?" are questions which will be asked whether we wish it or not. We need to be ready to speak of God's love in Christ from which not even death can separate us (Rom 8.38-39). If we do not offer Christ's answer to the questioner, in what sense has the funeral been a Christian one?

If we do not lead people to the love of God, where is that hope of which the scripture speaks?

While the resources and service texts provided in that book seek to address a range of circumstances in which funeral rites are required, the central text in each staged rite speaks of our common mortality in the light of the Paschal Mystery. Supplementary material is provided for specific cases, but the intention is to avoid the proliferation of possibilities which obscures the one thing that all funerals have in common: someone has died.

Whether my liturgical drafting is effective, I leave for others to judge. It would scarcely be fitting for me to comment. However, in that work I hope to have demonstrated that, while subjecting the work of others to scholarly scrutiny may be of some value, the primary task is to draw the liturgical assembly together for the worship and praise of God.

What does the funeral celebrate?

Many contemporary mourners in Britain look for a celebration of the life of the deceased. Tributes replace sermons, songs from tapes and CDs replace hymns, favourite poems and sayings replace scripture. In my judgement, the Christian minister who is asked to officiate at such a ceremony has the right to ask whether what is being sought is a Christian funeral. What has happened to the Christian funeral when all that is expressed is grief and loss?

Equally, there has been a move among some Christians so to celebrate the hope of the resurrection that the darkness of death is scarcely faced. Sorrow is expressed, but the keynote is joy. Grief is acknowledged, but the mourner is exhorted to be glad. What has happened to the Christian funeral, when grief is short-circuited?

Throughout this book, I have argued that death is real and that the Christian does not deny its pain but confronts it with the "word against death" of the Paschal Mystery. In the Trinity separation, transition and incorporation are experienced in the Cross,

Descent and Resurrection of Christ. The Christian funeral expresses grief, for in the death of a human there is an end to one made in the image of God. Yet our grief is not ours alone; it is the grief known within the Trinity in the dying of the Christ. The Christian funeral speaks of a journey moving not only from life to death, but from death to life. The journeying is not ours alone; it is the journey of Christ to the dead to whom the gospel is preached. The Christian funeral proclaims hope. It is a hope rooted in Christ whom death could not hold. What we have been, we have been in Christ; what we shall be, we shall be in him.

That is why at the Christian funeral we read the scripture, proclaim the story and make our prayers. There is more than a dignified farewell; there is committal to God. There is more than the tale of the deceased; there is the story of Christ. There is more than keeping our spirits up; there is the gift of the Spirit among whose harvest is "that peace which the world cannot give".

To the triune God be glory given in the Church and on the earth, as all creation joins the ceaseless praise of heaven. To the ages of ages. Amen.

Select Bibliography

An extended Select Bibliography is to be found in Volume I

Liturgical texts reviewed in the commentary

An Anglican Prayer Book (London: Collins *per* Claremont: Philip). 1989.

The Book of Alternative Services of the Anglican Church of Canada (Toronto: Anglican Book Centre). 1995.

The Book of Common Prayer (Oxford: Oxford University Press – 1982 printing). 1662.

The Book of Common Prayer (New York: Church Hymnal Corporation). 1979.

Book of Common Worship (Louisville: Westminster John Knox). 1993.

The Book of Common Worship (London: Oxford University Press). 1963.

The Book of Common Worship Supplement (Madras: The Christian Literature Society). 1966.

The Book of Worship (Delhi: ISPCK). 1995.

Common Order (Edinburgh: St. Andrew's). 1994.

Common Worship: Pastoral Services (London: Church House Publishing). 2000.

Enriching Our Worship 2 – Ministry with the Sick or Dying: Burial of a Child (New York: Church Publishing Corporation). 2000.

The Great Book of Needs (South Canaan, Pennsylvania: St.Tikhon's Seminary Press). 1999.

The Lutheran Book of Worship (Minneapolis: Fortress). 1978.

The Methodist Worship Book (Peterborough: Methodist Publishing House). 1999.

A New Zealand Prayer Book/He Karakia Mihinare o Aotearoa (Auckland: Collins). 1989.

Order of Christian Funerals (London: Geoffrey Chapman). 1990.

Order of Services (Tiruvulla, Kerala: The Mar Thoma Sabha Book Depot). 1988.

Our Modern Services (Nairobi: Uzima). 2002.

Patterns and Prayers for Christian Worship (Oxford: Oxford University Press). 1990.

A Prayer Book for Australia (Alexandria, NSW: Broughton). 1995.

Revised Funeral Rites 1987 (Edinburgh: The General Synod of the Scottish Episcopal Church). 1987.

Service Book (Oxford: Oxford University Press). 1989.

Uniting in Worship (Melbourne: Joint Board of Christian Education). 1988.

Non-liturgical texts referred to in the commentary

Chupungco, A. J. (ed.). 1997. *Handbook for Liturgical Studies – Volume IV: Sacraments and Sacramentals* (Collegeville: Pueblo)

Gitari, D. (ed.). 1994. *Anglican Liturgical Inculturation in Africa: The Kanamai Statement 'African Culture and Anglican Liturgy'* (Bramcote: Alcuin/GROW)

Martimort, A. G. (ed.). 1988. *The Church at Prayer – Volume III: The Sacraments* (London: Geoffrey Chapman)

Russell, J. K. 1996. *Men without God?* (Salisbury: Highway)

Sheppy, P. P. J. 2003a. *In Sure and Certain Hope* (London and Norwich: SCM-Canterbury Press)

Sheppy, P. P. J. 2003b. "Sterbebegleitung und Begräbnis in der anglikanischen Tradition", in Becker, H.-J., Fugger, D., Pritzkat, J., and Suss, K. (eds), *Liturgie im Angesicht des Todes.* Vol. 5: *Reformatorische Traditionen der Neuzeit* (Tübingen and Basel: St. Ottilien Press, Pietas Liturgica 13)

Sicard, D. 1978. "La liturgie de la mort dans l'église latine des orgines à la réforme carolingienne", *Liturgiewissencshaftliche: Quellen und Forschungen 63* (Munster: Aschendorff)

Spinks, B. and Torrance, I. 1999. *To Glorify God* (Edinburgh: T. & T. Clark)

Index of Scripture Passages

Index of Names

A separate Index of Names appears in Volume I.

General Index

A separate General Index is to be found in Volume I.